LITTLEJOHN'S BRITAIN

D0594433

Richard Littlejohn is an award-winning journalist and broadcaster, and author of two best-selling books. He has written for London's *Evening Standard* and *Punch* and is still a contributor to the *Spectator*. His twice-weekly columns in the *Daily Mail* and the *Sun* earned him a place in the inaugural Newspaper Hall of Fame as one of the most influential journalists of the past 40 years.

He has been Fleet Street's Columnist of the Year and was named Irritant of the Year by the BBC's *What The Papers Say* awards for his unrivalled ability to get up the noses of the Establishment. His extensive radio and television work has brought him both a Sony award and a Silver Rose of Montreux. Littlejohn's satirical novel *To Hell in a Handcart* was the fastest-selling fiction paperback on its release in 2001. His highly acclaimed non-fiction book *You Couldn't Make It Up* skewerd John Major's Conservative government – much the same as *Littlejohn's Britain* does for the Blair years.

Also available by Richard Littlejohn

LITTLEJOHN'S BRITAIN

BY
RICHARD LITTLEJOHN

arrow books

Published by Arrow 2007

2 4 6 8 10 9 7 5 3 1

Copyright © Richard Littlejohn 2007

Richard Littlejohn has asserted his right under the Copyright, Designs
and Patents Act, 1988 to be identified as the author of this work

This book is sold subject to the condition that it shall not, by
way of trade or otherwise, be lent, resold, hired out, or otherwise
circulated without the publisher's prior consent in any form of
binding of cover other than that in which it is published and without
a similar condition including this condition being imposed on the
subsequent purchaser

First published in Great Britain in 2007 by Hutchinson

The Random House Group Limited
20 Vauxhall Bridge Road, London, SW1V 2SA

www.rbooks.co.uk

Addresses for companies within the Random House Group Limited
can be found at: www.randomhouse.co.uk/offices.htm

The Random House Group Limited Reg. No. 954009

A CIP catalogue record for this book
is available from the British Library

ISBN 9780099509448

The Random House Group Limited makes every effort to ensure
that the papers used in its books are made from trees that have been
legally sourced from well-managed and credibly certified forests.
Our paper procurement policy can be found at:
www.rbooks.co.uk/environment

Mixed Sources
Product group from well-managed
forests and other controlled sources
www.fsc.org   Cert no. TT-COC-2139
© 1996 Forest Stewardship Council

Printed in the UK by CPI Bookmarque, Croydon, CR0 4TD

For Wendy, Georgina and William

Contents

Acknowledgements

Heartfelt thanks to Paul Sidey and Wendy Littlejohn for their invaluable help, support and patience in the editing and compiling of this book. Also to Deke Arlon, Jill Arlon, Alison Sloan, Terry Connolly, Eddie Young, Charles Boundy, Sinead Martin, Martin Soames, Roger Field and Peter Ward. Special thanks go to Chris Stevens, Mitch Symons, Martin Clarke, Leaf Kalfayan, Paul Dacre, Alistair Sinclair, Fergus Shanahan, Paul Hudson and all those at the *Daily Mail* and the *Sun* who have had a hand in the column over the years. There are many others without whom this book would not have been possible. I'm thinking in particular of the Wicked Witch, Two Jags, David Blunkett, the Mad Mullah of the Traffic Taliban, Mandy and Reinaldo and the thousands of unsung Guardianistas who have endlessly provided me with so much material.

Transport by Brian Duff. Soundtrack by Ray Davies, Madness, Billy Bragg, Squeeze, Warren Zevon, Randy Newman, Bruce Springsteen, Southside Johnny and Benny Hill.

Richard Littlejohn
London 2007

1 | A Straight Kinda Guy

Not long after the Tories won their fourth successive general election victory in 1992, I received a dinner invitation from an old Fleet Street mate, Alastair Campbell. We'd covered the 1987 election together from the vantage point of the Neil Kinnock battle bus. Although Alastair worked for the Mirror Group as a journalist, he assumed the semi-official role of Labour PR man (we hadn't heard of spin doctors back then) as Kinnochio stumbled from gaffe to catastrophe to landslide defeat. Ally was always on hand to explain to us what Neil 'really meant'.

No one took any notice of him, but if we had it would have come as no surprise when he eventually abandoned journalism and moved in to Downing Street as a full-time propagandist ten years later. Nor did we hold it against him. Everyone knew that Ally was more of a Labour cheerleader than a proper reporter.

And it was in that ad hoc capacity that he invited us to dinner at his home in North London. He thought it was time that I got to know a rising young Labour frontbencher, Tony Blair.

As it happened, I had met Blair of couple of times before in his role as shadow employment secretary under Kinnock.

Fleet Street's thirsty Labour correspondents, of whom I was one before I became an equally thirsty columnist, used to drink in Blackpool's last residential pub, the Empress, a former haunt of music hall and variety artistes tucked away in the warren of backstreets behind the Imperial Hotel, which served as Northern headquarters for the annual seaside political conferences. What attracted us to it was a flexible attitude to the then restrictive licensing laws, a decent jukebox, cask ales and a complete absence of politicians and trades union leaders, who didn't seem to know it existed. Which suited us just fine.

We were in there one lunchtime when a fresh, unfamiliar face turned up. He looked vaguely familiar but no one could place him.

The beaming newcomer bounded over to the veteran industrial correspondent of the communist *Morning Star* newspaper, Mick Costello, known to most of us as 'Elvis', who was quietly nursing his hangover.

He grabbed Elvis by the hand and started shaking it vigorously.

'Hi, Mick, good to see you.'

'Who the fuck are you?' growled Elvis.

'Tony Blair, shadow employment,' said Blair.

'Well you can fuck off.'

There was a brief, embarrassed silence, but Blair's rictus grin didn't crack. Without missing a beat, he walked over to the bar, bought himself a pint, and proceeded to introduce himself to the rest of us.

Ten minutes later he wished us all a cheery goodbye.

Missing you already.

'What was all that about?' we asked.

'Fuck knows,' was the general conclusion.

But we had to admit he had chutzpah. This boy was either going to vanish without trace or was going to go far.

Even though Blair is roughly the same age as me, back then he looked about twelve. This led me to christen him 'Doogie Howser MP' – after Doogie Howser MD, a character in an American TV show which ran from 1989 to 1993, based around a teenage prodigy who worked as a doctor. Blair even looked like Doogie.

I think he was flattered that someone had taken some notice of him at long last.

When Kinnock was beaten by John Major and succeeded by the late John Smith, Blair was hailed as part of the coming generation and appointed shadow Home Secretary – and along with Gordon Brown was being spoken of in some circles as a future Labour leader.

It was with this in mind that Ally decided to pin his colours to Blair and begin a charm offensive to win over those members of the press they thought could be useful to them.

By then I was presenting a three-hour morning show on London's LBC and Alastair was one of my regular political pundits. So was Charles Kennedy, then president of the Liberal Democrats.

It was no surprise, then, to find Charlie also on the guest list. This was when Blair was still buying into the 'Big Tent' view of politics as one big 'I'd like to teach the world to sing' Coke commercial.

Although Charlie was one of my radio pundits, politically the only big tent you would find the pair of us in would be the beer tent.

Charlie was there with his then girlfriend, the publisher Georgina Capel. I was with my wife Wendy and we were also joined by Ally's neighbour and my old friend and *Daily Mail* colleague Baz Bamigboye and his wife Tricia. I was sat in the middle of the table, opposite Tony, and next to his wife, Cherie, whom I'd never met before. (Years later, when I got to know more about the scary Mrs Blair, I christened her 'the Wicked Witch' – a nickname which seems to have stuck.)

Alastair's wife had prepared fish pie, and although Ally had foresworn the booze following his nervous breakdown a few years earlier, there was plenty of chilled Chablis on tap – which the rest of us (or at least Baz, Charlie and me) took full advantage of.

After a convivial couple of hours of small talk and laughter, things started to get serious over the cheese course.

Here was the big pitch. Tony fixed me in the eye and began to explain why Britain needed a Labour government. Only Labour could tackle welfarism, he explained. It had to come from the left because the Tories were so discredited and distrusted. Didn't I agree?

Oh, absolutely, Tone. Any more Chablis, Ally?

Did I have any thoughts? Blair wanted to know. He was fascinated to hear my take on the world.

'Well, it's like this,' I explained. 'You need a totem, you need to set an example.'

'Great. What did you have in mind, Richard?' he asked.

'Liverpool,' I said, taking another glug of white.

Baz started spluttering with laughter. I looked down the table for Charlie Kennedy's reaction, but observed that he was fast asleep, face down in his fish pie.

'Er, Liverpool?' Blair replied, his face freezing.

'Yep, Liverpool,' I said.

(This was not long after the BBC series *Boys From the Blackstuff*, which made Liverpool a byword for economic depression, unemployment, a rampant black economy and welfare fraud – a reputation no longer deserved, I should add, lest the wacky Scousers overreact in the same way as they did when Boris Johnson questioned their rectitude in the *Spectator* in 2005.)

'Why, um, Liverpool?'

Simple, I explained. Merseyside was well known for welfarism. If Blair could tackle the problem there, he could beat it anywhere.

He seemed to accept my thesis, but wondered what exactly I had in mind.

By this time, warming to my theme, I decided to spell it out, ignoring my wife's apprehensive expression across the table.

'It's like this. You put tanks on the East Lancs Road, submarines in the River Mersey and then surround the place with barbed wire. Then you send in the bombers and turn the place into a car park. When the dust settles, you invite the Hong Kong Chinese to take over. Job done.'

The more absurd and extreme my argument became, the wider became Blair's eyes and grin. He started nodding vigorously, maniacally almost.

I was joking. (I think. It seemed like a good idea at the time, as these things generally do after a few bottles of wine.)

Ally had his head in his hands. Baz was convulsed with laughter. Charlie was still asleep. Wendy gave me one of those resigned looks she's thrown me so many times over the past thirty-odd years of marriage.

Next to me, from the direction of Mrs Blair, I was aware of a certain *froideur*. It was like sitting next to Ice Station Zebra.

'Um, well, I hear what you say. Interesting,' said Tony, darting glances between Ally, me and his sub-zero spouse.

'I think it's time we were going,' said Cherie – from what I remember, about the only thing she said all night.

And with that – 'Lovely evening, so good talking to you' etc – they were gone.

In the cab on the way home, Wendy asked me what was with all the Liverpool stuff. Didn't I know who she was?

Who?

Mrs B.

Some stuck-up, left wing Islington brief, isn't she?

You do know who her dad is?

Not a clue.

Wendy explained that Mrs Blair was, in fact, Liverpool-raised Cherie Booth, daughter of the actor Tony Booth, star of *Till Death Us Do Part*.

So while I'd been banging on about scrounging Scouse gits, the father of the woman I was sitting next to was famous not just for playing a Scouse git but for playing the most famous Scouse git in Britain.

And I'd also managed, albeit in jest, to advocate the total destruction of the city she had grown up in. (Maybe I should read the weekend supplements more often. Then I might have stumbled across the profile of C. Blair which my wife had read while I was checking out the football pages.)

Oh well. That's us off the Christmas card list, I figured.

Then I wondered: why the hell didn't he say something? Why did he sit there grinning and nodding instead of saying something like: 'Look, I know you're only joking, Rich, but I think I should point out that, er, actually, ha, ha, Cherie's from Liverpool . . .'?

Blair would rather risk a night in the spare bedroom than stop in full flow a half-pissed hack whom he hoped to impress.

I think that was the night I worked Blair out. Whenever I met him subsequently, he always agreed with me on just about everything. Not that he meant it, just that his career has been built on being all things to all men.

This isn't meant to be a political book with a capital 'P'. It's designed as a series of snapshots, part caricature, of the Blair years.

Before I hit the wordface I thought it would be instructive to dust off the cuttings book and revisit what I said about Blair before he became prime minister.

A year before the 1997 election it was obvious that Blair would be the next occupant of 10 Downing Street. The Tories had imploded and had been reduced to a sleazy, undisciplined rabble, completely spent after a decade and a half in office and bereft of fresh ideas. Blair could have been custom-designed to mollify Middle Britain, guaranteed not to frighten the horses. He seemed to offer conservatism with a caring face. But what did we really know about him? Everything and nothing.

In June 1996 it was revealed that while Blair was an Anglican, he was also taking Holy Communion at a Catholic church near his home in Islington. No big deal as far as most of us were concerned. After all, his wife is a Catholic and he would naturally want to accompany her to church. It was also rumoured he was taking instruction from a priest with a view to converting. But the moment the story was published, Blair announced immediately that he would stop attending Mass.

Just like that.

It struck me then that the only reason he reacted as he did was because he feared Protestant Britain would never elect a Catholic prime minister.

It was a telling insight into the real soul of the man and prompted me to comment in my *Daily Mail* column on 6 June, 1996:

Tony Blair appears not to have a single shred of principle in his entire body.

If he wants to become a Roman Catholic that is entirely a matter for him, his wife and the Holloway Road branch of the Glasgow Rangers supporters club. But the speed with which he then offered to give up taking Holy Communion was the act of a gutless opportunist. In his desperate attempt to be all things to all men, he ends up being nothing to anybody.

If it's Tuesday this must be the Church of the Sacred Bleeding Heart of Jesus, located in a marginal seat somewhere near Milton Keynes. If it's Wednesday, it's time to break bread with the provisional wing of the Tabernacle of Jah Rastafari (Bob Marley Chapter). If there's a by-election in Bradford, Blair would convert to Islam for the day. Blair is a Scotsman who pretends to be a Newcastle United supporter when he's in his constituency in the North-East. He's a Catholic in the Irish Republic of Islington, an Anglican in Stuff the Pope country.

In Washington, he's a free-trade Clinton Democrat. In Frankfurt, he's a European federalist. In the Home Counties, he's the royalist, tax-cutting Son of Thatch. In Scotland, he's the devolutionist heir of William Wallace. At the Brighton conference, he's a card-carrying member of the TGWU. In Sydney, as a guest of Rupert Murdoch, he's the anti-establishment satellite kid. When he's lunching at the *Guardian*, he's a fibre-enhanced, soak-the-rich, Meat Is Murder socialist. When he's supping with the Tory press he brings a short-handled spoon and devours British beef as if it's going out of fashion, which, thanks to him and his scaremongering sidekicks, it is.

In the Far East, he's the son of Adam Smith. In East Lothian, he's the son of John Smith. He's the believer in council-run comprehensives who sends his son to a grant-maintained school.

He's the man who tore up Clause Four yet wants to renationalise the railways.

He's the Universal Soldier and he's fighting for the Queen. He's a real Nowhere Man. He's Misstra Know It All. He's a Dedicated Follower of Fashion.

And if he's the rock and roll fan he pretends he is when he's not at the opera or attending finger-in-the-ear Lindisfarne revivals or fiddly-diddly night at Minogue's, he'll know what I'm getting at.

But where do you go to, my lovely, when you're alone in your bed?

Not exactly Nostradamus, but I can't see much there that needs revising a decade on. Do we really know any more about Blair today?

Everything and nothing, even after the Formula One affair, the Dome, the dodgy dossier on Iraq, the death of Dr Kelly, the Hinduja affair, cash for passports, cash for peerages, Connaught Square, fill in your own outrage.

What's changed is that the rest of the world finally caught up with me.

But where does he go to when he's alone in his bed?

God knows.

2 | The Which Blair Project

Is this the scariest movie ever? That was the question being asked about *The Which Blair Project*, released in May 1997 to huge popular acclaim.

Critics said the film has no discernible plot, shaky presentation, banal dialogue and nothing much actually happens. It follows the adventures of three overgrown students – Tony, Mandy and Ally – who can't see the wood for the trees. While Tony is the main character, the production values come from Mandy, who once made a few minor television documentaries, and Ally, who used to write soft-porn stories.

The success of the film-makers was in convincing the public that the story was actually real, rather than a complete figment of their imagination.

Although *The Which Blair Project* promised much, it delivered very little.

The dialogue seems to have been made up as they went along and, if there ever was a plot, it was lost early on. It tries hard to be sinister, but after only a few scenes descends into complete farce.

However, experienced reviewers who should have known better swooned over the film, seduced by the handsome leading man. Their fawning enthusiasm and clever hype from the film's ruthless publicists kept *The Which Blair Project* at number one at the box office.

For those few of you who haven't yet seen the movie, it takes its title from the contradictions within the main character, Tony Blair, who leads his followers into the woods, where he keeps them in the dark. They never know what is going to happen next.

Which Blair is the real Blair?

Is it the Blair who loves the pound, or the Blair who wanted to scrap the pound? Is it the Blair who backs small businesses, or the Blair who introduced 3,000 new regulations on businesses?

Which Blair?

Is it the Blair who believes in low taxes, or the Blair who put up taxes faster than in any other country in Europe? Is it the Blair who was all for abolishing selective schools, or the Blair who sent his children to (selective) faith schools?

Which Blair?

Is it the Blair who believes in one man, one vote democracy, or the Blair who uses trades union block votes and ballot-rigging when it suits him? Is it the Blair who locks up right-wing tyrants, or the Blair who lays out the red carpet for left-wing tyrants?

Which Blair?

Is it the Blair who thinks the bombers of Baghdad should be punished, or the Blair who thinks the bombers of Belfast should be rewarded? Is it the devout Anglican Blair or the Blair who worships at a Roman Catholic church?

Which Blair?

Ten years on, none of us are any the wiser.

Scary, or what?

3 | Blair Force One

Tony Blair always resented the fact that his buddy George Dubya Bush was whisked round the world on Air Force One, the presidential jet, and ferried to and from the White House lawn in a personal helicopter, while Blair had to make do with scheduled airlines or bumming a lift from the RAF.

After nine years of pestering, Blair finally persuaded Gordon Brown to finance Blair Force One, his own prime-ministerial plane, at a cost of £30 million to the British taxpayer. Welcome to the inaugural flight.

Good morning, ladies, gentlemen and members of the trans-gendered community. This is your captain speaking. Blair Force One especially welcomes passengers regardless of ethnicity, religion, disability, sexual orientation or criminality. Today, we will be flying by the seat of our pants. We are not anticipating any resistance or turbulence, although there may be some spinning.

Our chief stewardess in our First Class cabin is Mandy, who will be assisted by the lovely Reinaldo. First Class customers will also have access to Ayurvedic massage from Carole and exclusive in-flight hairdressing facilities by Mr André, stylist to the stars and the captain's wife. Tantric massage with ylang-ylang oil and aromatherapy is also available.

Our purser in Business Class is Patricia, who will be patron-ising you throughout your journey. Please be aware there is a waiting list of up to eighteen weeks for service in this cabin. We would like to apologise in advance for any inconvenience, which is caused by unforeseen staff redundancies and the closure of some of our delivery units.

In Premium Economy, Gordon will be offering our patented Stealth service. For your comfort and convenience, there is a twenty per cent supplement payable on all drinks, crisps and inheritance trusts in this section. Customers may also be required to pay an additional insurance premium and a special arrivals tax, details of which are hidden in the small print on the back of your ticket.

Just a reminder that our menu is available in twenty-eight different languages. However, we must apologise for the fact that, for your safety and convenience, our award-winning beef on the bone has been withdrawn from the menu until further notice.

In our Admiralty Class cabin, chief steward John will be inviting female passengers and stewardesses to join him in the Mile High Club, which is located in the restroom next to the galley at the rear of the aircraft and features a complimentary chipolata buffet.

Those of you wishing to join the Mile High Club are advised that condoms, Viagra and the morning-after pill are available free of charge.

It is an offence under international law to smoke in the restrooms. Cottaging is permitted for passengers over sixteen. Please ask your cabin staff for our exclusive range of complimentary lubricants.

For your health and safety, we remind you that this is a no-heckling flight. Anyone caught jeering the captain or any members of our crew will be arrested under the Public Order Act and their passport will be confiscated.

Passengers are also strongly recommended not to consume more than twenty-seven units of alcohol and to eat at least five portions of fruit and vegetables during this flight. Passengers who decline to co-operate with healthy eating guidelines may be refused service.

Smoking cigars, pipes and cigarettes is strictly prohibited on Blair Force One, unless of course you happen to be a member of Mr Ecclestone's Formula One party, in which case an exception will be made. However, smoking cannabis is encouraged. Please choose from our selection of spliffs on the duty-free trolley.

Your comfort and safety are our top priority. Customers are

advised that failure to comply will result in a smack in the mouth from John.

Firearms are strictly prohibited on this flight, except for Yardies travelling to Britain from Jamaica and members of the Irish Republican Army.

Our customer liaison manager Charles will be passing through the plane distributing visa applications and copies of the Human Rights Act.

If you have joined Blair Force One via a connecting flight from Mogadishu, Kabul, Tirana, Tehran, Baghdad or Algiers, we advise you to destroy your papers and claim to be fleeing oppression. You can then use the fast-track lane at Heathrow, before boarding our executive coach service to Croydon, where our representatives will be happy to find you free accommodation and other benefits.

If you are a foreign criminal or an Islamist terrorist, please ask for our in-flight lawyer, Cherie, who will be pleased to advise you how to settle permanently in Britain at no cost to yourself. You may also be entitled to compensation. Blair Force One is proud to be the only airline in the world currently offering this service.

If you are a British citizen travelling in our Middle Class and Working Class cabins, we would ask you to remain seated throughout, keep your mouths shut and go to the back of the queue on arrival.

If you look out of the left side of the aircraft you will be able to spot a number of landmarks of New Britain. In particular, take time to admire the Millennium Dome, which is currently being turned into a supercasino by our chief steward's friend, Mr Anschutz.

Before deplaning, please put all your loose change and foreign currency into the envelopes provided. Gordon also accepts cheques, credit cards, watches, wedding rings, jewellery, IOUs, false teeth, family heirlooms and the deeds to your home. In fact, we would ask that before you depart Blair Force One, you remember to leave all your personal wealth and belongings behind.

Ladies and gentlemen, I'm aware we are experiencing some turbulence, losing altitude fast and appear to be in freefall. But I still can't give you an estimated time for my departure.

Got that, Gordon? And in case any of you are thinking of storming the cockpit, I remind you that the door is locked and our air marshal, Sir Ian, has instructions to shoot on sight.

Thank you for choosing Blair Force One.

4 | There'll Always Be an England

There's a chance that you're reading this book in an airport departure lounge or on a plane bound for more agreeable climes.

I was going to say sunnier climes, but the temperatures in Britain over the past few summers have been the kind we spend a fortune each year seeking out abroad.

Still, there's a world of difference between lolling around in the sun wearing shorts and T-shirts and sweltering in an office with no air-conditioning or crammed into a crowded commuter train doing a passable imitation of the Black Hole of Calcutta.

After two weeks of living *la dolce vita*, most of you won't want to come back. As the ghastliness of your life in Blair's Britain gradually recedes, you get used to the caterpillar pace of life, the cheap wine and afternoon siestas and begin to think to yourself: 'I could suffer this all year round.'

Strolling on the beach, dangling your toes in the pool or relaxing over an exquisite and inexpensive seven-course menu gastronomique, your mind irresistibly begins to embrace the prospect of your number coming up on the escape committee.

Every year hundreds of thousands of us decide to up sticks and emigrate. Close to four million British passport holders now live permanently overseas, if you don't include the Hong Kong Chinese.

The numbers are rising fast, according to the latest figures. Migrationwatch calculates that as many as 340,000 people are turning their back on the United Kingdom each year.

America, Australia, South Africa and New Zealand have always been favourite destinations, and France has now overtaken Spain as a sanctuary from the madness of modern, multicultural, morality-free Britain. There are also significant settlements of expats in

Yemen, Libya and Sierra Leone. I guess most of the British contingent in Libya must be involved in the oil industry, but it's come to something when people would voluntarily live under Colonel Gadaffi rather than the Blair Terror.

Many emigrate because that's where their work takes them. But once there they tend to stay put.

My own family is a case in point. My late father was transferred to America thirty years ago. My mum still lives there and my younger sister, who went with them, is now a US citizen. They enjoy a much better quality of life and standard of living than England has to offer them.

There's nothing new in this. My dad's brother became a 'Ten Pound Pom' almost half a century ago and never came back. My grandparents followed him to Australia when grandad retired from the docks. Both lived well into their nineties, not the kind of longevity they could have expected if they'd stayed in East London.

What's new is the sheer scale of emigration and the reasons for it. Of course, we've always had sixtysomethings sitting around on the Costa del Crime lamenting that fings ain't what they used to be back home.

I thought it was just my age. On turning fifty, I became aware of the number of conversations with my peers who were all thinking of getting out for good. You can't hail a cab in London without the driver regaling you with his plans to retire to a villa in Spain or Tenerife.

But it's not only the baby-boomer generation cashing in their chips and moving abroad. I've been struck by emails from young couples in their twenties who have concluded there's nothing for them here and are seeking a new life elsewhere.

It's profoundly depressing that so many energetic, qualified young people feel they have no future in the country of their birth – a nation supposed to be the fourth (or fifth) richest nation on earth. And it's equally depressing that even larger numbers of older people believe that staying put is a sure-fire recipe for a miserable old age.

This isn't all down to economics, although exorbitant housing and transport costs, suffocating taxation and rip-off pricing are major factors.

People look around them and see a country in which nothing seems to work properly, where they are paying through the nose for incompetent and indifferent public services; where they stand a good chance of catching a fatal infection while they're in hospital, simply because those in charge can't be bothered with even the basic principles of hygiene; where an education system once the envy of the world has been sacrificed on the altar of social engineering and experimentation; where crime is rife and the law seems always to side with the criminals; where trying to get anywhere is a costly ordeal; where the streets are flooded but there's a hosepipe ban.

They see government which, at every level, seems to despise them. They tire of being told to be ashamed of their nationality, that their traditions are worthless, that they are all closet racists.

Over the past nine years, much of Britain has been utterly transformed. At the heart of it has been Labour's deliberate decision to abandon our borders and encourage mass immigration from all over the world. This country has always had a proud record of accepting and assimilating newcomers, but this process has been overwhelmed by the millions who have arrived in the past few years.

You don't have to be a card-carrying BNP Neanderthal to worry about the consequences of this sea change in our society. It is simply impossible to absorb and assimilate this many people from a myriad of cultures in such a short space of time – that's always assuming they want to assimilate, which in the case of many Muslims they don't.

Neighbourhoods have been transformed almost overnight. Long-standing residents, including – often especially – those from the settled immigrant communities, feel threatened. They become strangers in the place they grew up. They're not 'racist' – that hackneyed, catch-all slander levelled at anyone who voices any misgivings about the level of immigration. They just didn't vote for this and weren't told it was going to happen.

The new immigration has arguably brought economic benefits, especially if you're in the market for a nanny or a plumber. But, unarguably, it has also brought problems with rising social tensions, pressures on housing and services and newcomers undercutting wages and pricing indigenous workers out of a job.

Is it any wonder so many people are turning their backs on Britain? They are convinced Britain has turned its back on them.

At the 1987 Labour Party conference, in the wake of Margaret Thatcher's third election victory, the penny finally dropped. Neil Kinnock got to his hind legs and asked a trades union-dominated audience: 'What do you say to a docker who earns £400 a week, owns his own house, a new car, microwave, as well as a small place near Marbella? You do not say,' he continued in a cod Cockney accent intended to mimic Ron Todd, then leader of the transport workers, '"Bruvver, let me take you out of your misery."'

Labour's defeat had been secured by the votes of millions of aspirational working people, whom the party had taken for granted. But although Kinnock had identified the problem he clearly didn't have the answer. In 1992, John Major's Conservatives swept back in to Downing Street.

That was the point at which Labour realised they could never again rely on the support of Britain's traditional working-class voters. For a start, the working class were moving upmarket, thanks to the economic reforms of the 1980s. Demographically, the country was becoming more Conservative.

So Labour struck on a twin strategy. It would woo the middle classes by putting as many of them as possible on the public payroll. It would then set about importing a brand new working class from overseas, who would show their gratitude by voting Labour in all those run-down inner constituencies which had once been socialist citadels.

And while Labour set off in pursuit of Mondeo Man and Waitrose Woman, the white working class could go hang. The new breed of Labour politicians, the assorted lawyers, lecturers and researchers have never had much time for them, anyway. They despise their tastes, the houses they live in, the cars they drive, the food they eat, the clothes they wear, the newspapers they read, the television programmes they watch, the places they take their holidays, the names they give their children. If Wayne and Waynetta couldn't be relied upon to vote Labour, they could go to hell. Amazingly, some Labour politicians have always believed that, come election time, the white working class would come home with their tails between their legs. In spite of all the evidence, they figure they have nowhere to go.

Since 1997, Gordon Brown has spent billions hiring hundreds of thousands more civil servants and bureaucrats. At election time, they're warned if they don't vote Labour their cushy jobs will be lost to the 'Tory cuts'.

Simultaneously, Labour ruthlessly abolished border controls, opening the door for hundreds of thousands of immigrants to come here both legally and illegally. In the fullness of time, all these new arrivals have, or will, become naturalised. And the vast majority of them will be Labour voters.

Most of these immigrants have moved to constituencies which were once white working-class strongholds, or have a settled population of an earlier wave of immigrants. You didn't have to be Sir Oswald Mosley to predict that there would be tensions.

Mind you, those of us who dared to warn of the potential problems were routinely smeared as racists. I've lost count of the number of times some self-righteous, smug git from the fascist left has called me a recruiting sergeant for the BNP.

They typically missed the point. Most of us who were saying there would be trouble ahead abhor the thuggish BNP and all its works. We desperately wanted to stop them getting a foothold.

This was never about race, never about immigration. I'm passionately in favour of immigration, but it has to be managed. This has been about numbers, pace of change and the government's insistence that British citizens always have to adapt to new-comers, not the other way round.

By the time Labour woke up, it was too late. In all the kerfuffle over the reshuffle, the BNP's success in the local elections of May 2006 seems to have got lost in the flood. The BNP became the second biggest party in Barking and Dagenham and made break-throughs across the North. Fortunately, most people weren't taken in by this bunch of Toytown Nazis. But even one BNP councillor is one too many.

Many of those who voted for the BNP in East London come from the families of former dockers and car workers referred to by Kinnock and represented by the late Ron Todd, once a shop steward at Ford's now defunct Dagenham works. They're not all virulent racists, although some probably are. They just want some-one to listen to them, not treat them like second-class citizens. They hear politicians talking about diversity and inclusion and then wonder why nobody ever wants to include them. Rather than listen to them, Labour ignores and insults them. The Tories, who liberated the working class in the 1980s, have nothing to offer them. I don't suppose the ozone layer plays big in Barking. The Liberals are too busy chasing the votes of disaffected Muslims.

It's tempting to dismiss those local election results as a blip and hope that the BNP will crawl back under their stone. But they're not under a stone, they're in the town hall. And the blame for that lies with all the main political parties and specifically with the anti-English policies pursued by Labour.

There's no more glaring example than the so-called West Lothian Question.

The Scots have their own parliament, the Welsh have their own assembly. Some time before the start of the third Millennium, the Northern Ireland Executive may even get around to sitting.

So why should Scottish and Welsh MPs get to vote on English affairs in the House of Commons? English MPs don't get a say on domestic issues in Scotland and Wales. There are no logical or democratic reasons why MPs from outside England should have any influence whatsoever on what happens there.

Let's get one thing straight. The Scots and Welsh voted for devolution. The English weren't even consulted, let alone given a chance to vote in a referendum on such an important constitutional matter. Nevertheless, the vast majority of us have gone along with it. If that's what the Scots and the Welsh want, fair enough.

There hasn't even been that much bridling until fairly recently at the fact that the English have to keep picking up bills worth billions of pounds for substantially higher public spending in Scotland and Wales.

We put up with the Scots and Welsh being over-represented at Westminster. It takes thousands fewer votes to elect an MP in Scotland and Wales than it does an English MP.

You might have thought that Scottish and Welsh politicians would be happy with their lot. They've got their own playgrounds now. But they're not content with that. They want to run England, too. We're not talking about defence or the economy, or anything else which affects the whole of the United Kingdom. They want to interfere in schools, transport, health and suchlike. Frankly, none of this is any of their damn business any more. They opted out. Not us.

The Scottish Parliament has the power to raise income tax by up to 3p. They won't do it. They want to keep on spongeing off the English. Slowly but surely, the English are beginning to stir.

Belatedly, Labour is waking up to the dangers. Why should the English accept as a cabinet minister, let alone prime minister, an MP who has no powers over what happens in his own constituency?

Yet, up until now, Labour has been content to ignore legitimate concerns and dismiss everyone expressing them as a knuckle-scraping Little Englander.

Sure, there are a few shaven-headed plankton on the far right who drape themselves in the flag of St George. But why is English nationalism always 'ugly and dangerous', when Scottish nationalism, Welsh nationalism and Irish nationalism is romantic, worthy, to be applauded and rewarded?

I haven't noticed much anti-Scots, anti-Welsh or even anti-Irish sentiment in England. But there is plenty of anti-English racism in Scotland, Ireland and Wales. Nationalism doesn't come much more 'ugly and dangerous' than the blood-stained Irish variety.

So why is English nationalism, uniquely, something of which to be ashamed and which must be contained? And, by extension, English patriotism?

I'm an Englishman and proud of it. I'm also a fervent supporter of the Union. And, I suspect, so are most of my fellow countrymen and women. Not for us the petty, insular sectarianism of the Celtic fringes.

If the English have tended to think of ourselves as 'British' it's because we're not hung up about clinging on to a tribal identity. We've been prepared to see our taxes siphoned off in subsidies to Scotland, Wales and Ireland because we recognise that the Union as a whole is greater than the sum of its parts. But we do have a sense of fair play. And we also have a breaking point.

Frankly, we are beginning to tire of the racist abuse and 'extremist' jibes being levelled at us. And the fact that English taxpayers are seen as mug punters north and west of the border.

The break-up of the Union has not been our doing. The momentum for devolution came from Scotland and Wales. It has been cynically exploited by an unprincipled Labour government which wants to have its cake and eat it. Labour needs its legions of Scottish and Welsh MPs if it wants to form a majority government. The Tories actually won the popular vote in England in 2005. Labour's original aim was to break up the United Kingdom into regions subservient to Brussels. Two Jags was charged with setting up regional assemblies in England, but like everything else Two Jags touched, it turned to dust. When the scheme was piloted in the North-East, the people said enough.

The English haven't yet reached the point where we are mad as hell and we're not going to take it any more. But there's a deep well of anger and frustration at Labour's venality, incompetence and cultural vandalism. Labour has a fanatical determination to change irrevocably the face of England.

I say England specifically because although Labour's policies impact on other parts of the kingdom, it is England which is the main target and has taken most of the collateral damage. Blair's government has been firing cultural Katyusha missiles into Middle England since May 1997. The social engineers in charge of the national curriculum have even removed the requirement on schools to teach British history. Do you think this is going to stop teachers in Scotland eulogising William Wallace or Robert the Bruce? Or prevent Welsh pupils being taught about their Celtic heritage?

But in England, many schools are already neglecting our proud history – or else distorting the past to portray us as worthless, war-like racists whose only contribution to the world was to exploit its ecology and enslave its aboriginal peoples.

In some London primary schools, children are bombarded with lessons about Islam, Sikhism and Hinduism but nothing about their own culture.

That's par for the course in state schools today – and has been for years. A friend of mine took his daughter out of a council-run primary school in North London when he discovered that although she could sing the anthem of the African National Congress, she didn't know the words to 'God Save the Queen'. Now that they've got the thumbs-up from government, the Guardianistas running the education system will probably drop British history from the syllabus altogether.

From day one – or Year Zero as I christened it back in 1997 – Labour has set out to destroy England as we knew it. While the Welsh and the Scots have been given their own parliaments and the IRA encouraged to take over Northern Ireland, the English have been subjugated, abused and ignored. Mass immigration – legal and illegal – has transformed parts of England into foreign countries.

Labour MP Frank Field compares it with Stalin's forced migration in the Ukraine.

Entire neighbourhoods are being ethnically cleansed – and it's the English who are getting out of town.

But as I keep stressing, this is not about race, it's about numbers. It concerns earlier generations of immigrants and their descendants as much, if not more, than anyone else – as an email I received from reader Cassandra Gosai to a column I wrote on the subject in the *Daily Mail* illustrates graphically:

As an ethnic minority English woman living in Newham, East London, your article struck home. My husband (a British Indian from East Africa) and myself have seen our borough change beyond recognition in the last five to six years. Now it could be Cairo, Pakistan or Yugoslavia. I hate feeling like this. No, it isn't racism, this is a dreadful warning of what could happen – is happening to Britain – unless immigration is curbed.

There were plenty more in that vein. The reasons people are getting out are partly economic but primarily because they feel they no longer belong in their own country.

Even some Labour figures admit immigration is in meltdown. Home Office minister Joan Ryan admitted that the arrival of the next wave of Eastern Europeans – including at least 45,000 'undesirables' from Romania and Bulgaria – will cause 'chaos'. What the hell does she think we've got already?

Some commentators put this down to Labour not having a coherent immigration policy. They're well wide of the mark.

This *is* Labour's immigration policy. The plan from the off was to create as many new British citizens as possible in the shortest period of time in the hope that they would return the favour by voting Labour.

It's why leading Labour politicians argue for an amnesty for illegals – or 'undocumented' immigrants, as they prefer to call them. It's the quickest way of getting them onto the electoral roll.

This is all part of a twin-pronged attack on the natural Conservative majority in England, together with Gordon Brown putting hundreds of thousands more people into nonjobs on the public payroll and making millions of others dependent on welfare and tax 'credits'. Labour has created a vast client state, to be cowed by the threat of losing their jobs and benefit payments – or of deportation in the case of recent arrivals – should they ever be rash enough to vote Tory.

Ministers pretend that they are going to get a grip of immigration, but only because they can't admit the plain and simple truth that everything is going exactly to plan.

And as for the hundreds of thousands of British citizens selling up and emigrating every year, so much the better. That's part of the plan, too. They were only likely to vote Conservative, anyway.

So if you are contemplating emigration, there's no reason to feel guilty.

It's what the government wants.

Chesterton's 'secret people of England' have not spoken yet.

But they're voting with their feet.

5 | They Are the Masters Now

> The people are the masters. We are the servants of the people. We will never forget that.
>
> – Tony Blair, 7 May, 1997,
> addressing Labour MPs at Church House, Westminster.

You could have fooled me.

We now live in a punishment culture, where the most trivial rules are enforced to the letter by an army of petty officials and gauleiters and penalties are out of all proportion to the seriousness of the crime.

In 2006, parking fines topped £1.2 billion. Enforcement ranges from merely overzealous to demanding money with menaces. In some areas, drivers are 400 times more likely to be punished for a minor parking infringement than they were when Labour came to power.

That's right – 400 times. And the amount extorted in fines and clamping charges has doubled.

Ever since the Tories stripped the police of responsibility for parking enforcement and handed it over to local authorities, the number of tickets issued has gone through the sunroof. This was done in the name of 'decriminalising' minor parking offences. Decriminalisation? It certainly doesn't feel like it. If paedophiles were pursued with the same ruthlessness as drivers who pull up on a double-yellow for thirty seconds, there wouldn't be a child-sex offender left on the streets.

Councils have recruited ruthless private firms to issue penalty notices and collect the cash by the vanload. Dubious methods, deception and downright illegality is the order of the day. One in five tickets has to be cancelled because of 'irregularities' by traffic wardens – in other words, handing out tickets which should never have been issued in the first place and hoping that the mug motorist won't have the time or inclination to appeal.

Is it any wonder, when wardens are offered incentives from flat-screen televisions to foreign holidays to ticket every car in Christendom? We'd be outraged if we thought the police were being bribed to frame certain types of criminals (although most of us wouldn't object to the odd iPod or plasma TV if we thought it might persuade the Old Bill to take burglary and car theft seriously).

Yet councils have colluded in this semi-criminal enterprise. As long as the town hall gets a fat slice, they'll turn a blind eye to the widespread abuse. They will also make parking restrictions as arcane and perverse as possible to maximise revenues. No two yellow lines are ever the same. The time of day you can park, the side of the road you can park: it changes from week to week, with the expressed intention of tricking motorists. It is entrapment, pure and simple. And if these weren't crimes of strict liability, a court would throw them out.

Red routes, temporary parking bays, cameras. As soon as we get behind the wheel, we put ourselves on offer. And the penalties bear no relation to the so-called 'crime'. Fines of £60 are commonplace for infringements which cause absolutely no obstruction to anyone, merely for stopping in a 'restricted' area drawn up on a whim by a bored council official with a box of crayons, simply to justify his miserable existence. Cowboy clampers demand up to £350 – more than a week's take-home pay for many people – to release confiscated (i.e. stolen) cars.

And, of course, none of this money goes towards mending the roads or making journeys any easier. It's frittered away on humps, chicanes, little red bricks, barriers and bare metal road-width 'restrictors' designed to rip the paintwork and wing mirrors off anything wider than a bubble car. Most of it goes on wages. Town hall traffic departments are stuffed with scruffy cycling enthusiasts, sexual inadequates, otherwise unemployable polytechnic graduates and certifiable, tree-hugging 'environmentalists'.

Their policies are dictated by misanthropic megalomaniacs such as Red Ken (London Mayor Ken Livingstone) and madwomen who believe everything they read in the *Guardian*. They have turned the streets of Britain into a giant crazy golf course, specifically designed to milk motorists and cause the maximum possible inconvenience to people trying to go about their lawful daily business.

How do these people sleep at night? Take officials like those in Derby who decided to prosecute Josephine Rooney for non-payment of council tax and the magistrates who thought it appropriate to send her to prison. Did they bask in the warm glow of satisfaction at a job well done, of law upheld, of justice triumphant? As they settled down with their families to watch the 2006 World Cup, did they for a moment spare a thought for the sixty-nine-year-old spinster thrown into prison alongside prostitutes, drug dealers and other common criminals?

You can argue that Miss Rooney didn't have to go to jail. She'd made her protest against the callous indifference and incompetence of her local authority, she'd got the publicity she craved. What useful purpose was served by getting herself incarcerated? The easiest thing would have been to pay her council tax and walk free to fight another day. But that's not always how it works. Logic and common sense go out of the window when someone is bent on martydom. Intransigence morphs into insanity.

So Miss Rooney got her day in court and her night in jail, until a benefactor paid her £798 arrears. No one with a shred of decency wants to see an elderly woman behind bars, especially when she was morally right (if legally wrong). I'd like to have thought that an anonymous Derby councillor, or council employee, would have paid her fine out of a deep sense of shame.

In case you missed it, Miss Rooney ended up in prison after witholding her tax because of the council's refusal to clean up her neighbourhood. Over the past few years, Hartington Street, Derby, a once respectable, clean-living district of working families, had been transformed into a boarded up, drug-infested hellhole; its traditional red-brick terraces reduced to stinking squats; its needle-strewn streets patrolled by crack-addict prostitutes desperate to earn a few quid for their next fix.

Like hundreds of other Hartington Streets all over Britain, Miss Rooney's inner-city sanctum was simply abandoned by the authorities, who compounded the problem by throwing money at absentee slum landlords, who exploit the misery of those who can find nowhere better to live. The police, as usual, have more pressing priorities.

There'll be a Hartington Street in your town, too, a place that society forgot. Think yourself lucky that, unlike Josephine Rooney, you don't have to live there.

For years, she had implored the council to do something – anything. They chose to do nothing. Eventually, in the only gesture she knew was guaranteed to attract their attention, she refused to pay her council tax. She played the Go Directly to Jail card.

And go to jail she did.

Derby Council could have sent a man round with a broom and a bin to sweep up the litter and collect the spent needles. They could have dispatched a squad to powerjet the graffiti off the walls. They could have had a word with the borough commander and asked him to send a panda car round to Hartington Street once in a blue moon. Miss Rooney would have paid up.

Instead they decided to take her to court. There's nothing these people like more than to make an example of a white, middle-aged member of the awkward squad. Look at us, they can argue, we uphold the rules without fear, favour or prejudice. No one is above the law.

If Miss Rooney was determined to play the martyr, the magistrates were happy to oblige. There's no conditional discharge for non-payment of council tax. No probation officer's reports, no community service, no suspended sentence, no automatic reduction in penalty for pleading guilty. No mitigating circumstances, no compassion, no second chance. If Miss Rooney had told the court lies, peddled them some sob story about being too hard up to pay, she'd have walked.

The council says it had no alternative but to prosecute.

Really?

The previous year, Derby Council failed to collect £3,777,000 in unpaid council tax. How many other defaulters have been dragged before the court? How many more have been sent to jail?

Precisely.

Across Britain, around £700 million is owed in council tax, especially in the Midlands and the North. Half the time, councils make no attempt to collect it. A baseball bat and a Rottweiler is usually sufficient to deter the collection process.

How many of the druggies, vagrants and prostitutes in Hartington Street are being pursued for non-payment of council tax?

Correct.

Miss Rooney's bad luck was to have a fixed abode, to have lived a blameless life, always previously having settled her bills on time. She is a net giver, both in the taxes she has paid and the voluntary service she has performed for the community, for which she has won an award from the Home Office. She is also a devout Christian. Would they have taken her to court had she been a devout Muslim?

Her crime was to challenge the powers that be, to demand that they keep their side of the social contract. And to refuse payment when they failed to live up to their end of the bargain. She was punished not for the sake of a few quid in unpaid council tax but to show her, and us, who's boss. How dare she tell Derby Council how to do their job? How dare she demand they clean up her street? Just pay up and shut up, pet.

Increasingly the law only applies to those who agree to live within the law. Much easier to prosecute a frail old lady than go after a violent crack addict.

Josephine Rooney was an embarrassment, a living, breathing reminder of the criminal neglect of the system. The old biddy just wouldn't keep her mouth shut, would she? Put your pinny on, luv, you're bleedin' nicked. And don't forget your toothbrush.

So she was handcuffed – *handcuffed* – and dragged off to jail to teach her a lesson. What did they think she was going to do: pull a knife, stab a guard and have it away over the wall?

Then there was the case of eighty-one-year-old Beryl Withers, fined £50 for the heinous crime of feeding the birds. Mrs Withers was scattering a few breadcrumbs for the pigeons in her home town of Nottingham (is there something in the water in the East Midlands?) when she was upbraided by two council wardens.

Mrs Withers had just finished her lunchtime sandwich and rather than throw away the morsels which remained, she decided to throw them to the birds. Having done that she even put the bag in the nearest litter bin. The wardens demanded her name and address, told her she was breaking the law and threatened her with a £2,000 fine. Two days later she received a fixed penalty notice in the post, alleging that she had been 'seen emptying the contents of a bag to feed the pigeons'. She said the birds cleared up the crumbs in the time it took the wardens to take down her details.

Mrs Withers, a policeman's daughter, was outraged, having never been in trouble with the law in her life. Understandably, she said it would break her late father's heart to see 'the powers that be concentrating on defenceless people like me instead of tackling proper crime'.

Mrs Withers is a paragon of selfless service, who skippered a naval postal vessel in the Channel during the war. Not that any of that would cut much ice with the charmless gauleiters of Nottingham. The council stood by its decision to punish her, claiming: 'Dropping food represents a health risk. It attracts rats.' She'd hardly strewn half-eaten pizza over the pavement. And if there were any rats around, they were out of luck. The pigeons beat them to it.

Nottingham is the murder capital of Britain and plagued with burglary, robbery, rape and gun crime. Yet the council choses to concentrate its 'resources' on bullying little old ladies. Where do they find these wardens and what, exactly goes on in their heads? Have they no sense of discretion or natural justice?

Some people complain that all this is 'unBritish'. Sorry to shatter your illusions, but this is very British indeed. Very New Labour British. As British as shopping your neighbours for breaking the hosepipe ban and as British as Eastbourne Council fining shop-keepers £75 if a seagull tears open their rubbish bags. It wouldn't occur to the council to provide more dustbins. Punishment is always the weapon of first resort. It's about showing us who's boss.

Since the collapse of socialism, all those who once thought they could rule us through nationalisation and trades union bullying have decamped into local government, the health service, 'safety camera partnerships' and dozens of other agencies which they manipulate to control our lives by other means.

As I said, we now live in a punishment culture, established to feed the voracious appetite of politicians and public sector employees for power and privilege. In another time and another place, jobsworths like this would have been making sure the cattle trucks to Auschwitz ran on time.

They must have missed that bit about being the servants, not the masters.

6 | And Coming Up After Tony Blair

Blair has always been obsessed by television. In February 2005, channel Five gave over a whole day to Blair. He turned up on *The Wright Stuff*, the *Five News* lunchtime bulletin and the *Five News* programme at 5.30pm. There was also an hour-long special, *Talk to the Prime Minister*. This got me wondering what the TV listings would be like if every other network fell into the hands of New Labour.

BBC1

6.00am   Breakfast with Blair

In this special Vote Labour edition, Tony is joined by the prime minister. Not for viewers of a weak disposition or those nursing a hangover.

10.00am   Mandy Pandy

Mandy arranges passports for his funny foreign friends, the Hinduja brothers, with hilarious consequences. Also starring Reinaldo as Teddy and Alastair Campbell as Looby Loo.

11.30am   Treasure Hunt

Continuing the search for weapons of mass destruction in Iraq.

1.00pm   BBC News

Live from Millbank. Your newsreader is Tony Blair, producer Peter Mandelson.

1.40pm   Neighbours

Grumpy Gordon fails in his attempt to get the troublesome family next door evicted.

2.35pm   Murder, She Wrote

Feature-length edition. The curious case of Dr David Kelly, a government scientist who is found dead in a rural beauty spot. Everything points to suicide, but Jessica suspects foul play.

5.35pm   Neighbours
Tension mounts as Gordon tells Tony that he doesn't believe a word he says any more.

6.00pm   BBC News
Includes a special report on how the Tories cause cancer.

7.00pm   Holiday 2005
A perfect vacation for a hard-up family with four children and a live-in mother-in-law. Tonight the Blairs from London sample a five-star hotel in Egypt and stay at the castle of an Italian count, all for nothing.

7.30pm   EastEnders
A knees-up in the Queen Vic as Tony unveils his bid to bring the 2012 Olympics to Walford, only to discover his moment of glory has been scuppered by Dirty Ken, who compares the Israeli IOC delegate to a 'concentration camp guard'.

8.00pm   Ground Force
Charlie Dimmock leads the assault on the 'holy city' of Fallujah and builds a new gazebo in the central mosque.

9.00pm   Have I Got News For You
Presented by Boris Johnson. Ian and Paul are joined by Kimberly Quinn and Petronella Wyatt.

9.30pm   Life of Grime
A fly-on-the-wall look at how the Conservatives are to blame for the germs and disease which lurk inside Britain's hospitals, killing thousands of patients every year. Presented by a fly on the wall.

10.00pm   BBC News
Featuring a special investigation by Alastair Campbell into secret Tory plans to slaughter the firstborn.

10.35pm   Question Time
Chaired tonight by Alastair Campbell. The prime minister faces a series of tough questions from carefully selected members of the Labour Party.

12.05am   Badger Watch
Live from Clapham Common, your host is Ron Davies.

BBC2

6.00am   **CBeebies**
Presented by Tony Blair and the Koala Brothers.

7.45am   **Looney Tunes**
More wacky emails from Alastair Campbell. Today, Alastair tells everyone to f*** off.

7.55am   **Newsround**
Everyone's favourite uncle, Peter Mandelson, presents a special edition in which all Tories are exposed as child molesters.

11.00am   **Young Indiana Jones Chronicles**
Tony Blair as Indiana saves the world from international terrorism and the Tories.

12.30pm   **Working Lunch**
Cherie Blair explains how you can make a bundle from a children's cancer charity simply by giving a short after-dinner speech.

2.00pm   **FILM: Doctor In Trouble** (1979–97)
Every hospital in Britain is closed down due to Tory spending cuts. Starring Charles Clarke as Sir Lancelot Spratt, the evil pizza-loving consultant surgeon.

4.35pm   **Snooker**
Tony Blair executes the perfect 147 break before beating Jimmy White to become world champion.

8.00pm   **Top Gear**
Presented by Richard Brunstrom, chief constable of North Wales. In tonight's 'star in a reasonably priced car' John Prescott road tests the latest £70,000 saloon from Jaguar, which is being delivered to one of his four homes next week.

9.00pm   **The Million Pound Property Experiment**
Cherie Blair explains how it is possible to lose a fortune simply by selling at the bottom of the market and buying at the top. Tonight's edition features a house in central London which has dropped £500,000 overnight. Presented by Two Poofs and a Paintbrush.

10.00pm What The Tories Did For Us

In this edition, Alan Hart-Milburn explains how Mrs Thatcher bankrupted Britain, closed thousands of schools and hospitals, burned down council estates and put up income tax to 105 pence in the pound for the poor, while letting the rich get away with paying nothing at all.

10.30pm Newsnight

Presented by Tony Blair, who interviews Peter Mandelson, Alastair Campbell and Alan Milburn about why no one should ever vote Conservative again.

ITV1

6.00am GMTV

Tony Blair and Lorraine Kelly are joined on the sofa by the prime minister's wife, who talks about healing crystals and how a positive approach to cancer can make you better off.

9.25am Trisha

Presented by Patricia Hewitt. Today's topic: How The Wicked Tories Killed My Baybee.

10.25am This Morning

A celebrity edition, presented by husband and wife team Tony and Cherie Blair. They are joined in the shower by Carole Caplin, who gives them a rub-down with magic mud from the Amazon delta.

12.30pm ITV News

Alastair Campbell introduces a special report on how voting Tory will lead to your children being eaten by giant snakes.

1.00pm Everything Must Go

A leading politician's wife shows you how you can make money flogging unwanted gifts on eBay.

2.00pm I Want That House

A lady barrister walks round central London pointing at houses she can't afford. Presented by Cherie Blair and Andy from *Little Britain*.

3.00pm Hot Property

The perils of buy-to-let. How using a convicted conman to pay through the nose for two flats in Bristol can come horribly unstuck. With Peter Foster.

3.45pm   **My Parents Are Aliens**

Damien (Leo Blair) begins to wonder if there is something a bit strange about his mum and dad.

5.00pm   **Today with Des and Mel**

Sitting in for Des and Mel tonight are celebrity couple Tony and Cherie Blair. They will interview themselves. Their fee will not be going to charity.

6.30pm   **ITV News**

With Alastair Campbell and Fiona Millar. Reporter Alan Milburn investigates how Conservative economic plans will lead to ten million unemployed and your house being repossessed the day after the election.

7.00pm   **Wish You Were Here**

Cherie Blair and her mum sample the delights of Cliff Richard's home in Barbados. Peter and Reinaldo fly to Brazil, where they practise the ancient ritual of choking the chicken.

8.00pm   **Who Wants To Be A Millionaire**

Special celebrity husband and wife edition. Tony and Cherie Blair answer difficult questions, including 'Any chance of exempting Formula One from the tobacco advert ban?'

9.00pm   **The Bill**

The fraud squad are called in to Sun Hill to investigate a £373,000 mortgage scam involving a well-known politician. Starring Peter Mandelson as himself.

10.00pm   **Neighbours From Hell**

A family with four children living in a central London terraced house tell of their ordeal at the hands of the deranged Scotsman next door, who paces the floor all night and keeps trying to force them to move out.

10.30pm   **ITV News**

Alastair Campbell presents an exposé of Michael Howard's secret life as a pimp, drug dealer and mass murderer.

11.00pm   **I'm A Prime Minister, Get Me Out Of Here**

Tony Blair has a panic attack after ordinary voters infiltrate a studio audience and start asking awkward questions. (Pick of the day.)

CHANNEL 4

6.05am   Mandy's Muppets

6.10am   The Dupes

7.30am   Friends of Peter

8.00am   Everybody Loves Reinaldo

8.25am   King of Queens

8.55am   Grace and Favour

9.30am   FILM: Passport to Pimlico (2005)
Crazy crime caper which follows the progress of a busload of Albanian gangsters posing as asylum seekers who obtain fake UK passports and set up a brothel and protection racket business in a Pimlico council house, courtesy of British taxpayers. Directed by David Blunkett.

2.15pm   Name Your Price
How two Indian businessmen came to receive British citizenship after making a sizeable donation to the Millennium Dome.

4.00pm   A Place In The Sun
Tony and Cherie Blair explain how you can beat those airport queues and save a fortune by using the RAF to fly to your holiday destination.

5.00pm   Richard and Judy
Standing in tonight are Tony and Cherie Blair. See all other channels. Cherie asks: 'Can you make the cheque out to cash?'

7.00pm   Channel 4 News
With Jon Snow. No change to scheduled programme.

8.00pm   Property Ladder
Kirsty and Phil follow one lucky couple who have managed to trade up from a humble Islington terrace, which they sold at a loss, to a magnificent £3.5 million mansion in exclusive Connaught Square – even though they have no money to pay the mortgage and can't find a tenant mug enough to cough up the extortionate rent.

10.00pm   Desperate Housewives

Tonight the housewives are desperate to get their children into the exclusive London Oratory school, only to find that all remaining places have been filled by the offspring of Labour politicians.

11.00pm   Shameless

A couple freeload their way around the world, even accepting money from a children's cancer charity to help pay their mortgage. Yet Tony still insists he's a pretty straight kinda guy.

Once again, I should have known better.

A few weeks later, the Right Honourable Anthony Charles Lynton Blair, First Lord of the Treasury and Prime Minister of the United Kingdom, successor to Walpole, Pitt and Churchill, graciously consented to appear on ITV, where he was to be interviewed by Little Ant and Dec.

Not even Ant and Dec – Little Ant and Dec, a pair of ten-year old boys best known for asking smutty questions of celebrities such as Pamela Anderson, of *Baywatch* and Internet porn fame.

Not only that, but the interview was actually requested by 10 Downing Street.

The most charitable explanation is that when Alastair Campbell suggested *Saturday Night Takeaway*, Blair thought he was going to ring out for a curry.

More likely, the Koala Brothers turned him down.

So Blair prepared to fire the starting gun for a crucial general election by exposing himself not to John Humphrys or Jeremy Paxman but to the forensic interrogation of two Year Six pupils from Gateshead on a teatime variety show.

I give up.

Just the previous Friday, I imagined it was only a matter of time before Blair jumped on the Jamie Oliver school meals bandwagon. *Sun* cartoonist Dave Gaskill drew Blair as the celebrity chef, whizzing round the country force-feeding healthy meals to unsuspecting schoolchildren. By the following Wednesday, Oliver had been invited to Downing Street to break croissants with Blair, who sat there chatting away in his best estuary and mugging for the cameras. He probably had to be restrained from slipping on a parka and a chef's hat.

Prime ministers have always gone in for phoney populism. More than thirty years before Blair invited Oasis to tea, Harold Wilson handed MBEs to the Beatles because he thought it would make him appear groovy.

But you can't imagine Darling Harold being interviewed by Pussy Cat Willum and Olly Beak on *Five O'Clock Club*. Jim Callaghan may have had a few problems with the press, but at least he didn't ring up *Tizwaz* and ask if he could go a couple of rounds with the Phantom Flan Flinger and Spit the Dog. And for all her media savvy, Mrs Thatcher managed to win three elections without the help of Tucker and Pogo off *Grange Hill*.

If Blair had been around in the 1960s he'd have turned up sitting in a flowerpot, chatting away with Bill and Ben.

On the Saturday before Blair was due to appear, Ant and Dec were hammered in the ratings by the return of *Doctor Who*. Despite this runaway success, actor Christopher Ecclestone said he wouldn't agree to a second series and the hunt was on for a new Doctor.

It wouldn't have surprised me if the BBC had received a call from Number 10 offering the services of You Know Who.

Or if Blair had turned up in a long scarf on the doorstep of the Tardis and announced that the next election was going to be held in the year 2525.

7 | What Do You Think Of It So Far?

Time was we put our rubbish out once a week, the dustmen took it away. End of story. Not any more. We now live in a brave, new, ozone-hugging, 'green is the new blue' world, in which every one of us is an Enemy of the Earth.

At least, that's how the politicians and the 'environmental services' Gestapo see us. In their lunatic zeal to establish their green credentials, the authorities have chosen to forget that their primary purpose is to empty the bins and take the refuse away. They are all Green Avengers now, self-righteous defenders of the environment, with grandiose titles plucked from the *Guardian*'s jobs pages.

Householders are not regarded as paying customers – we are all potential polluters. Inside every dustbin lurks not just the remains of last night's dinner, or an empty sauce bottle, but a clear and present danger to the future of the planet.

We are all criminals. And we must be punished severely, just like Donna Chalice, who found herself facing a £1,000 fine for not separating her household waste properly.

Mrs Chalice, a harassed mother of three young children, from Exeter, committed the heinous crime of mixing her paper waste and her aluminium foil in the same bag. Or was it her cereal packets and potato peelings? It doesn't matter, madam. Take your pinny off, you're bleedin' nicked.

Mike Trim, from Exeter Council, said Mrs Chalice had been warned before about chucking everything in the same bin. He said they were reluctant to prosecute, but had no choice in this case.

Rubbish. They love it. There's nothing these tinpot tyrants enjoy more than throwing their weight about, showing us who's boss. Dragging Mrs Chalice before a court like a common criminal was the crowning achievement of Mike Trim's career. Whenever and wherever environmental health officers gather over half a pint of organic ale, the toast will be 'Mike Trim'. He really showed the bastards, didn't he?

Take the case of TV editor Alison McNally who wanted to know what she was supposed to do with the carcass of a roast chicken she'd just eaten, given that the dustmen had been and wouldn't be back for another fortnight, because her council, like hundreds of others, had halved the number of refuse collections to concentrate on recycling – in line with government targets laid down by the EU.

After all, if she left it in the bin for two weeks it would soon smell worse than Mark Oaten's briefcase. If she put it outside, the place would be crawling with vermin in about five minutes. Foxy-woxy would think Alison had opened a KFC especially for him. Soon the wheelie bin would be lying on its side and there'd be bones everywhere – not to mention everything else she'd thrown out being strewn all over the shop.

So Alison rang the refuse department. She got through to 'environmental services officer' Paul Redmond, at Waverley Council, in Surrey. He told her that perhaps it wasn't such a good idea to eat fish or chicken so soon after the dustmen had called. However, he added, helpfully: 'If you find yourself having a roast dinner right after a collection, you can put the carcass in the freezer and move it to the bin when collection day comes around again.'

Brilliant. If we all took his advice and filled our freezers with perishable leftovers, there'd be no room for anything else.

He didn't quite say: 'Don't you know we've got a planet to save, you stupid, selfish woman?' But he might just as well have done. If he had, he'd only have been articulating official policy.

Now, I'm not opposed in principle to recycling, even though I used to drive round Crouch End in a Citroen Dyane with a 'Nuclear Power, Yes Please' sticker in the back window, just to wind up the local branch of Greenpeace. (The 'Nuke the Whales' T-shirt worked, too.)

Most of us do our bit, to a greater or lesser extent. We accept that recycling is desirable, even though less of it would be necessary were it not for the excessive packaging insisted upon by another branch of government in the name of protecting the public. We never had all this junk when we bought our groceries loose and our screws by the pound, not in hermetically sealed packets of five.

We try to remember to put paper and glass in the receptacles provided. I throw out enough newspapers every week to keep all the members of London's rough-sleepers community in bedding for a year. And I'm their best customer down at the local bottle bank.

But we're all fallible. Harassed mums haven't always got the time to sift through the contents of their pedal bins. Older people get confused, especially when there are different rules for papers, magazines and cardboard.

Councils should make allowances. Instead, they employ inspectors to sift through our rubbish and hand out on-the-spot fines to anyone who mistakenly or otherwise puts a tea bag in the wrong sack. Some councils issue transparent refuse sacks so they can spot in an instant a rogue nappy or wine bottle. They then tear open the bags and scatter the litter all over the street to gather the evidence to confront the offender. Most of this is just posing, although you should never underestimate the sheer, almost sexual excitement public 'servants' get from punishing the people who pay their wages. If they really cared about pollution, they'd make more effort to clear up all the fridges, mattresses and burned-out cars dumped everywhere and take a tougher line on illegal Gipsy sites and their ubiquitous, attendant rubbish dumps, which scar our green-and-pleasant. They might even get round to sweeping the streets once in a while.

But they don't. That would be too much like hard work. So they do what government always does, whether it's the Traffic Taliban or the Child Support Agency – they go after the law-abiding majority, they police those who consent to be policed.

Environmentalism has been elevated to the status of a new religion. It allows people to behave appallingly in the name of a good cause. There's a nutter living near a colleague of mine who takes a knife to everyone's bin bags to inspect them for the 'wrong' kind of refuse. If he finds any of his neighbours trying to sneak an empty bottle of washing-up liquid in with their biodegradable waste, he goes berserk and reports them to the council. Someone like this should be sectioned, not encouraged. Either that, or dragged into the street and clubbed like a baby seal. The current obsession with environmental issues borders on mental illness. Stupidity and bloody-mindedness is the default setting. It's glaringly obvious that cutting rubbish collections is not only a gross dereliction of duty but a serious threat to public health and comfort.

The refuse department used to come under 'sanitation' for the simple reason that leaving leftover food and assorted detritus hanging around is unsanitary and creates a breeding ground for germs and disease. Even in a sealed plastic sack, a few days is about the optimum time it's sensible to leave household waste before its starts to putrefy, giving off noxious smells and attracting maggots, flies and rats. That's why we had weekly collections in the first place, back when councils employed sanitary inspectors in peaked caps to ensure the rubbish was picked up and disposed of as quickly and hygienically as possible.

Today, the town halls are packed with graduates of pretend 'universities' who think merely emptying dustbins is beneath them. They produce strategies and leaflets. They look on themselves not as public servants, but as our masters.

The current obsession with recycling is just another manifestation of our punishment culture. The paying public are there to be regulated, bossed around and fined at every available opportunity. They're even putting microchips in our wheelie bins to keep tabs on us.

Councils need to be reminded that they work for us, not the other way round. The system should be run for our convenience, not theirs. If they want to be certain that everything that can be recycled is recycled, they can take their 'environmental services officers' off fatuous hotlines, give them a pair of rubber gloves, overalls and a mask and send them down the tip to make themselves useful picking out anything we may have missed.

But it ain't gonna happen. What we've got instead is a recipe for filthy streets full of chicken bones and an epidemic of fly-tipping.

The tragedy of all this is that it has soured relationships between the public and the dustmen, genuine public servants who perform a real service, who through no fault of their own have been forced into the frontline. More than one in five dustmen say they have been verbally or physically abused on their rounds. In 2005, they were on the brink of a national strike.

Rose Conroy, of the dustmen's union, the GMB, said: 'More binmen are getting beaten up and the incidents are getting more violent. People are ending up in hospital now. The binman's job used to be so straightforward. Rubbish wasn't divided and you could leave what you liked. People get angry when rubbish is left behind, because they've paid their tax.'

Precisely.

Collecting the rubbish at least once a week, every week, should always, always, take priority over the notion of recycling. Refuse collection should be the horse, not the cart.

Mandy Gregory became so sick of staring at her overflowing dustbins that she bought her own dustcart. It cost her £8,000 and she decided to offer a private refuse service to hundreds of friends and neighbours in Telford, Shropshire. Mandy was livid at her local council's refusal to collect household rubbish more than once a fortnight. So she and her husband, Gordon, took matters in to their own hands and plan to charge residents £3 a week to empty their bins.

Mandy said: 'People resent paying the council for a service that is not good enough. There have been loads of complaints. Bins are overflowing and people are having to bag up their own rubbish and take it down to the tip themselves. There are huge queues and you sometimes have to wait an hour to dump it.'

And how did Telford and Wrekin Borough Council react? As soon as the town hall heard about Mandy's little scheme, they sacked hubby Gordon, who had been working as a council binman and banned Mandy's new firm from handling council-issue wheelie bins.

You might have thought that the chief dustman – who probably calls himself something like Director of Environmental Enhancement and gets paid around £75,000 a year – would have resigned in shame.

You couldn't be more wrong. To justify his salary, the Director of Environmental Enhancement has to come up with a grand strategy. When the job was chief dustman or clerk of works, his only role would be to make sure the dustbins got emptied.

But now he's far too important for that. There are consultative groups, heads-up meetings, pie charts, working parties, action plans, implementation procedures, targets to be monitored, risk assessments to be carried out and environmental impact studies to be commissioned.

That's before the gender assertiveness training and the diversity and inclusivity programme to ensure best practice across a range of accountability modules in a barrier-free, no smoking workplace situation. Actually emptying the bins once a week – which is what he's paid for, after all – only gets in the way of the grand design. Burbling on about landfill and recycling targets, a council spokesman said: 'Initiatives like this really undermine what we are trying to do.'

This madness has crept up on us by stealth. No one voted for it. Can you imagine any party standing for election on the pledge: Vote for us and we'll double your taxes and halve your rubbish collections?

Of course not.

This policy has never been through a democratic process, it's designed to give 'environmental services officers' in non-jobs something to do, while at the same time showing us who's boss.

It means that instead of flipping burgers, which is about all most of them would otherwise be qualified for, they can go home at night feeling good about themselves.

This is how government evolved in Blair's Brave New Britain. Those who run what are laughably called the public 'services' have forgotten what they are there for in the first place.

You'd get better service in an Albanian airport cafeteria.

If you want anything done you either have to do what Mandy Gregory has done and do it yourself, or pay someone for a service which you are already paying your taxes for but no one can be bothered to provide.

What do you think of it so far?

Rubbish.

8 | A Land Fit for Jobsworths

Ever since the end of the Second World War and the defeat of Nazi Germany, we've liked to comfort ourselves with the thought: it couldn't happen here.

Oh yes it could. In a heartbeat.

Britain is crawling with the kind of people who would have been queuing up to collaborate had the Germans successfully invaded. There are some stories which make me so angry, I want to fix bayonets and charge. This was one of them.

In 1940, a flotilla of small ships set sail from Britain to rescue 340,000 Allied troops trapped on the beaches at Dunkirk. Sixty years later, John Everett, a boat owner on the River Thames, decided that he too wanted to commemorate the heroism of the men and women involved in the evacuation. Without them, the Second World War would almost certainly have been lost in 1940. Mr Everett planned to erect a plaque in honour of the late Douglas Tough, a Teddington boat builder, who commandeered over a hundred private boats and sent them to Dunkirk.

But when he submitted his plans to the Environment Agency, they were rejected on the grounds that any wording referring to war or victory was 'inappropriate'.

Some ludicrous jobsworth who signed himself 'CJ Woodward, Recreation Officer', informed Mr Everett that the inscription could offend foreigners.

It would have read: 'This operation was called Dynamo. It saved our country, enabling us to go on to victory in 1945.' CJ Woodward also ruled that the proposed heading on the plaque, 'Second World War', was 'not acceptable'.

I have no idea what the C in CJ Woodward actually stands for. I shall leave it to your imagination.

'Inappropriate' is one of those weasel words bureaucrats and politicians, particularly on the fascist left, use when they want to smother the truth and censor free speech. I'm certain CJ didn't get where he is today by using 'inappropriate' language. But I'd love to know what was 'inappropriate' about the wording on the plaque. And precisely why the words 'Second World War' were 'not acceptable'.

Not acceptable to whom, exactly? Given that Dunkirk not only took place during the Second World War but actually affected the outcome of the war, I would have thought that a heading 'Second World War' was accurate, acceptable and wholly appropriate.

But CJ refused permission because: 'Teddington is an important arrival point from foreign ports.'

No it's not.

And anyway, who could possibly be offended by a memorial to the men and women involved in the Dunkirk rescue? Is there a cell of former members of the Waffen SS living on a houseboat in Teddington?

I was about to ask where they find berks like CJ, but I already know the answer. They get them out of the jobs pages of the *Guardian*.

There are legions of people on the public payroll who seem to do nothing else except seek out and take offence on behalf of others, where no offence exists. They appear to hate their own country and miss no attempt to rewrite or erase our history.

CJ is out of the same mould as the Havering Council flag police, who the same week banned the Union Jack from buildings in the borough. I am delighted to report that traders on Romford market decided to respond to that ban by flying the flag from every stall.

John Everett eventually reached a compromise deal with CJ and the plaque, in watered-down form, was officially unveiled in time for the anniversary. They should have marked the occasion by chucking CJ in the Thames.

Sometimes I can't help wondering what the men and women who went through the last war make of what has happened to the country and freedoms they fought to preserve. Did they really go through six years of hell to build a land fit for the likes of CJ Woodward and the flag police?

9 | A Private Matter

Labour used to scream to the high heavens about 'Tory sleaze'. And in the terminal years of the Conservative government there was plenty to scream about – the Mellorphant Man, Archer, Aitken and a few other long-forgotten miscreants.

But once Labour came to power, it was a different story. When a Tory minister was caught shagging his secretary it was always a resignation affair. But when the late Robin Cook, New Labour's first Foreign Secretary, was ordered by Alastair Campbell to choose between his wife and his parliamentary assistant – Glorious Gaynor, as I will always think of her – Downing Street insisted it was a 'private matter'.

In case you forgot, Cookie chose Gaynor. He dumped his wife in the departure lounge at Heathrow. Who said chivalry was dead?

When a Conservative MP was caught with a rent boy (or a woman other than his wife) it was a national disgrace. When the same thing happens with a Labour (or Liberal, for that matter) member, it's a 'personal tragedy'.

Blunkett and Two Jags get chapters of their own, but they weren't the only ones.

There could have been no more graphic illustration of the new climate of hypocrisy than the reaction when it was revealed the Labour MP Clive Betts was having an affair with a rent boy called José Gasparo, whom he picked up in a smelly homosexual brothel called Villa Gianni and was employing him as a parliamentary researcher. It ranged from indifference to indignation.

Predictably, the BBC – which filled its boots with stories about 'Tory sleaze' – ignored it completely. The *Guardian* even cited it as grounds for a new privacy law.

Now there's a surprise.

I couldn't care less what consenting adults get up to behind closed doors, provided I don't have to watch, participate or pay for it through my taxes. This case breached the third of those cardinal principles. Betts put his rent boy on the public payroll as a researcher. He also tried to get him a Commons pass. That is a fundamental abuse of office by an MP. Just as it was when Tory MP David Shaw hired hooker Pamella Bordes as his researcher a few years ago.

There was all hell to pay over the Shaw story. And rightly so. Yet many of the same people who were screaming blue murder about 'Tory sleaze' back then either kept their mouths shut or attacked those newspapers for having the audacity to publish the Betts revelations.

They tried to turn this sordid tale into an issue about Betts' sexuality – just as they did when George Michael was arrested for masturbating in a public toilet in Los Angeles.

(As I asked at the time: what if George Michael had done it in the ladies?) But this wasn't about sexuality, it was about proper behaviour and morality. Did Betts' constituents want their MP shacked up with a Brazilian rent boy, thirty years his junior, whom he picked up in a filthy knocking shop in one of the less salubrious parts of London? Is it right that an MP should employ his rent-boy lover as a researcher at taxpayers' expense and attempt to get him a Commons security pass?

There were other legitimate questions, too. On what grounds was Gasparo living in Britain? Are we so short of rent boys that we have to import them? Did Clive Betts make any attempts to pull strings to gain permission for Gasparo to stay here?

And while we're at it, what is it about Brazilian boys? I've always associated 'having a Brazilian' with Essex wives, not Labour MPs.

All of these questions we were perfectly entitled to ask. We had a no more satisfactory answer than we did to the question about whether Peter Mandelson's Brazilian boyfriend was given special treatment because he was the lover of a prominent Labour politician.

I said time and again that I would have been asking the same questions had Mandelson been a Tory minister and Reinaldo a Brazilian flamenco dancer called Reinalda.

The same applies to Betts.

Can you imagine how those who claimed 'it's all about his sexuality' would have been howling if this were a fifty-three-year-old Conservative backbencher and a scuzzy, twenty-year-old hooker he picked up at the back of King's Cross station?

Then there was Ron 'Badger' Davies, once a power in the land of his fathers. Secretary of state for Wales, leader of the Welsh assembly, member of the Welsh assembly. He had it all. If ever a man was the product of his genes, it was Ron. And, yet, in a moment of madness, he threw it all away.

At the height of his powers, Ron went for a walk on Clapham Common and ended up having sex with a Rastafarian. Later he was to be found cruising a notorious gay pick-up spot off the M4 and was photographed fondling a forty-eight-year-old Scouse builder. Ron insisted that he wasn't looking for love, he was spotting badgers.

Even today, you can't mention either Clapham Common or badgers around Westminster without bringing the house down.

Ron then got caught for a third time, looking for rough trade in a park in Wales. He claims to have been birdwatching. The one thing he wasn't looking for was birds. And it wasn't a woodpecker he had in his hand.

Three strikes and he was out. Shortly afterwards, he announced he would not be seeking re-election in Caerphilly. Ron eventually made a comeback, as director of the Race Equality Council in Pontypridd. Lovely, tidy, smashing. Perhaps his brief encounter with Rastafarian Donald Fearon on Clapham Common will help him get to grips with the ethnic minorities.

But it's not as if he's got his work cut out. Pontypridd is hardly a seething cauldron of racial turmoil. The constituency is 98.8 per cent white. Still, he'll have plenty of spare time to check out the local badger community.

A couple of years later, we discovered that Ron wasn't the Only Gay in the Valleys. Chris Bryant, Labour MP for Rhondda, posted a picture of himself, wearing only his underpants, on a homosexual dating agency website. It was a self-portrait taken in his bathroom using a digital camera. Bryant sent the picture along with a string of obscene emails to a man he had never met and whose name he did not know.

One of the messages read: 'I'd love a good long f***.' Another said: 'Horny bastard – u interested in playing around?' Another: 'Oi, mate – so you want to come and f*** around?'

All right then, you smooth-talking devil. Bryant described himself as:

> Fit bloke here. Gym 3x a week – bright, solvent, single, very versatile – 32w 42c, 5'11" – 41 yo – look younger (yeah, they all say that) – live maida vale w9 – u?

The emails became more explicit, as Bryant discussed sexual preferences and arranged to meet the man in a gay bar in Soho. He said the man will probably have another 'mate' with him, but says he 'will be looking for a shag'. Bryant adds: 'If my mate does show, don't you get pissy!'

Nice to know the art of romance isn't dead.

Bryant eventually invites the man to his home. And that, children, is where we will draw a discreet veil over the relationship.

There's nothing illegal about this curious, cold-blooded form of courtship. I've no doubt thousands of people are at it. But they're not Members of Parliament, who should be held to a higher standard. MPs are lawmakers and their private behaviour matters.

Call me old-fashioned, but is this really a way for an MP to behave?

Yet again, I must emphasise that I'd be saying the same thing if it were a heterosexual or woman MP. Can you imagine the unimpeachable Ann Widdecombe posing in nothing but her bloomers on a dating agency website and sending a stream of 'take me now, big boy' emails to a complete stranger? Or Bunter Soames looking for love in cyberspace buck naked but for a posing pouch in the regimental colours of the Hussars?

Precisely.

Chris Bryant always struck me as personable but precious. What he gets up to on the keyboard of his laptop or behind the closed doors of his Maida Vale love palace is arguably his own business, provided it doesn't involve children or farm animals. He's as entitled to a sex life as the next man.

Where his sexuality does have an impact is on his professional behaviour. Bryant was one of the most vociferous campaigners for the legalisation of 'cottaging' – gay sex in public toilets. Given his own predilection for picking up complete strangers for casual sex, he clearly has a vested interest in the matter.

How would Bryant have reacted, for instance, if a Tory MP who happened to be, say, a property developer, was campaigning actively for special tax concessions for the building industry?

I think we can guess.

*

There have been some priceless 'private matters' and 'personal tragedies' over the years – most recently the antics of Liberal Democrat MP Mark Oaten.

It's difficult to get too sanctimonious when you can't stop laughing. And whatever else there is to say about the Oaten affair, it was hilarious. I defy anyone to discover that an MP has been indulging in a 'bizarre sex act too revolting to describe' and still manage to keep a straight face.

It's best not to speculate. What we do know, courtesy of one of the rent boys involved, is that Oaten was already taking part enthusiastically in a three-in-a-bed gay sex session when he decided to ask his partners in passion to 'degrade' him.

Call me naive, but in these circumstances where, precisely, on a scale of one to ten, does degradation kick in? Some of us might think that a seedy threesome with two male prostitutes in a squalid south London flat was pretty degrading to begin with. Apparently not. It was merely an 'error of judgement'.

No it wasn't. An error of judgement is leaving home without an umbrella when the weather forecast predicts an eighty-five per cent chance of rain. It's taking a corner ten miles an hour too fast and scuffing your alloys on the kerb.

What it isn't is paying £140 to be humiliated by two rent boys, especially if you plan running for the leadership of one of the three great parties of state.

You might venture the opinion that it is no way for any married father of two to behave, let alone a prominent MP who trades on his commitment to family values. Once again we were told this is a private matter and we mustn't be judgemental.

For once, just once, wouldn't it be refreshing to hear an MP caught with his trousers down or his fingers in the till coming straight out with a statement along the lines of:

> My behaviour has been an absolute disgrace. I am thoroughly ashamed of myself. I am offering no excuses. What I did was despicable. I am resigning from my seat and you will never hear from me again.

Instead we get weasel words about lapses of judgement and 'personal tragedy'.

A personal tragedy is something you are powerless to prevent, such as losing a loved one – not paying rent boys for sex.

You might have thought that someone in Oaten's position would have crawled off into a hole, never to be seen again. Or at least done a bit of penance.

There's never any question of disgraced modern politicians doing a Profumo and disappearing from public life to devote themselves to good works. Needless to say, within a few weeks, he turned up on *Newsnight*, riding round London in the back of a taxi talking about his 'error of judgement' and appearing on daytime chat shows.

His wife ended up selling her side of the story to the newspapers. She turned her husband's 'shame' into – dare I say it? – a cottage industry and seems to consider herself some kind of freelance agony aunt.

(Incidentally, a reader from Corby wrote asking me to settle a bet. They were having a sweep in his local on what the 'bizarre sex act too revolting to describe' could possibly be. I wrote back saying that I couldn't be too specific but Oaten had fallen between two stools. 'Thanks, Richard,' he replied, 'you've just won me £30.')

★

One of the funniest 'scandals' involved old Labour stalwart Joe Ashton, former MP for Bassetlaw, who was caught with his trousers down in an East Midlands brothel miles from his constituency when it was raided by police and immigration officials.

He claimed he was driving home when he got a stiff back and pulled off the motorway for a massage.

Joe maintained his presence was entirely innocent. In which case, I wondered, why didn't he take his back trouble to an osteopath, rather than a Thai knocking shop called the Siam Sauna? He refused to elaborate on reports that he engaged in the 'body to body' massage which was the speciality of the house. Perhaps he pulled off the motorway in search of bang-bang chicken and stumbled mistakenly into the wrong establishment. Maybe he thought the 69 was beef satay.

When he was offered 'two together' he may have thought he was being invited to buy a couple of tickets for Northampton Town's next home game.

We have it on the word of no less an authority than the former receptionist at the Siam Sauna, Miss Laura MacNess, that Mr Ashton had visited the establishment not once, but seven times. He always requested the £40 'naturist massage'. This involved sharing a bath with one of the girls, followed by a quick rub-down. Miss MacNess was unable to confirm whether or not any extras were involved.

So only Mr Ashton and the masseuse in question know exactly what happened behind closed doors – and she legged it back to Thailand. Mr Ashton would not enlighten us, although he insisted that nothing sexual had occurred. I suppose it all depends on how you define 'nothing sexual' and whether having a bath with a naked young Thai prostitute falls into that category.

He went to extraordinary lengths to conceal the truth. He even issued a statement blaming absolutely everyone but himself – the press, the police, the Data Protection Agency, Uncle Tom Cobbleigh. It concluded: 'I have nothing more to say and I hope this will now bring the media harassment to an end.'

Of course, it didn't.

As sleaze scandals go, this one fell a long way short of the standards set by Profumo and the Duchess of Argyll in the 1960s.

Labour's sexual miscreants are so unimaginative. You might just have forgiven Joe if he'd been discovered trussed up in a Belgravia dungeon, being whipped with a copy of *Tatler* by a minor member of the aristocracy. At least it would have shown some initiative.

Joe Ashton always struck me as a fairly preposterous figure. He might be Two Jags' long-lost brother. There are similarities between them, most notably the complete absence of any sense of the ridiculous. This is a man who was happy to take money off a downmarket tabloid for what passed as a column, yet was constantly demanding laws restricting what he defines as media intrusion.

One thing Ashton never struck me as was an innocent abroad, although I may have misjudged him. Perhaps he's the sort of man who rings a woman advertising French lessons on a card in a phone box and turns up expecting her to help him conjugate a few verbs. He might dial a Danish dental nurse, operating out of a tenement in King's Cross, in the naive hope that she will give him a good flossing.

Then again, he might hand over £40 in used notes to a woman specialising in punishment and correction and ask her to give him a hundred lines.

I remember remarking at the time that Joe must be the only man who ever went to a Thai massage parlour for a massage.

Eventually he did issue a statement in which he admitted lying to the police. He told them he was sixty-four, when his true age was sixty-five.

'I did knock six months off my age. I had just become an old-age pensioner and like other well-known faces who get to sixty-four and are still working I decided to stay there.'

You know where this is going, don't you? I couldn't resist it.

When I get older
Losing the plot
Any moment now,
Will you still be sending me to Parliament?
Select committees?
Paying my rent?
If I'm discovered down on all fours
With a Siamese whore,
Would you believe me?
Would she still knead me?
If I say I'm sixty-four.

If I'm arrested
During a raid
By the CID,
I could always offer them a false address
That might get me
Out of this mess.
Then if the story appears in the *Sun*
I could blame the law,
They shouldn't have leaked it
'Cos nobody tweaked it
The member for Bassetlaw.

10 | Underneath the Archer

After a decade of Labour lies, deceit and downright corruption, it's almost enough to make one nostalgic for the good old days of Tory sleaze, Tory sleaze, Tory sleaze. Not that Tory sleaze ever went away completely, as we were reminded when Jeffrey Archer got himself sent to prison for perjury after being convicted of lying in court during his libel action over newspaper revelations about his relationship with the prostitute Monica Coghlan – who worked under the nom-de-tom Debbie Nipples.

It was a denouement worthy of one of Archer's potboilers.

J EFFREY ARCHER took a sip from a Waterford crystal flute of his favourite vintage Krug and placed the glass gently on the polished surface of his Chippendale trophy cabinet. His lifetime achievements were arrayed before him. His Nobel Peace Prize, his Rugby World Cup winner's medal, the small urn containing the Ashes presented to him after his series-winning double century and 10 for 0 in the Sydney Test. He picked up the Oscar he won for his starring role in *Chariots of Fire* and placed it closer to the silver-framed photograph of Marilyn Monroe, with its passionate dedication: 'To Jeffrey, the greatest lover I ever had,' written in lipstick across her ample bosom. Jeffrey turned away and gazed out over the spectacular 360-degree panorama from his apartment – to the north, the Houses of Parliament; to the east, the Eiffel Tower; to the west, the Statue of Liberty; to the south, Sydney Opera House.

He thought back to that steamy night in Barcelona, when his late hat-trick had secured an historic treble for Manchester United. He treasured that holy trinity of medals almost as much as the Victoria Cross he won at Dunkirk and the nine golds he brought home from the Tokyo Olympics.

Jeffrey topped up his drink and plucked a Twiglet from the golden urn given to him by a grateful Aga Khan after he had ridden his horse to victory in the Derby. He remembered his elation as he crossed the finishing line at Epsom. It had been almost as satisfying as the memorable night at Madison Square Garden when he knocked out Muhammad Ali in three rounds to take the world heavyweight title, before adjourning to the Rainbow Room in Manhattan to play trombone with the Duke Ellington Orchestra and sing a duet with Frank Sinatra. That had given him as big a buzz as the afternoon at Buckingham Palace in 1966 when Her Majesty the Queen had touched him lightly on each shoulder and commanded him: 'Arise, Sir Jeffrey' after he had captained England to victory in the World Cup Final at Wembley.

Oh, how they partied that hedonistic summer, Jeffrey, John, Paul, George and Ringo, Mick, Keith, Bill, Raquel, Ursula and Marianne. Thank God that business with the Mars Bar never came out, he smiled to himself.

Jeffrey thought back to the long nights at Abbey Road when he wrote, produced and performed every single track on *Sgt Pepper* because the rest of the Beatles were all out of their heads on acid. The tricks he had learned at Sun Studios, back in the days he discovered Elvis, were not forgotten.

And still today, where would Oasis be without him? Very few people knew that Noel wrote 'Wonderwall' in honour of the picture gallery on the wall of Jeffrey's oak-panelled study – Jeffrey with Gandhi, Jeffrey with Roosevelt, Jeffrey with Stalin, Jeffrey with Churchill. And, slap bang in the middle, pride of place went to Jeffrey with Tom Hanks in Los Angeles on the set of the hit movie based on Jeffrey's own life story – *Forrest Gump*.

Now here he was on the brink of his greatest political triumph. He had guided Attlee to a landslide victory in 1945, served under Winnie, Eden, Macmillan, Douglas-Home, Wilson, Heath, Wilson again, Callaghan, Thatcher, Major and had practically invented New Labour on his own. Soon the ultimate prize would be his – Mayor of London.

And yet, and yet. Maybe it was the champagne kicking in on an empty stomach, but he suddenly felt queasy. Why had he gone to such extraordinary lengths to impress? Why had he told so many lies? He really had been Britain's youngest Tory MP, at twenty-nine. He really was an Oxford blue and had recovered from financial ruin to become one of the world's best-selling authors. His books had brought pleasure to millions. He had a saint of a wife – 'fragrant', a judge had called her – a loving family, great wealth, beautiful homes, a peerage, more than enough for one man in one lifetime.

Yet he wanted more, always more. And the fools, the fools. They bought it. Even the Great Lady herself.

He never ceased to be amazed what people would do, what they would believe, in exchange for a glass of bubbly and a plate of shepherd's pie.

As he flipped open his mobile to call his broker and check his Anglia share portfolio, there was a ring on the doorbell. He could hear Liz Hurley pleading from the bedroom: 'Don't answer that, Jeffrey. Take me now big boy. Just once more, I beg you.' But he knew time was running out.

Jeffrey walked slowly across the Persian rug, pulling his silk Ralph Lauren dressing gown round his perfectly sculpted torso, honed by a personal trainer who had served under him in the SAS on the Iranian embassy siege.

As he opened the door, two men stood there. He could tell by their shiny suits, their grubby collars and their stale whisky breath they were either from Fleet Street or Scotland Yard.

'Lord Archer, Lord Jeffrey Archer?' said the older of the two.

'No,' said Jeffrey. 'Not me, guv. Never heard of him.'

11 | www.wwww.com
(The Wonderful World of the Wicked Witch)

'I want a word with you,' said the scary, familiar-looking woman bearing down on me under full sail.

It had been a decade since I'd bumped into the Wicked Witch socially, chez Campbell. I've tried to make it a rule to steer as clear as possible of hobnobbing with politicians once they achieve high office. In any event, for some unfathomable reason, my name seemed not to be on the Number 10 guest list after the Blairs moved in. Not that I'd ever been invited there by John Major, either.

Was it something I said?

In the normal course of events I give politicians a wide berth, but this was one of those occasions when fraternising with the enemy becomes unavoidable.

The occasion was the leaving do for David Yelland, who was off to America after five years editing the *Sun*, where I was writing a column. He'd invited along a couple of hundred of his closest friends from the worlds of media, politics and the used-car business.

While he was running the *Currant Bun*, David had inevitably become close to the Blairs (it was an occupational hazard for *Sun* editors after 1997), so I knew they'd be there. No problem. I'd seen Tony a few times since he became prime minister, and despite the bucketloads I'd tipped over his head in the column, he never seemed to take it personally. Even if he hated my guts, he kept it to himself. We're all grown-ups and we've got our jobs to do.

The foyer at the Commonwealth Foundation, off Pall Mall, was the usual scrum of sweating, braying hacks and politicians, throwing back cheap champagne, working the room. For a brief instant, I was alone. The Wicked Witch seized her opportunity. The conversation went something like this:

'I've been waiting to catch up with you,' she said.

'How very nice to see you again, Cherie,' I replied.

'Now then. Why are you so horrible to my husband?'

'Someone's got to do it,' I said, grabbing another glass of pop from a passing waiter.

'You don't have to be quite so nasty to Tony,' she came back.

'I'm not always,' I said, trying to be emollient. 'I've been sticking up for him over his support for George Bush.' At this, she formed the fingers of her right hand into a prong, like someone making the shape of a kestrel's beak at a magic lantern show. She then prodded me in the heart and made a buzzing sound, like an electric charge.

BZZZZZZZZZZZZZ.

I could see Tony watching what was going on with increasing alarm. He broke away from whoever he was talking to and hurried over, arriving at the same time as my wife, Wendy.

'Hi, Tony,' I greeted him with a warm handshake.

'Hi, Richard,' he said, before smiling at Wendy, shaking her hand and saying: 'Hello again, long time.'

The WW looked at Wendy and barked: 'Who are you? Are you something to do with him?' (Meaning me.)

'I'm his wife,' Wendy told her.

'Er, you remember, Cherie, we met . . .' Tony interceded.

'No,' said the WW.

'Good to see you again, really must be, er, you know. Shall we go upstairs to the reception, Cherie?'

'I'll join you up there,' she said dismissing him and turned back to me.

BZZZZZZZZZZZZZZZ.

It hit me again.

'Well, bye then.'

'Bye, Tony.'

As Blair was hustled away up the stairs by his security men, he turned back to me, shrugged his shoulders and rolled his eyes to the heavens, as if to say: 'Sorry, but you know what she's like.' The WW returned to the job in hand. By now I was aware that the three of us were on our own. The crowd had parted and a circle had formed around us, like a fight in a school playground.

Turning to Wendy, with all the warmth of a polar ice cap, the WW asked: 'Have you got a family?'

I could see where this one was going. Her eldest, Euan, had just gone to Bristol University and the WW had become involved in a scandal over using a convicted conman to strike a cut-price deal on a couple of flats near his college.

Needless to say, I'd had a field day. The WW has always jealously guarded her children's privacy and I'd ruthlessly lampooned her.

I was also led to believe that she wasn't exactly thrilled when I christened her late-in-life fourth baby 'Damien' (his real name's Leo). People had assumed that I got the name Damien from the spawn of the devil in the movie, *The Omen*. Actually, I got it from Del Boy's son in *Only Fools and Horses*. Still, why spoil a good story?

'Have you got a family?'

Wendy explained that, yes, we had two children.

'Don't you find it expensive, you know, putting them through education?' Wendy said that our daughter was already out at work and that because our son had trained as a chef and paid tax for a few years before going back into education, he qualified for a grant, so it wasn't a great burden on us.

'Which university is he at?' the WW asked.

'Cambridge,' said Wendy.

The WW gave her daggers.

'Yes,' I interrupted. 'He was offered a place at Bristol, but he turned it down because he had his heart set on Cambridge. And when they offered him a place, well, it would be rude not to, wouldn't it? There's no comparison.' Talk about a dagger to the heart.

BZZZZZZZZZZZZZZZZZZZZZZZZZZZZZ.

'But it still must have been expensive.'

'I can see how you would find it a bit of a struggle, what with the mortgage on those flats in Bristol,' I said. I couldn't resist it.

The WW jabbed me again. And this time she really meant it.

BZZZZZZZZZZZZZZZZZZZZZZZZZZZZZZZZZZZZZZZZZZ.

If her right hand really had been plugged in to the mains, I'd have been thrown back through the wall and would have ended up lying in a smouldering heap in Pall Mall. This time she left it there, pressed against my chest. I took her prong between my thumb and index finger and handed it back to her.

'Nice talking to you,' I said. And with that she turned on her chunky little heels and was gone.

'She thinks she's put a hex on you,' Wendy said.

Eh?

'She'll have got that from Carole Caplin, all that buzzing and poking. It's to transfer negative energy to you.' So there you have it, The Night The Wicked Witch Tried To Put A Spell On Me.

The nickname must have gone to her head.

*

When the story broke about the Blairs buying a couple of flats in Bristol, there were only two things which could have made it newsworthy.

One, did they 'do a Mandelson' and cut a deal designed to save thousands in stamp duty?

Two, did they use a convicted fraudster, Peter Foster, as their financial adviser?

On the first count, they paid more than the £250,000 stamp duty threshold for each of the flats, so there was no bent deal.

On the second, Downing Street categorically denied that Foster had acted as an adviser. A series of devastating emails proved that Foster did broker the deal. He viewed the properties, negotiated a discount of £69,000, found a letting agent and gave advice on every aspect of the transaction. Foster even warned the WW about trying to knock down the price to just below the stamp duty threshold because the Inland Revenue were keeping their eye on all such deals.

So why on earth did an educated, learned QC involve a man who has been to prison on three continents in what was a routine purchase of two flats, one for Euan to live in while he was at Bristol University and the other as an investment?

There was nothing remotely sinister or underhand about

buying the properties. The Blairs aren't short of a few bob, had no mortgage (this was before the £3.7 million loan on Connaught Square), live for nothing, take free holidays. It's not as if they've ever spent anything on school fees. Why didn't she just go to an estate agent or ask one of her clerks at her legal chambers, Nonces 'R' Us, to act for her?

To understand why you have to peer inside the wonderful world of the Wicked Witch. Behind the painted smile, she has always struck me as completely tonto – part ruthless feminist, part New Age loony, part bunny-boiler. After moving in to Number 10 she seems to have convinced herself that the usual rules didn't apply to her.

Whenever there's been any criticism of her and her husband over whether Damien had the MMR jab, their freeloading holidays, the way they played the education system, she has managed to use her children as human shields.

When this story broke, it was suggested that anyone running it would be compromising Euan's security and invading the Blair family's privacy. And they would have had a point, were it not for the involvement of Foster. He was the boyfriend of the WW's 'lifestyle guru' Carole Caplin, a former soft-porn model. The WW was close to both Miss Caplin and her mother Sylvia, a self-appointed medium. Cherie was paying Mrs Mad the thick end of £4,000 a month for her 'advice'. That's almost fifty grand a year.

Miss Caplin, who now works as an agony aunt, specialises in 'alternative' therapies (the WW and Caplin took showers together to scrub out harmful toxins) and was once a trainer for a mind-bending cult called Exegesis, which was condemned in Parliament. Her mother claimed to receive messages for the WW from the dead.

Both mother and daughter are clearly bonkers. But not half as potty as the women who rely on them for everything from spiritual guidance to what kind of shoes to wear.

What was worrying is that a woman married to the prime minister and said to wield more influence in the government than most cabinet ministers was in thrall to this mumbo-jumbo. And that someone tipped to become a High Court judge should show so little judgement as to use a convicted fraudster as a go-between in a property deal. This incident alone should have disbarred her from ever sitting on the bench.

When the truth came out she utterly humiliated herself, her husband and his staff at Downing Street. If they'd all come clean from the start, not fallen back on their usual evasion and smears, it would never have got so far out of hand. It was a full ten days before Tony Blair made a personal statement sticking up for his wife and even then only for political advantage before Prime Minister's Question Time. Any decent husband would have been out in front of his wife, all guns blazing, from day one. If you want to take her on, you've got to get through me first. Men, would you allow your wife to be hung out to dry and subjected to relentless personal attack for a week and a half? Women, how would you feel if he did?

After all, this started, remember, over a property deal from which they stood to benefit as a married couple, using money which belonged to them both, part of which was intended to provide their eldest son with a place to live while at university.

Frankly, I have never accepted that Blair knew nothing about it. But his tactic was to hide under the bed and hope it would all go away, while his wife was put through the bacon slicer.

That's not to say I have any sympathy for the Wicked Witch. She's deserved everything she's got. But I was appalled at the behaviour of her husband in letting her go through it alone. Whatever happened to 'for better, for worse'?

What all this illustrated is that the Project, the naked pursuit of power, the image of the Blessed Tony, must take precedence over everything. And if that means his wife getting ripped to shreds while he cowers behind the cupboard with his hands over his eyes, so be it.

Anyone with half a brain could see from the off that Foster was trouble. It stretches belief that the Funny People hadn't tipped Blair the wink that his wife was keeping some pretty rum company. I know he was a busy man, but his wife is his closest confidante. You'd have thought she might have mentioned over the cocoa that she'd just spent over £500,000 on two flats, one of which their eldest son was going to live in.

Get anything at the shops today, dear?

Not much – new pair of knickers, new frying pan, two flats.

That's nice, dear.

This all rumbled on for a couple of weeks and in the end we all got bored. So, as usual, they got away with it, even if the WW had to take her turn in the ducking stool.

Serial fraudster Peter Foster was given a one-way ticket back to Upsidedownland and we assumed Caplin would get the Siberia treatment and be forced to while away her days peddling ylang-ylang oil and ashtanga yoghurt from a bedsit above a kebab shop on the Finchley Road.

But it turned out we didn't know the half of it. While all this madness was going on, Caplin had invited another friend of hers to make a fly-on-the-wall documentary for the BBC. In the middle of the media circus, it emerged that Tony Blair, whom we were assured hardly knew Caplin and had never met Foster, goodness me no, was ringing her up every night and leaving messages on her answering machine. It was all captured on tape.

'Hi, it's Tony calling.'

Sod off, Tone, I've told you not to call me at home.

Why would the prime minister interrupt his busy schedule to call a madwoman? Did the WW know that the film was being made? Was Blair aware that every time he called her answerphone the cameras were rolling?

The film also revealed that Caplin's flat was decorated with dozens of photographs of the Blairs and that Carole's nickname for Tony was Toblerone. (Eventually the WW and Caplin parted company, as everyone does with the Blairs. See 'Carol Caplin's Diary' elsewhere in this book.)

★

I first realised the Blairs had gone completely mad back in 2002, when I was sent a cutting from the *Edmonton Journal*, in Canada.

It was headlined 'Tolerance for Mayan Paganism'. Here are the highlights.

'In August, during a family holiday on the Mexican Riviera, British Prime Minister Tony Blair and his wife Cherie went through a 'rebirthing ritual'.

Dressed only in bathing suits, Britain's first couple stood outside a brick pyramid and bowed toward each point of the compass while chanting to the four winds. The spiritual leader of the ceremony encouraged them 'to feel as one with Mother Earth and experience inner feelings and visions'.

The Blairs then moved around the outside of the pyramid, praying first to the Mayan symbols of the sun and baby lizards, signifying spring and childhood. They then prayed to another wall, on which a bird was painted, representing adolescence, summer and freedom. On the third was a crab, for maturity and autumn, and finally a serpent, for winter and transformation.

Moving inside, Tony and Cherie immersed themselves in the herb-infused mist of a Mayan steam bath to sweat the physical and spiritual impurities from their bodies and to balance their energy flow.

Mayan holy songs were incanted and they meditated and attempted to conjure up visions of animals in the steamy air. Before emerging from the pyramid the Blairs said a prayer for world peace and then underwent a 'rebirth'.

This involved smearing one another with papaya and water-melon, then with mud from the Mayan jungle outside.

Finally, while exiting the womb-door of the pyramid, the Blairs were told to scream out loud to signify the pain of birth. They then walked hand-in-hand for a dip in the Caribbean.'

This is the man who took us to war in Afghanistan and Iraq.

Nurse!

Their raid on the dressing-up box for their state visit to Pakistan and India was another dead giveaway. The prime minister turned up dressed up like Peter Sellers in *The Party*. I half expected him to start singing 'Goodness Gracious Me' or set off dancing down the street with bells between his fingers chanting 'Hari Krishna, Harry Ramsden's, Harry Corbett, Harry Potter'. What did he think he

looked like in his Nehru jacket, hands pressed together like the
Maharishi?

We'd come to expect the full ethnic rig from the WW at the
drop of a turban. Any excuse to doll herself up in a sari. This time
she even went in for the red dot between the eyes.

Why, for heaven's sake? She's a Roman Catholic from
Merseyside, not Mrs Gandhi.

Of course, the red dot could have meant a sniper had her in his
sights, but that's unlikely.

In America, a red dot on goods in department stores indicates
an extra ten per cent off. Certainly, the WW looked a few rupees
short of a dowry. The Wicked Witch wouldn't dream of pulling on
a short denim skirt and white stilletos when she visits Romford.
Probably wise with her ankles. Blair doesn't wear a See You Jimmy
bonnet, a kilt and a skean dhu when he goes to Scotland.

So why did they feel it necessary to go native when they visited
the subcontinent?

There's nothing especially unusual in Western women togging
themselves up in ethnic garb. My sister-in-law used to do it when
she lived in Luton.

But she was eight at the time.

*

Tired of being on the rough end of the pineapple, from her lofty
perch astride her high horse the Wicked Witch declared that all
criticism of her is sexist.

It was only a matter of time. Smearing critics is what Labour
does. They never address their own behaviour. Instead they attack
their opponents' motives, falsely accusing them of being variously
sexist, racist, homophobic, xenophobic, blah, blah, blah.

I wonder if she had anyone in mind.

I'd heard all before, pet, and it didn't wash then. I can do sexist,
if that's what you like. For instance, by drawing attention to the
WW's saddlebag hips and legs like Popeye's trousers.

That would be sexist.

But generally I prefer to leave that kind of stuff to the women's pages, where they do it so much better.

Nothing I've aimed in the direction of the WW over the years has been motivated by sexism. It has been driven by pure disgust at her freeloading, exploitation of her position and her chronic lack of judgement.

She even had the gall to complain that the late Sir Denis Thatcher never had to endure the kind of scrutiny she has. But Denis was a model of propriety who made his money before his wife became prime minister, shunned the limelight, and never once tried to exploit his marriage to the Iron Lady for personal gain.

If he had behaved like the WW, he would have been slaughtered. Labour would have been screaming 'Tory sleaze' and calling for the fraud squad.

Imagine that, in 1979, Denis had campaigned for, say, the privatisation of British Telecom and immediately after being elected Mrs Thatcher had duly obliged. Then he had set up a telecoms consultancy to cash in on that privatisation and immediately had been awarded a £5 million contract out of public funds.

What would the world have made of that? It would have been enough to bring down the government.

Now consider that the WW was one of the noisiest campaigners for the introduction of the catastrophic European 'Human Rights' Act into British law. Shortly after entering Downing Street, Blair rushed through the Act, proclaiming it was one of his proudest achievements in politics.

Then the WW set up Nonces 'R' Us (aka Matrix Chambers), specifically to exploit the 'Human Rights' goldmine. Matrix has received millions of pounds of taxpayers' money in the form of legal aid – some of which found its way back into the Blair household coffers.

Yet apart from my column and a couple of honourable exceptions, no one uttered a dicky bird.

The Tories kept schtum. Many of Fleet Street's finest, who would have been screaming blue murder if this had happened under a Tory government, fell silent. And most of them remained silent as the WW tumbled from conman to free holiday after free holiday to the lucrative lecture circuit.

The first widespread grumblings of discontent came when it was discovered that the WW was to be paid £30,000 for a lecture in Washington, which just happened to coincide with Blair's visit to the White House. She was billed as: 'The First Lady of Downing Street'.

This inspired one previously sympathetic sage to declare: 'Oh, Cherie, you've gone too far this time.'

This time? What about last time? And the time before that? And the time before that, too? And that other time?

What about all the money she earned from a children's cancer charity in Australia? The figure has been widely reported as £100,000 – though estimates range from £17,000 to £102,600. You pays your money and takes your choice. True to form, she's never confirmed or denied any of it.

Tony Blair did say at one stage he would include his wife's public speaking earnings in his Commons' register of interests declaration.

Curiously enough, he didn't. Actually, the amount is irrelevant. After her Antipodean expedition, this is what I wrote:

The Wicked Witch flies out on Monday for a series of dinners aimed at raising money to fight cancer in children.

She's being billed as 'the most powerful woman in Britain' which sounds about right – and will also be plugging her book *The Goldfish Bowl: Married to the Prime Minister*, which is already destined for the bargain bucket in Oxfam.

Mug punters are being asked to fork out more than £4,000 for a table. That guarantees them pre-dinner cocktails and a Polaroid for the mantelpiece.

Roll up, roll up for a Wicked Lady with the Wicked Witch.

Although she insists on using her maiden name of Booth in her professional capacity, on the trip Down Under she's listed as: 'Cherie Blair, wife of the British prime minister'. The organisers won't discuss her fee for 'contractual reasons' which means it's true. Downing Street says it's a 'private matter' which is what they always say when any of them is caught bang to rights.

This Australian jaunt follows a recent lecture tour in the USA, which netted her £30,000 from a crowd of insurance salesmen. If private individuals want to pay through the nose to listen to a few self-aggrandising platitudes from the WW that's entirely a matter for them. It's their money.

You might think it's bad enough that the wife of the prime minister is cashing in on the gullibility of American businessmen. But accepting money from a charity is despicable. The whole point of working for charity is that you give your services free, gratis and for nothing. Some celebs may expect a cab to and from the event or their overnight hotel bill to be picked up. But that's about it. I know quite a few high-profile individuals who work tirelessly for charity and wouldn't dream of asking for a penny.

So what are we to make of the prime minister's wife filling her boots at the expense of a children's cancer charity? We're not talking Mother Teresa here, are we?

For a start, it's a disgraceful exploitation of her position. And when it's abroad, she doesn't only demean herself, she demeans us all.

This should do wonders for our image Down Under, as if the Aussies haven't got a low enough opinion of us already.

The last time the WW was there, she staged a *Supermarket Sweep*-style raid on a clothing shop after being invited to pick a couple of free gifts to take home. She emerged with sixty-eight – SIXTY-EIGHT – items, including jumpers, tops, underwear, pyjamas, jackets, jeans, belts, bags, even an alarm clock. Total value: £2,000. Eventually, she was shamed into paying for it all, but not before the damage was done.

Well, I say 'shamed'. The WW is utterly shameless when it comes to getting her snout in the trough. Ever since she moved into Downing Street in 1997, she's been using it as a meal ticket. Free holidays, free frocks, designer discounts – you name it, she expects a deal on it.

Can you imagine Norma Major, Denis Thatcher or Audrey

Callaghan behaving in such a brazen, money-grubbing fashion? Of course not. And imagine the outcry if this had been a Conservative prime minister's wife.

Yet there hasn't been a peep from Labour's backbenches or any of Blair's celebrity supporters. If this was Princess Pushy or Fergie they'd be screaming blue murder. And rightly so. But the Wicked Witch can cruise the world with impunity, Hoovering up freebies, racking up speaking fees and exploiting her husband's position.

A hundred grand isn't pin money. I'm assuming the Blairs have a joint account. Even if they don't, this money adds to their overall wealth. So he benefits, too.

Blair should be forced to explain to Parliament and to the electorate why he thinks his family should profit from a foreign children's cancer charity. This isn't a private matter. The Wicked Witch is trading as Mrs Cherie Blair, wife of the prime minister. She's not only acting in his name, she's acting in our name. And it stinks.

But Blair must shoulder his share of the blame, too. After all, he shares in the profits.

That trip to Washington was virtually an uncanny rerun of the Beckhams' grand tour of the USA the previous week.

It was all about establishing Brand Blair, to be exploited ruthlessly once the prime minister leaves office. They've always had one eye on the money-spinning American lecture circuit and the multimillion US book rights. America is where the real money is to be made and the Blairs intend to milk it to the full, with the WW playing Posh to Tony's Becks. He's even picked up the lingo, telling the Commons on his return that he didn't intend to negotiate a cut in Britain's EU rebate – 'period'. Don't you mean 'full stop', old boy?

How long before the WW launches her own range of designer jeans for the American fuller-figure market?

Or would that be sexist?

Frankly, I've never thought there was a cigarette paper between

Blair and his missus. Tony is merely the frontman for Brand Blair, a voracious, power-grabbing, money-grubbing machine. They need all the money they can get after the WW lumbered them with a £3.5 million mortgage on a house in Connaught Square. They are the BOGOF Blairs. Buy One Get One Free.

Complaining about their venality makes no difference. They are beyond shame. He's Becks to her Posh, although she probably sees herself as Hillary to his Bill. Last autumn she embarked on a lecture tour with Bill Clinton.

(Ah did not have lectural relations with that woman.)

She was wringing the last drops of blood out of the First Lady of Downing Street and was reportedly paid £30,000 a pop.

This is where we came in.

I've been on the receiving end of the wit and wisdom of the Wicked Witch.

And believe me, it ain't worth thirty grand.

BZZZZZZZZZZZZZZZZZZZZZZZZZZZZZZZZZZ.

12 | Summer Holiday

For the past few years the Blairs have taken their summer holidays as guests of Cliff Richard at his homes in Portugal and Barbados. Cliff said he felt sorry for the prime minister after the invasion of Iraq and decided he needed a break.

Was that the real story? Or did the Wicked Witch just turn up on his doorstep unannounced, with Damien, her mum, a couple of suitcases, a pushchair, a carrycot, a week's supply of Pampers, one of those bottle-sterilising kits and a team of bodyguards?

*

'Hello, Cliff, remember me? Cherie. Cherie Blair. That's right, we met at Wimbledon last year. Or was it Queen's Club? Anyway, you know you said that you had this place and that if we ever found ourselves in the area we should come over and say hello? Well here we are.

'I know I should have called first, sorr-ee. I meant to give you a ring from the airport but Damien was sick down the front of my Donna Karan blouse and I had to go to the ladies and change and then Mum needed the toilet you know what they're like when they get to that age and they called the flight before I had the chance and they won't let you use your mobile on the plane something to do with interfering with the equipment and there were some Gipsies who'd had too much to drink fighting in the aisles and trying to open the emergency exit.

'Anyway to cut a long story short when we got to Faro there was a bit of a mix-up because Mum had forgotten her passport and we had to wait in this room until the man from Special Branch had sorted it out and I had to change Damien this packet food goes straight through him and then when we got to the baggage carousel one of our cases had gone missing they think it could be in Buenos Aires I've asked them to send it on here I hope you don't mind.

'By the time we got in the taxi the battery on my mobile had run out and Mum hasn't got one can't figure out how they work she's useless really and the man from the Special Branch was in the car behind and I didn't want to make the driver stop you know how fast these Portuguese cabbies drive on these twisty roads it scares the life out of me to be honest and we were late enough already as it was and I wanted to be here in time to have a swim before dinner.

'That's the trouble with scheduled airlines you have to mix with all the ordinary people and some of them are really unspeakable and they pack you in on these holiday routes and they don't care if I don't get my suitcase back I'm going to sue them for every penny did I mention I'm a top lawyer? We didn't have any of this trouble last year when we flew with the RAF but the newspapers got hold of it and started saying things like who do they think they are the bloody Royal Family and then Gordon told Tony that he wasn't going to pay for the air force to fly us all over the world and we could buy our own tickets.

'Well it's so expensive what with Mum and the three kids and now we have to buy a ticket for the bay-bee even though he sits on my lap most of the way and you have to pay airport tax I think it's disgraceful on top of everything else you know the price of petrol and all that.

'So I'm just glad to get away for a few days it was doing my head in I can tell you so I've left Tony in charge of the other three they can't get up to much while I'm away Euan's doing his GCSEs.

'Say hello to Mr Richard Mum don't be shy she's come over all silly she's always been a big fan of yours go on Mum don't be daft you don't mind if she calls you Cliff do you Cliff? Would you like to hold the baby while I go for a dip thanks ever so. "Congratulations" is one of Tony's favourites and we all thought you were brilliant in Summer Holiday we were singing it at home the other day.

"'We're all going on a summer holiday,

"'No more spinning for a week or two.

"'Something, something on a summer holiday

"'For me and yoooouuu!"

'Come on Mum sing along you know the words you've seen it about 200 times you took me to the Gaumont remember?

"'We're going where the Sun can't find us

"'We're going where the food is free

"'We've seen it in the movies

"'So let's see if it's truuuuuuuuue!"

'This is great. We're not putting you to any trouble are we Cliff?'

*

But although Blair was clearly grateful for the hospitality, with opposition to the war mounting and bombs now going off in London, he decided he didn't want the British public knowing where he was going.

So in 2005, he tried to keep his holiday destination a secret on 'security' grounds. Under an unofficial agreement between Fleet Street and Number 10, newspaper editors reluctantly agreed to comply with his respect for privacy.

Which meant columnists like me could only speculate.

From a distance it's difficult to work out where the prime minister is taking his summer holiday. Downing Street won't say and Tony didn't confide in me where he was going. It's so funny, but we don't talk any more. I did hear a rumour that the Blairs' host is a confirmed bachelor boy. And judging by the photos in the Sun, it's a wonderful life – wherever they're staying. Good times are clearly being had by all. Congratulations on keeping it a secret.

They're obviously travelling light. When reporters went looking for him on the beach he wasn't there. As soon as he got wind that the press was on his tail, he put on his dancing shoes and decided to move it.

A spokesman for Number 10 would only say that if we were

lucky we were going to find him way out in the country. Please don't tease, we said, but they were having none of it.

Some photographers hired a boat, but blue turns to grey so quickly on that part of the ocean that even spotting a big ship can prove difficult. Eventually the snappers did manage to take some grainy pictures of Blair as he stepped out of the shadows, sipping an expresso bongo. He was so close to the edge of the deck that there were concerns he could easily fall.

Then the photographers spotted the Wicked Witch. They'd got themselves a living doll – of the Cabbage Patch variety.

When the girl in your arms looks like that in a swimming costume, you would try to keep the reptiles at bay.

Talk about a devil woman. Blair's gotta do his best to please her. At one stage there was even talk of locking her up in a great big trunk, so no big hunk could steal her away.

Still, I've heard she's got lucky lips.

Later in the day, one reporter got close to the Blairs' yacht and almost persuaded a crew member to throw down a line. But staff were told: don't talk to him.

It's all in the game.

Given the time Blair has been spending giving power to all his friends, it's hardly surprising security is tight. The couple are surrounded by men wired for sound, packing evil automatics.

No sign of the young ones, although there were unconfirmed reports of Euan Blair being seen propping up the bar in a local pub called the Honky Tonk Angel.

Despite the ring of steel, it's been a hectic social whirl, with friends coming and going so fast it's been a case of goodbye Sam, hello Samantha.

Downing Street refused to confirm when the prime minister would return to Britain, but sources said there would be no more working for a week or two.

Although he stayed away from Robin Cook's funeral, Blair is scheduled to deliver the keynote speech at the mistletoe and wine festival at the Winter Gardens in Blackpool. He is also due to present the prizes on Saviour's Day at the London Oratory.

Hurry home, Tony, wherever you are. These miss you nights are the longest.

Try not to fall off a cliff.

*

On one of his free holidays in Barbados, Tony Blair was photographed playing the ukulele – more George Formby than Ugly Rumours, the pop group he sang in while at university.

It was reported that he entertained fellow guests at his mystery Caribbean villa with his very own version of Formby's 'When I'm Cleaning Windows'.

Lay-dee-z and genn-ul-men, it went something like this:

> Now I go taking freebies,
> To save a tidy sum,
> With Cherie and the kiddies,
> And Endora, her mum.
>
> There's always lots of suckers,
> Who let us stay for nowt,
> And burly, Ray-Banned minders,
> To keep the reptiles out.
>
> We stay at least a fortnight,
> We always eat our fill,
> We swim and surf and sunbathe,
> But we never see a bill.
>
> In my profession I work hard,
> I have to take a break,
> So why should you expect me,
> To pay the going rate?
>
> When I'm floating on the sea,
> Arm in arm with my Cherie,
> You must respect our privacy,
> When we're taking freebies.

(Ukulele break)

Now when I'm taking freebies,
I leave Two Jags in charge,
He can have the aggro,
So I can have it large.

We had to ban the papers,
It simply isn't right,
For them to print those pictures,
Of Cherie's cellulite.

She's still a handsome woman,
She's big on human rights.
And back in our cabana,
It's five times every night.

We like to take our freebies,
On the Caribbean sea,
But if Cliff's got other guests there,
We'll go to Italy.

We love the clear blue ocean,
Though we'll settle for a lake,
But this year, I think we'll give,
A miss to Sharm el-Sheikh.

The cares of office melt away,
When the sun is on your back,
And when I'm taking freebies,
I'm a long way from Iraq.

I know the bombs in London Town,
Give you the heebie-jeebies,
But I'm well out of the firing line,
When I'm taking freebies.

There's nothing like Barbados air,
When you're living like a millionaire,
Miles away from Connaught Square,
When I'm taking freebies.

13 | Carole Caplin's Diary

Carole Caplin, resident 'lifestyle coach' at Number 10 until she fell out with the Wicked Witch, is said to have kept a diary of her life with the Blairs. Reports suggest it has been hawked around publishers and could be worth as much as £1 million. Which may explain how this ended up in a plain brown envelope on my desk.

MONDAY

Got back from rebirthing seminar in the Maldives feeling energised. It was amazing. Must tell Cherie, she'll love it. Sat under pyramid made from palm fronds, smothered from head to foot in mud, seaweed and goat dung, howling at the sun like a stuck pig. The tantric healer said this would release all the bad karma pent up inside me. To tell the truth, I've had more than my fair share of bad karma these past few months.

I can't understand why Alastair is so hostile towards me. What have I ever done to upset him? He is a man with some serious issues. I mixed him a ylang-ylang smoothie to calm him down but he threw it across the room. His wife, Fiona, is even worse. I don't think she's ever forgiven me for that botched Brazilian.

There was something peculiar about the flat when I got back. I can't put my finger on it but the door was open and the furniture was all over the place. Trying to remember whether I'd asked the feng shui people to give the place a makeover while I was away.

When I picked up the phone to call Cherie, there was a strange clicking noise. Then a voice came on the line and said 'How's your boyfriend, sweetheart?' Before I could say anything, he laughed and rang off.

I made myself a cup of nettle and cumin tea and started sorting through the post. One letter caught my eye. It consisted of letters cut out of the newspapers, pasted onto 10 Downing Street headed notepaper and underlined in lipstick. All it said was YORE FINISHED, YOU MAD COW.

Took a cab to Number 10. So much to catch up on. My swipe card didn't work. Funny. That nice young policeman let me in, the one I gave the Vulcan mind massage after the Christmas party.

'Hello, anyone home?' I called out, but no one replied. I made my way upstairs, carrying all the bags of clothes I'd blagged for Tony and Cherie.

Laid them out on the bed. A Peruvian peasant frock for Cherie and a simple Moroccan goatherd's singlet for Tony. I knew they'd love them.

In the bathroom, I prepared for Cherie's colonic irrigation. This was our weekly ritual. We'd both strip off in the shower and rub each other down with a scrub made from yam tree extract and finely ground toenail clippings from a specially bred herd of Andean llama. Then I'd hook her up to the cold tap and let the toxins flush out.

Once, when I was giving Peter Mandelson his pedicure and bikini wax, I forgot all about poor Cherie. Not a pretty sight, I can tell you. That certainly put a strain on our relationship. She didn't speak to me for days, not until she could sit down properly again. No sign of Cherie, though. On the stairs I bumped into her mum, Endora, but she completely ignored me. After all the astrological readings I've given her for free, too. She's never forgiven me for my boyfriend Peter, ever since he persuaded her to join that pyramid selling scheme. 'Gordon Brown's had half my pension and now you've cost me the other half,' she shouted at him. Some people.

Things started going wrong after Cherie asked Peter to buy those two flats in Bristol. I can't see what all the fuss was about. He saved her sixty grand. So what if he'd spent time behind bars? That was all a long time ago. He's no worse than some of those dodgy characters Tony has round for drinks so they will write out large cheques to the Labour Party.

Anyway, where was Tony? I know there's supposed to be a war on but it was time for his massage. He gets really tense, you know. He says the only way to release the tension is for me to walk up and down his back in my stilletos. It's all perfectly innocent but that didn't stop someone at Number 10 (no name, no pack drill) popping his head the door and remarking: 'When you've finished in there, I wouldn't mind giving you one.' What do they take me for?

The mobile rang. It was my bank manager wanting to know what I intended to do about my overdraft.

Overdraft? What was he talking about? I paid in Cherie's monthly cheque shortly before I went off to the Maldives. It had bounced.

I took that letter out of my hand-stitched, Ibis-skin clutch bag, and looked at it again. There was something about that shade of lipstick. It was just like the one I used on Cherie in that photoshoot.

'Getting the message now, are we?' Standing right in front of me was that man from MI something – Captain Scarlett, I think his name is. 'If I were you, darling, I'd pack up your pills and potions and disappear back to the Maldives, pronto. And make sure you step over Geoff Hoon on your way out.'

I was speechless. Where was Cherie, where was Tony, what was going on? Had I offended them?

Captain Scarlett scowled: 'What are you waiting for?'

I looked round for the nice young policeman who'd let me in.

'You won't find him,' Scarlett said. 'He's on his way to Elstree, where he'll spend the rest of his career wearing a pointed hat and directing traffic.'

'I don't suppose you fancy a Vulcan mind massage?' I asked.

'You taking the p***?' said Scarlett, relieving me of my security pass. 'And we don't want any of this turning up in the newspapers, do we? Dangerous places, alternative therapy spas. People can get hurt. Run along now, there's a good girl.'

I stumbled, crying, into the street, clutching my Tibetan worry beads. I looked up at a second-floor window, where two familiar faces were grinning from ear to ear.

They won't get away with this, I vowed, searching through my bag for the number of that nice woman I met at Madonna's book launch.

14 | Psst, Wanna Buy a Squirrel?

'Norman Stanley Fletcher, you are charged that on or about the 23 July you did offer for sale one grey squirrel, contrary to the provisions and statutes pursuant in the Natural Environment and Rural Communities Act 2006. Furthermore, you are charged that on or about the same date, you did also offer for sale five pounds of Polish potatoes in contravention of both the Weights and Measures (Packaged Goods) Regulations 2006 and the Polish Potatoes (Notification) (England) Order 2004. How do you plead?'

Daft as it sounds, cases like this could be coming soon to a magistrates' court near you. The Metric Mullahs are already using weights and measures legislation to persecute recalcitrant traders who insist on selling their various goods in imperial units.

In the case of greengrocer Steve Thoburn, he was hounded into an early grave because of his local trading standards Taliban's determination to prevent him using pounds and ounces.

I shouldn't be surprised if the same zealots are mounting dawn raids on fruit and veg stalls to search for any trace of illicit Polish potatoes.

Under the aforementioned Act, 'No person shall, in the course of business, import into England potatoes which he knows to be or has reasonable cause to suspect to be Polish potatoes.'

Why?

This is just one of more than 3,000 new laws introduced since Labour came to power ten years ago. It is also a criminal offence to sell a grey squirrel, or a ruddy duck, for that matter. I don't remember that in the manifesto. Who thought it was worth the time, effort and expense to outlaw the sale of grey squirrels? Is there a black market in squirrels out there? Can you buy squirrels on eBay? I've paid good money to get rid of squirrels. What happens to them after that is none of my business. I neither know nor care. Just so long as they don't come back.

The squirrel catcher claims he's going to drive them out into the countryside and release them. I've always assumed he gassed them and dumped them in a skip. Could it be that he's actually knocking them out to a butcher in Cottenham, Cambs., to meet the culinary requirements of the hundreds of 'travellers' who have colonised the village?

I can't think of anyone else who would want to buy a squirrel. Over the years, door-to-door hawkers have tried to sell me all sorts of rubbish – chamois leathers, pens, encyclopaedias, lucky heather. But no one has ever offered me a brace of grey squirrels – not even those who just happen to be working in the area and find themselves with an excess of Tarmac and wonder if I'd like it laid on my drive.

In addition to trafficking in squirrels, you can now be arrested for grubbing up an orchard, impersonating a traffic warden and offering air traffic control services without a licence.

Who in their right mind would want to impersonate a traffic warden? They're among the most hated people on earth. You might just as well walk through Walthamstow wearing a George Bush mask.

Who is going to offer air traffic control services without a licence? And more to the point, who is going to buy them? Admittedly, British Airways has fallen out with BAA over the security chaos. But I can't imagine the BA board deciding that in future they will be dispensing with the services of air traffic control at Heathrow and instead entrusting the take-off and landing of their aircraft to a minicab firm above a kebab shop in Staines.

'Roger, Charlie Echo Delta Niner, you're cleared to land. Once you've dropped off, could you do a pick-up in Hillingdon, a Mrs Chaudhary, going to the station, for cash? Madam, I know I said five minutes, the pilot is turning into your road now.'

Seriously, this is what you get when a control-freak government hires hundreds of thousands of people with nothing better to do than dream up exciting new ways of meddling in our lives in order to justify their own pathetic existence.

Labour has busied itself criminalising the law-abiding while failing miserably to tackle real crime.

Britain must by now be about the most regulated, inspected, restricted, nannied, spied-upon country on earth which still pretends to be a democracy. It's all part of the punishment culture ushered in by Labour, with the sole aim of showing us who's boss and parting us from our hard-earned. Exorbitant fines bear no relation to the scale of the offence. Speed cameras now outnumber police patrols by two to one.

Downing Street claims all its 3,023 new laws are essential. 'Crime has fallen by thirty-five per cent since Labour came to power precisely because we have given the police and criminal justice system the modern laws they have asked for to tackle crime effectively.'

Does anyone actually believe that? Do you feel safer than you did nine years ago? We are being stripped of our civil liberties, and for what? We've got surveillance on every street corner, yet our city centres resemble the Klondike on a bad night. The Home Office has passed sixty new bills, but violent criminals – both foreign and home-grown – are free to walk the streets. Feral youngsters run wild while decent taxpayers are fined for putting their rubbish in the wrong kind of sack. While our borders are porous and we face a clear and present terrorist threat, the government still finds time to legislate against selling grey squirrels.

Meanwhile unemployment is rising sharply, in large part because of the government's decision to encourage cut-price Eastern Europeans to take the jobs of British workers. Since Poland acceded to the EU, hundreds of thousands of Poles have come to Britain. The more the merrier.

Just so long as they don't bring any potatoes with them.

*

As if 3,023 new offences weren't enough, the government soon came up with a 3,024th – cycling without a bell.

You know a government is at its fag end when it can think of nothing better to do than introduce a new law making it compulsory for all bicycles to be equipped with a bell.

In a written answer to MPs in September 2006, the transport minister, Stephen Ladyman, said: 'New harmonised European construction standards for bicycles come into force in November this year.' (You just knew Europe would be behind it.) 'Although they do not cover bicycle bells, the introduction of these standards makes this a sensible moment to review our current policies on cycle construction, including the question of bells.'

In other words, we've found an exciting new way to punish people.

Is this really what Mr Ladyman went into politics for? It's hardly the Beveridge Report.

But what's even more astonishing is that the offence of cycling without a bell carries a fine of up to £2,500 and up to two years in prison. Who the hell thought that was an appropriate punishment for such a piffling crime? Two years in jail for cycling without a bell? I thought our prisons were supposed to be overcrowded already.

This presumably has been through seried ranks of civil servants, Whitehall committees, amended by lawyers and signed off by Ladyman himself. Didn't anyone pause and say, 'Steady on, old chap, two and a half grand or two years in chokey is a bit stiff'? Which chief constable will be the first to set up road blocks to conduct random bell checks? My money's on the Mad Mullah.

I'm reminded of that old joke from my schooldays.

Knock, knock.

Who's there?

Isobel.

Isobel who?

Isobel necessary on a bicycle?

Put your trousers on, you're nicked.

15 | Elf 'n' Safety

On 5 November, 2006, a crowd of more than 2,000 people assembled in a field in Ilfracombe, Devon, to watch a virtual bonfire on a big screen. Heaters were arranged strategically around the field to give the sensation of the warmth of a real bonfire and loudspeakers played the sound of wood crackling.

The organisers decided on this performance after concluding it would be uneconomic to comply with precautions insisted upon by local council health and safety officers. They would have to hire steel safety barriers, an army of stewards and first-aiders, and have the fire brigade on standby. They concluded it wasn't worth it.

Elsewhere, at Upton Park, in Slough, Berks., uniformed elf 'n' safety officers were busy confiscating sparklers from five-year-olds at a bonfire party, even though they were being supervised by their parents.

In Watford: 'It goes against one of the council's key objectives of having a smoke-free town by causing air pollution and scorching surrounding trees.'

Thus did Dave Cobb, Watford Council's 'service manager' justify banning the town's traditional bonfire. 'It takes significant staff resources to build and steward the fire and reinstate the area afterwards. It is extremely difficult to put out, in the case of over-crowding or crowd surges.'

So which is it – elf 'n' safety or because it contravenes the 'smoke-free' policy? I don't suppose it matters to the Dave Cobbs of this world. Any excuse to ban something will do.

Where do they find these people? Silly question, yet again they find them in the *Guardian* jobs pages. So we end up with a 'service manager' whose idea of serving the public is banning a bonfire on Bonfire Night.

Guy Fawkes Night is just one of the traditional British pursuits to fall foul of the elf 'n' safety Nazis. No aspect of human activity is considered safe unless it has been subjected to rigorous risk assessment, regulation and enforcement.

There's an entire puritanical, purse-lipped industry dedicated to finding out what people like to do and stopping them. All at public expense. The Health and Safety Executive long ago lost all touch with reality. They even wanted the army to put handrails on the side of the Brecon Beacons to stop soldiers falling over on training exercise.

Warden Hodges, from *Dad's Army*, you should be alive today.

Some of it borders on clinical insanity. Take this, for example: 'It's a bit like keeping tigers – they are beautiful to look at, but you wouldn't want them wandering the streets.'

That was Torbay councillor Colin Charlwood talking not about lions, or crocodiles, but palm trees. He was defending the council's decision to declare the English Riviera's famous palm trees a danger to the public. Charlwood, a Liberal Democrat (now there's a surprise) explained: 'What if one of those leaves caught a child in the eye, for example?'

If you require any further evidence that those responsible for the 'health and safety' racket are in the collective grip of advanced mental illness just consider that opening sentence. 'It's a bit like keeping tigers.' No it isn't, not even a little bit. Palm trees are not likely to roam the streets of Torbay attacking innocent holiday-makers. Neither are tigers, for that matter. You don't get a lot of tigers in Devon.

Perhaps Charlwood would care to consult the animal-tamer Roy Horn, of the famous Las Vegas double act Siegfried & Roy, on the relative risks of tigers and palm trees. Despite all the palm trees in Vegas, there is no recorded incident of anyone being savaged by one or being hospitalised by a frond-related injury. It was a tiger which mauled Roy, almost killing him.

Why do we allow these deranged 'health and safety' obsessives to rule our lives? Cllr Charlwood clearly belongs in a padded cell wearing a jacket which does up at the back, along with the rest of the safety Nazis. After all, you wouldn't want them wandering the streets.

If they were wandering the streets, mind you, they could be at the most dreadful risk.

For instance, the sign might read:

CHARNWOOD BOROUGH COUNCIL
CONKER COLLECTION
Do not throw sticks etc. into this tree
as it could cause injury to people walking below

That was Lowdham, in Nottinghamshire, a few years ago. Since then, acting on the orders of elf 'n' safety, councils all over Britain have been ruthlessly chopping down chestnut trees and hiring cherry pickers to remove killer conkers, lest passers-by slip on them.

Suffolk County Council banned hanging baskets from 'lighting pillars' – what jobsworths call lamp posts these days – during the Bury St Edmunds In Bloom festival, for fear they might fall on someone's head.

We've had a village in Gloucestershire banning swings in a children's playground, and health and safety officers in Bognor Regis insisting kiddies wear crash helmets on donkey rides on the beach. Football in school playgrounds has been given the elbow, in case anyone involved scrapes a knee simulating a Ledley King tackle. Ditto firework displays, bouncy castles, boating lakes, hopscotch, slides and roundabouts. If there's the slightest risk of anyone getting hurt, it's banned.

And they wonder why youngsters spend hours stuck in stuffy bedrooms playing video games. The authorities wring their hands about childhood obesity, while at the same time outlawing just about every form of physical activity from French cricket to egg and spoon races.

Schoolchildren are being forced to wear heavy sweaters in the playground during heat waves in case they get skin cancer. We've had schools banning children throwing paper planes in case they get injured; teachers being told not to apply sunscreen to pupils for fear they are accused of abuse; councils knocking flat cemetery headstones considered to be unstable for fear they could injure a mourner; a lifeguard instructor and her husband being prevented from taking their own three children into a toddlers' pool – because health and safety rules decreed there should be one adult per child.

They're stealing childhood.

Councils have turned towns and cities into fun-free, soulless, no-go areas. They're so scared of being sued that they'd rather kids sat around shopping centres shooting up heroin, smoking dope, sniffing glue and supping Special Brew than playing hopscotch.

There is no more depressing sight than walking through a once immaculate public park, past drained paddling pools, decommissioned swings and slides, padlocked roundabouts and boarded-up climbing frames plastered with graffiti and fly-posters.

And why has it come to this? Simple. It's a combination of brain-dead bureaucrats and greedy spiv lawyers. The 'where there's blame, there's a drink in it' culture has spawned an epidemic of bogus and excessive compensation claims, costing local authorities hundreds of millions of pounds every year – much of it going into the pockets of ambulance-chasing briefs.

We moan about vandalism, but we've abandoned our public spaces to the vandals. The Old Bill have withdrawn to the nick to spend more time with their gender-equality advisers. The uniformed presence of parkies, which used to deter hooligans, has gone the way of the penny chew.

Had I been a young boy today, I'd have cleaned up. Hardly a week went by without me coming home with a grazed knee, a sprained wrist or a lump on my head as a result of recklessly attempting to emulate Jimmy Greaves or the Lone Ranger. Did I get legal aid to sue the council? No, I got a bollocking for ripping my only good pair of trousers or scuffing my new Start-rites.

But, despite our cuts and bruises, my generation was a damn sight fitter than today's pasty-faced, flabby breed. We lived outside – climbing, brawling; exploring disused air-raid shelters and derelict houses; piling fifteen to the dozen onto rocking donkeys; ploughing home-made carts with pram wheels into walls; trying to make park swings loop the loop; slide-tackling on cinders; attempting diving slip catches on concrete; and trying to dunk each other in ponds. And, yes, smashing each other round the knuckles – and sometimes the head – with conkers, which we had assiduously gathered by throwing sticks up into trees.

My mum should have taken out shares in Elastoplast. We had no one to blame but ourselves and we wore our bandages as badges of honour. These days, Rodney, we'd be millionaires – especially if we became com-pen-say-shun lawyers or found a way of suing for a real or imagined injury.

Consider the case of Susan Storer, a deputy headmistress, who sued her former school for £1 million. What awful injury could she have suffered which caused her to believe only such an enormous sum could be considered appropriate compensation?

Had she slipped on a wet changing-room floor and sustained irreversible brain damage? Had she been pushed downstairs by a gang of thugs from the Lower Fourth and left a quadriplegic? Had she suffered such dreadful abuse and mental torture at the hands of pupils and her fellow teachers that she ended up on suicide watch in the local puzzle factory?

Er, not quite.

Mrs Storer was upset because the school failed to replace a chair which made 'flatulent noises' when she sat on it. It became something of a standing joke and she frequently had to apologise to parents, pupils and colleagues alike. What compounded her grievance was that the other two deputy heads, both male, were issued new, executive-style chairs, without the whoopee-cushion feature.

As far as Mrs Storer was concerned this was an open and shut case of sex discrimination. Call it a cool million for cash.

So she took her former school, Bedminster Down Secondary, to an industrial tribunal in Bristol. Asked why she just didn't sort out the problem chair herself, she replied: 'It's a health and safety issue for an employer to ensure you have a comfortable chair.'

Soon you won't be able to fart in Britain without a chitty from elf 'n' safety. We have become infantilised into believing that we are unable to think or act for ourselves and that every perceived grievance can only be assuaged by a bucketful of taxpayers' money.

So we end up with a forty-eight-year-old, well-educated schoolteacher unable or unwilling to procure herself a new chair and working herself up into such a lather of indignation that she has convinced herself that the only way to kiss it better is to bank a cheque for £1 million, tax free.

That's why organisers of fêtes, gymkhanas and concerts increasingly decide the game's not worth the candle. Employers are terrorised by the safety Nazis. You can't get a satellite dish put up without a 'special heights team'. Window cleaners are told they must erect scaffolding before they can wash bedroom windows on the first floor. We have seen track workers at Wimbledon rail depot being issued with 500ml bottles of SPF30 suncream to be applied at all times. Now you might applaud this as a responsible employer's concern for the well-being of the workforce. And you might be right, until I tell you that all the workers in question are on permanent night shifts.

We're not even safe in our own homes. Since time immemorial, mothers have been using their elbows to test baby's bath water. Grown-ups dip a toe in the tub before getting in. If it's too hot, they add some cold. And vice versa.

Now, by New Labour edict, all that has been given the elbow. Two Jags has announced that in future the government will decide the temperature of bath water. New regulations from the office of the deputy prime minister specify that thermostatic valves be fitted to taps. Once the water hits 113°F (45°C) it switches off. If your bath goes cold and you want to top it up with some hot water, forget it. And all taps will be subject to a mandatory annual inspection to check they're still working efficiently.

We now live in a country where your bath taps are going to be subject to an annual MOT test. You already need a licence to move a light socket, followed by a visit from a town hall jobsworth.

Elsewhere, elf 'n' safety enforcers in Yorkshire told a village choir in Terrington to carry out a risk assessment before they are allowed to sing in the parish church. Local MP Robert Goodwill said: 'What's next? Bell-ringers having to wear helmets in case a bell falls?'

Sorry, Bob, they beat you to it, old son.

The Central Council of Church Bell-ringers has already issued safety guidelines to its members, including specific instructions on muffling of clappers (only when bells are down). All ringing rooms, bell chambers and bell towers have been designated 'no smoking' and a prominent red light must be illuminated above the outside door (like a broadcast studio) to indicate when bells are being rung. Presumably, just in case a deaf person is about to walk into the ringing room while peals are in progress.

Ding, dong.

Then there was the edict insisting that visiting Russian trapeze artists must wear helmets if they want to perform in Britain.

This is what I wrote at the time:

No industry escapes unscathed, even the circus where risk is the whole point of the act.

Why don't they insist that the tightrope is laid on the ground? That way no one would ever fall off.

Logically, jugglers will have to wear safety helmets, too.

Fire-eating's out, obviously, and lion-taming has to fall foul of some law or other on animal safety.

I wonder where the Rubber Johnny Police stand on the possibility of clowns being hurt by flying custard pies?

As for Charlie Cairoli's jalopy, that would never get an MOT certificate. And even if it did, it wouldn't be long before the ring was littered with traffic humps and speed cameras.

A few months later, seventy clowns at Zippo's Circus in Blackheath, South London, held a mass meeting over fears that they may be sued if they continued to throw custard pies and buckets of water at members of the audience.

Zippo – real name Martin Burton – said clowns are concerned that the public may be losing their sense of humour. 'I'm of the old school and think that if you're stupid enough to sit in the front row then you deserve it,' he said. 'But many clowns do not share this view and are worried that it is an increasingly litigious world.'

He's right. It can only be a matter of time before Blame Direct are on the case: 'Have you been injured in a custard pie incident? You could be entitled to com-pen-say-shun.'

Oh, what a circus. The safety Nazis have forced fishermen to wear hairnets and they want to make bar staff in noisy pubs wear earmuffs.

As I said, no aspect of human activity is immune. And I mean NO aspect.

There's no escape from the health and safety Gestapo, even in the smallest room.

On Tayside, the NHS has issued guidelines on how to use the bathroom. A four-page leaflet, entitled 'Good Defecation Dynamics' has been published in Dundee. It gives advice on the safest way to sit on the toilet. 'Do not slump down but keep a normal curve in your back. Make sure your feet are well supported.'

What was that I was saying about not even being able to fart without a chitty from the safety Nazis?

You couldn't make it up.

16 | Rum, Sodomy and the Life Jacket

It's two centuries since Lord Nelson's famous naval victory over the French and Spanish in the Battle of Trafalgar. To kick-start the anniversary celebrations, an actor dressed as Nelson posed for pictures on the River Thames at Greenwich. But before he was allowed to board an RNLI lifeboat, safety officials made him wear a life jacket over his nineteenth-century admiral's uniform.

This set me wondering how Nelson would have fared if he had been subject to modern health and safety regulations.

(The scene is the deck of the recently renamed British flagship, HMS *Appeasement*.)

'Order the signal, Hardy.'

'Aye aye, sir.'

'Hold on, that's not what I dictated to the signal officer. What's the meaning of this?'

'Sorry sir?'

'England expects every person to do his duty, regardless of race, gender, sexual orientation, religious persuasion or disability. What gobbledegook is this?'

'Admiralty policy, I'm afraid, sir. We're an equal opportunities employer now. We had the devil's own job getting "England" past the censors, lest it be considered racist.'

'Gadzooks, Hardy. Hand me my pipe and tobacco.'

'Sorry sir. All naval vessels have been designated smoke-free working environments.'

'In that case, break open the rum ration. Let us splice the main brace to steel the men before battle.'

'The rum ration has been abolished, Admiral. It's part of the government's policy on binge drinking.'

'Good heavens, Hardy. I suppose we'd better get on with it. Full speed ahead.'

'I think you'll find that there's a four knots speed limit in this stretch of water.'

'Damn it man! We are on the eve of the greatest sea battle in history. We must advance with all dispatch. Report from the crow's nest, please.'

'That won't be possible, sir.'

'What?'

'Health and safety have closed the crow's nest, sir. No harness. And they said that rope ladder doesn't meet regulations. They won't let anyone up there until a proper scaffolding can be erected.'

'Then get me the ship's carpenter without delay, Hardy.'

'He's busy knocking up a wheelchair access to the fo'c'sle, Admiral.'

'Wheelchair access? I've never heard anything so absurd.'

'Health and safety again, sir. We have to provide a barrier-free environment for the differently abled.'

'Differently abled? I've only one arm and one eye and I refuse even to hear mention of the word. I didn't rise to the rank of admiral by playing the disability card.'

'Actually, sir, you did. The Royal Navy is under-represented in the areas of visual impairment and limb deficiency.'

'Whatever next? Give me full sail. The salt spray beckons.'

'A couple of problems there too, sir. Health and safety won't let the crew up the rigging without crash helmets. And they don't want anyone breathing in too much salt – haven't you seen the adverts?'

'I've never heard such infamy. Break out the cannon and tell the men to stand by to engage the enemy.'

'The men are a bit worried about shooting at anyone, Admiral.'

'What? This is mutiny.'

'It's not that, sir. It's just that they're afraid of being charged with murder if they actually kill anyone. There's a couple of legal-aid lawyers on board, watching everyone like hawks.'

'Then how are we to sink the Frenchies and the Spanish?'

'Actually, sir, we're not.'

'We're not?'

'No, sir. The Frenchies and the Spanish are our European partners now. According to the Common Fisheries Policy, we shouldn't even be in this stretch of water. We could get hit with a claim for compensation.'

'But you must hate a Frenchman as you hate the devil.'

'I wouldn't let the ship's diversity co-ordinator hear you saying that sir. You'll be up on a disciplinary.'

'You must consider every man an enemy who speaks ill of your king.'

'Not any more, sir. We must be inclusive in this multicultural age. Now put on your Kevlar vest; it's the rules.'

'Don't tell me – health and safety. Whatever happened to rum, sodomy and the lash?'

'As I explained, sir, rum is off the menu. And there's a ban on corporal punishment.'

'What about sodomy?'

'I believe it's to be encouraged, sir.'

'In that case . . . kiss me, Hardy.'

*

Once again, I discovered that you couldn't make it up.

Shortly afterwards, the organisers of the official Trafalgar bicentenary celebrations decided that rather than reconstruct the battle in which the British fleet defeated a much larger Franco-Spanish fleet, they would simply stage a simulated confrontation between a Red Fleet and a Blue Fleet, so as not to upset the sensibilities of French and Spanish visitors.

A book published to coincide with the anniversary claimed that although Nelson won the battle without losing a single ship, the real 'victory of character' goes to the Spanish, who along with their French allies lost eighteen ships.

Of course it does. And Germany won the Second World War.

Elsewhere, Totnes Council in Devon announced it was refusing to mark the anniversary of the battle in case it upsets their twin town in Normandy, France.

If Nelson were alive today he'd wonder why he ever bothered.

*

Like 'ASYLUM! – the game show', 'Rum, Sodomy and the Life Jacket' took on a life of its own, turning up everywhere from Internet sites to *Saga* magazine. Not that I cared. Plagiarism is a form of flattery.

Then one of my friends in the political lobby at Westminster drew my attention to the maiden speech of Lord Steinberg, a recently ennobled Tory peer.

My friend had witnessed fellow members of the House of Lords congratulating Steinberg on his brilliant and original debut and decided to check it out in Hansard.

You know what's coming, don't you?

Steinberg entertained the House with an account of how Lord Nelson might have fared in the Battle of Trafalgar if he had been forced to fight it under modern health and safety restrictions.

Everyone agreed that a star was born. By general consensus it was hailed one of the best speeches heard in the Lords for many a long year.

Steinberg simply downloaded it, copied it and passed it off in the chamber as all his own work. Even when I pointed it out in print, he still didn't acknowledge it.

Lords ain't what they used to be in Nelson's day.

17 | Jingle bells, jingle bells,
Jingle all the way,
Oh, what fun it is to see,
Two Jags run away.

It was Christmas 2004 and the venue was the exquisitely restored Royal Opera House in Covent Garden. The occasion was the annual reception thrown by News International for the Great and the Good.

Because I was writing a column for the *Sun*, I got invited, too.

There were hundreds of people milling around when I arrived. It was a heaving, cacophonous scrum and the New Labour Establishment was out in force.

As I grabbed a glass of warm champagne, I could see the flame-haired tresses of Rebekah Wade, the editor of the *Sun*, radiating like a beacon in a bog on the far side of the room. She caught my eye and started waving frantically and beckoning me to join her.

Standing next to her was Two Jags, our esteemed deputy prime minister, self-styled salt-of-the-earth hard man and tribune of the people. There was no love lost between Prescott and me – he'd never forgiven me for christening him 'Two Jags' in the first place, and for not missing a single opportunity to lampoon him in print.

Still, it's always been a principle of mine that I won't say anything about anyone in my column that I wouldn't be prepared to say to their face. Steeling myself with another slurp of fizz, I began to advance towards them, even though I thought I could be risking a smack in the mouth.

After all, Two Jags is famous for his volcanic temper, his complete lack of a sense of humour and his appetite for retribution. It hadn't been long since he'd punched in the face a protester who threw an egg at him on the general-election trail. Could that be my fate, too? I've thrown a lot more than eggs at him over the years.

The closer I got, the more agitated Two Jags became. I could see him barking at Rebekah, while simultaneously glowering at me. Here we go, I thought. One for the diary columns – and if I'm not careful, one for the police.

As I got within a couple of yards of them, Two Jags slammed down his drink, turned on his heels and stomped off across the room like a turbocharged XJ6 accelerating away from the lights. Seconds later, Two Jags had left the building.

What was all that about, then?

Rebekah relayed the conversation. I've cleaned it up a bit.

'Who you wavin' to? That's chuffin' Littlejohn, isn't it?' He's not chuffin' coming over 'ere, is he? You're not wavin' 'im over, are you? Chuffin' hell, 'ere 'e comes. If 'e chuffin' comes over 'ere, I'm chuffin' off.'

And with one bound, he chuffed off. So much for tough guy Two Jags.

★

Rewind ten years and I'm sitting drinking white wine with Tony Blair, newly installed in the Westminster office of Leader of Her Majesty's Loyal Opposition, as he embarks on his charm offensive to get the press onside.

The talk turns to Two Jags – as he then wasn't – Blair's newly elected deputy. Wasn't it a big problem that such an unreconstructed Old Labour buffoon would be just a heartbeat away from Number 10 in the event of New Labour winning the next general election?

'Look,' Blair said, 'if anyone thinks that in the event of me falling in front of a Number 9 bus, John Prescott is going to become prime minister, they're kidding themselves.'

Maybe, but Blair needed Prescott to reassure traditional Labour voters – and especially the trades unions – that the party was safe in his hands.

So he was prepared to indulge him. And, boy, once Labour got elected, did Blair indulge him.

It is a measure of Blair's contempt for the electorate that Two

Jags not only rose to such high office, but was kept there for a decade and, instead of being fobbed off with some sort of quasi-ceremonial role and a fancy title, was given a real department, where he could do real damage. And he did.

As I said in the introduction, this isn't intended to be a forensic analysis of the Blair years from a purely political perspective. I'll leave it to the historians to detail the full extent of the havoc wreaked by Two Jags during his time in office.

But perhaps my part in how he is perceived, at least, deserves a footnote in more learned tomes.

I feel I should start with a formal apology. I'm as guilty as anyone of turning him into a figure of fun. I've always believed piss-taking is more effective than polemic. The very nickname 'Two Jags' sounds almost affectionate. I can assure you, it wasn't meant to be. This is how it came about.

Despite his carefully cultivated, horny-handed-son-of-toil self-image, Prescott has always had an exaggerated sense of his worth and an inflated view of his station in life. (Speaking of stations in life, not long after Labour was elected, Two Jags travelled to Scarborough to deliver a triumphalist speech to one of the transport unions, extolling Labour's intention to build a 'world class' rail and bus network for a grateful nation. To demonstrate his commitment to public transport, he was waved off boarding a train at Scarborough station, like an old-style American president on a whistle-stop tour. A couple of stops down the line, with the cheers of his socialist brothers and sisters still ringing in his ears, he got off the train – where his chauffeur was waiting to meet him with the Jag to drive him back to London in luxury.)

He has always justified the perks of the job by comparing himself to his Tory predecessor, Michael Heseltine.

Not long after the 1997 election, a mole in Downing Street told me that when Prescott became deputy prime minister and discovered that all he was entitled to was a Rover or a Vauxhall, he spat out the dummy and insisted that what was good enough for Heseltine was good enough for him and if he didn't get one he would scweam and scweam until he was thick.

Heseltine had a chauffeur-driven Jag, so Prescott must have one, too. To shut him up, Blair gave in and Prescott got a shiny new Jag to go alongside his own battered, old XJ6. And that's how I came up with the nickname 'Two Jags'. I'm delighted to say it stuck.

Much later, after Tarzan accused Two Jags of being a 'lager lout' and said he should be forced to give up his 214-acre, grace-and-favour estate at Dorneywood, following his spectacular fall from grace, Two Jags barked back: 'Heseltine already has a big house in the country and perhaps others in other parts of the world. I have one house and one car. I am getting the perks, but I'm getting no more than others got.'

Two Jags has always missed the point. Heseltine might be a spiv, but he bought his own big house – he never used Dorney-wood. He also supplied his own Jag and his own chauffeur out of his own pocket.

Alan Clark, a proper snob if ever there was, once sneered that Heseltine was the sort of man who bought his own furniture. Prescott doesn't even buy his own petrol, but he's obsessed with status and behaves like Henry VIII.

The fact is, Two Jags is the biggest snob of all, the very charge he throws at his critics to deflect attention from his own egregious shortcomings.

It all came spewing out when, hilariously, he was given the Global Award for the Betterment of the World Environment at an earth summit in India. Here he was, on top of the world, yet he still found time for a typically graceless sideswipe at 'snobbish, public school newspaper editors who sit on their arses, have their oysters and do bugger all about the environment' while attacking him for 'junketing'.

For the record, I didn't go to public school and the last time I ate oysters I was sick as a dog for forty-eight hours afterwards.

Still, Two Jags got it in to his mind that the only reason anyone in Fleet Street has a pop at him is because they think he's 'a former ship's steward getting ideas above his station'.

Not guilty, m'lud.

Like Two Jags, I started work at sixteen. I have nothing but admiration for those whose success has been achieved through their own talent and sheer hard work without the benefit of an expensive education.

But, unlike him, I don't hate on sight those who did go to public school. You can only play the hand you're dealt.

What a quaint, old-fashioned view of the world Two Jags still has. His is a fantasy straight out of the pages of the *Beano* – with Lord Snooty at one end of the social scale and the Bash Street Kids at the other. The toffs sit in splendour 'having their oysters' while the lower orders tug their forelocks and exist on bread and scrape.

These days there are few barriers to advancement. The fact that someone like Two Jags can ascend to the great height of deputy prime minister is living proof. You might have thought Two Jags would have reflected on that sometimes and bless his good fortune, instead of festering with resentment.

What was most absurd about his analysis was that it was delivered from the sumptuous surroundings of the kind of five star inter-national hotel, in Mumbai, India, which had by then become his natural habitat.

In the eight years after Labour was elected, he flew First Class to forty countries, where he has been treated like a rajah.

I'm only surprised they didn't sit him on a set of scales, like a Middle Eastern potentate, and present him with his own body weight in rubies. If you're going to have a laugh, you might as well do it properly. Giving Two Jags an award for saving the environment is like giving Myra Hindley first prize for child care.

Here is a man who has been single-handedly responsible for more pollution than Chernobyl. He consumes enough fossil fuels to keep a small Third World country in electricity for a year. His jumbo jet jaunts, his eleven-car motorcades, his 250-yard seafront limousine rides (Pauline might have got her hair blown out of shape), his helicopter excursions and RAF shuttle services are the stuff of legend. How much of the earth's resources did it take at the time to heat his four homes, fill up his two Jags or run the air conditioning in his hotel suites? His idea of energy conservation amounts to keeping coal in the bath at Dorneywood.

JINGLE BELLS, JINGLE BELLS | 107

We didn't dislike him because he's a jumped-up waiter with ideas above his station, but because he's a thin-skinned, self-important, stinking hypocrite, with the social graces of a pig at a Palace garden party.

And he knows it.

My guess is that Two Jags hates himself far more than the so-called 'snobs' he claims have got it in for him. Two Jags managed to become everything he effects to despise. He laid claim to the Dorneywood country estate, when the chancellor declared it surplus to his requirements. He has spent years swanning round the world, First Class, all expenses paid, waited on hand and foot.

I wonder if he remembered to tip the butler.

Two Jags achieved wealth and position beyond his wildest dreams, but managed to remain permanently angry, a walking inferiority complex, always spoiling for a fight.

Even though he rails against public schoolboys in Fleet Street, his real problems have always been closer to home. He's known that Blair and his inner circle laugh at him behind his back.

Two Jags was bought and paid for long ago. He sold his socialist soul for a meaningless title, a country estate, an XJ8 and a reserved seat at the front of the plane. His lot has been that of the organ grinder's monkey, his only role in life was to rattle the tin in front of his old comrades in the trades unions.

But in a delicious twist of fate, there's a new order in the TUC these days, a new breed of firebrand union leader who looks on Two Jags as just another class traitor.

The truth is, he must know he's been living a lie all these years. Though the voice of the manual unions, he's never done anything more taxing than serving gin and tonics on the cruise ships.

On reflection, maybe I should have concentrated more on his venality and less on his comic potential. Over the years, I've lampooned him as everything from Budgie the Helicopter to Vicky Pollard from *Little Britain*. He became a sort of honorary panto-mime dame, even regarded with a degree of affection in some quarters. Oh, how we laughed at his mangled malapropisms and chuckled when he threw a punch at a punter on the election trail.

'It's only John being John,' Tony Blair would laugh dismissively. And so Two Jags stumbled from one fiasco to another.

But behind the bumbling buffoon lurked one bad bastard. He's a Club Class warrior in a long-wheelbase limo – a resentful mediocrity with a wholly justified inferiority complex and an exaggerated sense of entitlement.

Two Jags has always had a particular hatred of the South of England, especially those Southerners he suspects of voting Tory. That's one of the reasons he opened the way for 'travellers' to ride roughshod over the planning laws in rural areas – or rather drive their expensive 4x4s and erect their jerry-built settlements on England's green and pleasant.

Every resident distressed by the caravans on the village cricket pitch; every mum with a baby in a pushchair who treads in a pile of excrement; every housewife whose washing is polluted by the acrid smoke of burning tyres; every home burgled, every lawnmower stolen; every local pub terrorised; all these represent another small victory for Two Jags over 'the snobs'.

When hard-working, law-abiding, tax-paying citizens have had the audacity to complain about their lives being ruined and their neighbourhoods being invaded illegally, he spat in their faces and threatened to have them prosecuted for 'racism'. Two Jags is the only man in the country who doesn't have to worry about being invaded by 'travellers'. When the *Sun* turned up on his doorstep in a caravan, its reporters were promptly moved on by the Old Bill on 'security' grounds.

Everything he has touched has turned into an unmitigated disaster. Remember his plans for a 'world class' transport system? Billions of pounds later about the only person in Britain with an integrated transport system was Two Jags, as he stepped seamlessly from the back seat of his limo to the front row of an aircraft of the Queen's Flight to whisk him to yet another lobster supper or rugby league match. The rest of us are left stuck in traffic jams or stamping our feet on frozen platforms waiting for the train that never comes. He did more to demoralise the railways than anyone since Dr Beeching. His legacy was the most congested road network in Europe.

After he was rumbled at transport, he tried to foist expensive and unnecessary regional parliaments on an unwilling electorate – and was told in no uncertain terms to sod off.

But not before wasting another small fortune, which could have been more profitably spent on schools'n'ospitals, or policing, or lollipops.

It's in the area of planning where he has done the most damage. Decisions have been taken away from democratically elected local councils and handed over to unaccountable quangos, packed with Labour placemen.

The result is that hundreds of thousands of new homes are to be built in ancient fields and woodlands, on flood plains, even in back gardens which have absurdly been designated 'brownfield' sites.

Two Jags is also responsible for bulldozing Liverpool's historic housing stock, even though these attractive terraces could be restored and made habitable for a fraction of the cost of demolition and rebuilding. Meanwhile, picturesque Middle England is to be turned into a giant Soweto for wealthy Gipsies.

All of this he did from the safety of one of his four homes, or from the luxury of a sunlit hotel suite where he is attending another five star fact-finding summit.

He was a cross between a Soviet commissar and Marie Antoinette – the champion of public transport who travels by chauffeur-driven XJ8; the defender of the environment swanning around in helicopters and private jets; the advocate of affordable housing who lived in a ridiculous turreted mansion and had grandiose accommodation in Admiralty House and at Dorney-wood, courtesy of those British taxpayers he so roundly despises.

Two Jags likes to think he's come a long way since he was serving gin and tonics on the ferries. He may have had the trappings of office, but all the while he was kidding himself if he believes anyone takes him seriously.

New Labour's educated elite have always treated him like a waiter. Unions playing up? Rank and file getting restless? Let's send Two Jags to soothe things over and reassure them we're still the party of Keir Hardie, instead of a bunch of chancers on the make.

Oh, and one for yourself, steward.

If that's as far as it went, perhaps it wouldn't be so bad. But they made the mistake of letting him actually do things. And Two Jags did to the people of Britain what 'travellers' are doing to the countryside – and what he was simultaneously doing to his secretary.

Only we didn't know it at the time.

18 | Say Goodbye to Dorneywood

Finally, we discovered why Two Jags has always had the tetchy air of a man about to have his collar felt, and why he reacted to even the most innocuous question with an invitation to step outside.

He'd been living in mortal dread of that moment when Fleet Street's finest knock on his door and ask him how long he's been cheating on his wife.

In April 2006, it was revealed that he was having an affair with one of his junior secretaries, Tracey Temple.

Oh, and before you take a swing, old son, we've got the boyfriend and we've got the pictures. This was my first reaction:

God, how I envy whoever broke it to him. I'd have given a small fortune to see the look on his face.

There have been times I've regretted ever inventing the nickname Two Jags. It helped turn Prescott into a figure of fun, disguising the fact that he is in reality a loathsome, Soviet-style political thug. The satirical version of 'The Red Flag' – 'The working class can kiss my arse, I've got the foreman's job at last' – could have been written for him.

In his ascent – if that's the word – to the office of deputy prime minister, Two Jags has jettisoned everything he ever claimed to believe in. He's betrayed his class, his principles, and now his wife.

He has greedily acquired all the trappings of a Tory grandee – the turreted mansion, the country estate, the posh flat in town, the chauffeured limos, the private helicopters, the liveried flunkies, the padded expense account. And now he's got his very own Tory sex scandal. With immaculate precision, the Great Man has been caught with his trousers down in the very shadow of Brian Rix's Whitehall Theatre.

Two Jags – scourge of Tory 'sleaze', guardian of the Old Labour conscience – captured bang to rights knocking off a junior secretary in his grace-and-favour apartment in the Admiralty.

Oh, what joy it is to be alive this day.

He's like some nineteenth-century mill owner, seducing the hired help. You can almost see him sweeping down to the village, cape swirling in the wind, laughing maniacally as he exercises his *droit de seigneur*. Not that forty-three-year-old Tracey Temple seems to have been your typical trembling factory girl – not if those pictures of her undoing Prescott's shirt buttons to the waist and being hurled over his shoulders like a Lindy Hopper throwing herself at a GI are anything to go by.

We're told that at a party in 2002, Two Jags lifted up Tracey's skirt to see if she was wearing stockings. Who says romance isn't dead?

That's one way of getting in touch with your feminine side, I suppose. I wonder what the sisterhood make of it.

Somehow I can't imagine Willie Whitelaw tweaking the suspenders of a secretary at an office party. Not in public, anyway.

But Tracey clearly wasn't offended. According to reports, she and Two Jags were at it like knives for the next two years. We are asked to believe that the affair ended in 2004. And this is where the story starts not to ring true.

This is what Two Jags said in his statement: 'I did have a relationship with her, which I regret. It ended some time ago.' The *Daily Mirror*, which broke the story, refers throughout to a 'two year' affair.

But it also says of Tracey: 'Recently she spent time alone with her boss at his luxurious 215-acre country retreat in Dorney-wood, Bucks.' How many people do you know who refer to something which happened two years ago as 'recently'?

Me neither.

The usual turn of events is that when one of these office affairs turns sour, the junior party (almost always the woman) is transferred out of the department. Last time anyone looked, Tracey was still working there.

No doubt all will be clarified in due course. But I wouldn't be surprised if the affair was still going on when the newspaper fronted him up on Tuesday. In exchange for Two Jags' formal statement, the paper probably agreed to his version of events – namely that it all ended two years ago.

Prescott is trying to placate Pauline. Downing Street is standing by him. For now. But we're nowhere near 'drawing a line' or 'moving on' just yet. Not by a long chalk. Tony Blair will insist it is a 'private matter' – until it gets awkward for him. There may even be an attempt to spin it as 'John being John' – just as they did when Two Jags punched out a punter during the 2001 election. 'He's always been a bit of a lad, you know.' 'You've got to hand it to him. At his age. Randy old goat.'

A cynic might even conclude that it was a put-up job to get the health-service crisis and the release of foreign criminals off the front pages. A cynic might be at least half right.

But that isn't going to make it go away. This isn't the end of it. This is your starter for ten.

Tracey Temple hasn't surfaced yet. But her story will be worth a lot of money and the Labour Party, in its current parlous financial state, can't afford to buy her silence. Don't be surprised if she turns up in one on the Sunday tabloids, sprawled across the bonnet of an XJ6, sporting a sailor's cap and telling all about 'love rat' Prescott. And even if she doesn't, there will almost certainly be others. Two Jags, a former ship's steward, comes from a culture of a girl in every port.

Experience suggests that a man doesn't suddenly start straying at sixty-three. How many more 'moments of madness' have there been? I'm prepared to bet that once Fleet Street's dogs of war start trawling through the Labour Party, the National Union of Seamen and the darker corners of the corridors of power, this will prove not to have been the first time Two Jags has dipped his fingers in the typing pool.

My bet is Max Clifford's phone was ringing off the hook yesterday.

A few more days of embarrassing front page headlines and

Blair's support will melt away. The prime minister won't have been thrilled to discover that he and the Wicked Witch were photographed with Two Jags and Tracey when Prescott flaunted his mistress in front of the Queen at a memorial service for our war dead in Iraq.

It's open season on Two Jags and it's not just his sex life under the microscope. Those 'second home' exes had better be watertight.

I'll leave it to others to do the 'poor old Pauline' routine and the magisterial moralising about how Two Jags has demeaned a great office of state. For now I'm just savouring the moment.

Needless to say, Tracey Temple did surface with lurid details of their liaison – including the wonderful revelation that Two Jags was hung like a cocktail sausage.

Still, disgracefully, Two Jags survived, yet another example of Blair's post-shame administration. But just as the heat was subsiding, along came a croquet mallet to smack him round the head.

The *Mail on Sunday* published pictures of Two Jags whiling away an afternoon on the lawn at Dorneywood, playing croquet with his civil servants and Special Branch. There was no holding me back. These are the edited highlights.

Orwell would have loved it. Two Jags good, Four Jags better. If Two Jags had been around in Orwell's day, *Animal Farm* would have been binned before it got published. You couldn't make it up.

Croquet. Dwell on that for a moment. Croquet. The sport of toffs. Sir Alan Fitztightly and Lady Magnesia Freelove. More tea, vicar? Mine's a large Pimm's, heavy on the Tanqueray.

There's an old Kris Kristofferson song which starts: 'Woke up Sunday morning with no way to hold my head which didn't hurt.' Yesterday, the *Mail on Sunday* came up with the cure. The moment I saw those pictures of Two Jags on the croquet lawn at Dorneywood, I knew nothing else was going to upset me all day. I was born for days like these.

Thank you, Jesus. Thank you, Lord.

The British Library has just held a contest to find the best front page in history. Sadly, entries closed before this weekend. Photos of Two Jags leaning on a croquet mallet topped even those of him hoisting Tracey Temple across his shoulders at the office knees-up.

Next week: Two Jags goes fox-hunting. There's a certain symmetry between Two Jags and the Berkeley Hunt, though for the moment it escapes me.

Had it been Call Me Dave, it wouldn't even have made the paper. You expect an effete Old Etonian, married to a woman whose dad owns Scunthorpe, to ponce around playing croquet on a Thursday afternoon. But Two Jags? Tribune of the People, ship's steward (second class). Another gin and tonic, Giovanni.

The only point of Two Jags being in this utterly discredited government is that he is the Missing Link between the posh lawyers, social workers, researchers and PR spivs who comprise New Labour and the 'working class' mugs who vote for them. The fact of the matter is that the heavy industrial class who Two Jags is supposed to represent sank without trace after Wapping and the miners' strike, and now works in call centres and has second homes in Kissimmee.

But it amuses Blair and Brown to have the old bruiser on the strength. Not that he's much of a bruiser and never has been. You're a big man, John, but you're out of shape. I do this for a living. His only remote connection to the *Get Carter* generation is that Pauline looks like Michael Caine's landlady.

Yet, instead of hanging out at the Legion and playing a game of arrows with the chaps over a few pints of mild, Two Jags is swanning around the croquet lawn with his principle private secretary, a couple of lads from the Funny People and a woman who rejoices in the title of assistant to the DPM's special adviser – which I thought was Whitehall-speak for Tracey-Temple-in-waiting.

When Two Jags' office was fronted up by the *Mail on Sunday*, this was the reply. A 'spokeswoman' said: 'We are restructuring the deputy prime minister's office, taking on new responsibilities and, as many departments do, we have away days to be able to concentrate on the issues.'

Stop it. Stop it. Enough already. How did this dopey bird keep a straight face long enough to read out that statement? At this stage of the game, it's time to get serious, even though I could run to another few thousand words taking the proverbial.

We're paying for all this. While you're sitting there wondering if the credit card will run to last night's chicken tikka masala, how you're going to find the money to pay your council tax, or whether you can afford the school fees, this overweight, semi-literate oaf is living the life of Riley at your expense.

Blair and Brown – and I refuse to accept that they are not equally responsible – dumped this grotesque clown on the people of Britain. Blair encouraged him, Brown bankrolled him.

It's fashionable to build up Brown to rubbish Blair on the 'my enemy's enemy is my friend' principle, but Gordon is as guilty as Kenny Boy Lay's co-conspirator at Enron.

After the Tracey Temple fiasco, Brown was absolutely onside with Blair in the 'John is John' camp. He described Two Jags as an indispensable member of the team.

Stubborn though Blair can be, Two Jags could not have survived without Gordon's support. So the question is not just what has Two Jags got on Blair, but what has he got on Gordon?

I could go on. I could ask what the Old Bill are doing playing croquet with a Les Dawson lookalike (without the jokes) while old ladies are getting raped in their parlours and QPR triallists are stabbed at the school gates.

This is a rotten government in every single interpretation of the word.

Two Jags, with his, er, two jags, his four homes, his concubines, his croquet lawns, his gutbucket waistline, his nasty politics of resentment and entitlement, his kleptomaniac approach to office; this disgusting, thick yobbo is the snarling, belching, wheezing, secretary-molesting incarnation of what

Blair and Brown and the entire corrupt cabal of 'New' Labour gangsters have done to Britain.

Things can only get better.

And get better they did.

19 | The Colorado Kid

Oh, give him a home where the buffalo roam and the deer and the antelope play.

Quite the most preposterous explanation for Two Jags' jolly in 2006 to the ranch of Colorado billionaire Philip Anschutz – the man bidding to turn the Millennium Dome into a supercasino – came during an interview on the *Today* programme on Radio 4. He said that he'd always been a fan of cowboy films and couldn't pass up the opportunity to visit a real-life High Chaparral.

Who did Two Jags think he was going to bump in to? Roy Rogers? Tom Mix? John Wayne? As I wondered at the time:

> Did he have visions of spending the day lassoing steers, taming buckin' broncos, dodging arrows from pesky Injuns and sitting round the campfire, chewing tobacco and chowing down on beef and beans from the chuck wagon?

Someone should have told him that if he really wanted a genuine taste of the Wild West he'd be better off visiting Hull city centre at chucking-out time.

If they ever remake *Bonanza*, Two Jags is a shoo-in for Hoss.

Did he for a moment think this absurd alibi was going to get him off the hook? Did he honestly believe the British taxpayer should foot the bill for him to fulfil the childhood fantasies he nurtured at Saturday morning pictures watching the Lone Ranger down the local bug hutch?

Just in case we didn't buy that, he threw in the Doha trade talks and tried to claim that it was essential he took this golden opportunity to canvas the views of cattle ranchers on the question of international import tariffs. Since when has it been the job of a British deputy prime minister to represent the interests of Colorado cattlemen?

He would have been better served listening to all those suicidal

British farmers who have been brought to the brink of bankruptcy because of his government's incompetent handling of the foot-and-mouth crisis and criminally negligent administration of the European agricultural subsidies scheme.

Two Jags then went on to claim that, of course, he hadn't discussed business with his host, Philip Anschutz. Goodness me, no. Perish the thought. The question of turning the Millennium Dome into a supercasino never entered the equation. On the contrary, they whiled away the wee small hours over bourbon and after-dinner mints with a discussion about the abolition of slavery.

As you do.

Are you calling me a liar, Humphrys? Right, outside.

You can just imagine Mr and Mrs Philip Anschutz drawing up the guest list.

'Honey, who shall we invite for the weekend?'

'How about that fat British politician, you know, the one who looks like Buzz Lightyear?'

'Jim Preston?'

'That's the guy, he's vice-president or something, I think. I can never understand a word he says.'

'Me neither, but he does seem to be in charge of casinos in Englandland.'

'Good idea. We'll put him in the Wild Bill Hickock suite.'

Two Jags' story added up about as well as Del Boy's Made In Albania pocket calculator. Why else would an American billionaire who wanted to build a casino at the Millennium Dome invite the British politician in charge of redeveloping the Dome to spend a couple of days on his ranch?

If it was all kosher, why didn't Two Jags enter the trip in the register of members' interests until after he was found out? His entry already read like the running order of *Wish You Were Here*. Over the past nine years, Two Jags has spent more time in exotic, five star foreign hotels than Judith Chalmers.

At the end of his political adventure, there's a whole new career opportunity for him and Pauline as the Frank and Nesta Bough of the twenty-first century.

In 2004, he visited a supercasino in Australia, although he entered it in the register as a 'regeneration' fact-finding mission.

> 'You off down the bookies again, John?'
> 'No, Pauline, luv. Just popping out for a spot of regeneration.'
> 'That's what you said about that Tracey woman.'

What other exciting excursions are hidden in the small print? What happens in Vegas, stays in Vegas. Two Jags insisted on the wireless that he was here for the duration and was getting on with his job.

What job?

The office of deputy prime minister had become little more than a £2 million face-saving operation. Two Jags' diary one day that week amounted to opening a memorial to William Wilberforce (maybe that's where he got the idea for the slavery alibi). You don't need a deputy prime minister to do that. I'm sure the Lady Mayoress of Hull would have been happy to oblige. Failing her, someone off *Big Brother* could have cut the ribbon.

His supporters (about as numerous as Cristiano Ronaldo fans in the Rooney household) insist he has a vital role to perform, chairing a few committees.

Big deal.

And for that we were supposed to fork out a small fortune on staff, chauffeurs, offices, a fat six-figure salary, an index-linked pension, free housing, a well padded expense account, extensive First Class foreign travel and all the Wagon Wheels he can eat.

Anyway, I wondered, why was it necessary to keep him in gainless employment? He was sixty-eight, for heaven's sake, long past the age at which most people retire. If he must have a job, couldn't they find him something on the tills at B&Q?

Forget all the guff about precipitating a constitutional crisis in the Labour Party. My hunch has always been that the only reason he survived was because he knows where any number of bodies are buried. And if he was taken down he would squeal like a stuck pig.

Two Jags won't take a bullet for anyone – just like he blamed his civil servants for the freeloading in Colorado.

Classy.

But the posse was closing in fast.

You're surrounded, cowboy. Come out with your hands up.

I don't know about the pesky Injuns, but a couple of days after I wrote the article, it emerged that lassoing cattle was precisely how Two Jags passed his time in Colorado's answer to Michael Jackson's Neverland ranch.

The *Mail on Sunday* reported that the deputy prime minister galloped round the 32,000-acre spread on a thoroughbred stallion. He was kitted out in ten-gallon hat, hand-tooled cowboy boots and a solid silver belt buckle – $20,000 worth of gifts from his host, Philip Anschutz.

Say what you like about Two Jags. He may be an odious liability, but he adds hugely to the gaiety of the nation.

Which is how I came to write:

 ## The Colorado Kid: The Musical

(SCENE ONE. Two Jags strolls on to the porch of a Colorado ranch, his best girl by his side.)

> Oh, give me a Dome,
> Where the Hindujas roam,
> And Reinaldo and Mandelson play.
> Where roulette wheels spin,
> The House always wins,
> And millions are lost every day.
>
> Oh, give me a horse,
> And a Stetson, of course,
> Saddle that fine palamino.
> A belt buckle, too,
> And a trusty lassoo,
> Now where did you want your casino?

(SCENE TWO. Breakfast round the chuck wagon. A cowboy strums a guitar, to the tune of 'Oh, What a Beautiful Morning'.)

> Oh, what a ludicrous moron,
> Oh, what a blithering clown,
> Lock up your wives and your daughters,
> Two Jags is coming to town.

(SCENE THREE. Two Jags on horseback, singing along to 'Wandrin' Star'.)

> I was born in the wrong country,
> I was born in the wrong country,
> Should have been a cowboy,
> Ridin' round the plains,
> Rounding up them dogies,
> Pulling on the reins.
> I was born in the wrong country,
> The wrong, the wrong country.
>
> Do I know where Hull is?
> Of course I bloody do.
> Hull's for representin'
> Not for going to.
> I was born in the wrong country.
> The wrong, the wrong country.

(SCENE FOUR. In a tepee in the hills, Two Jags meets a tribe of Red Indians. To the tune of 'Running Bear', they serenade him.)

> Oompah, oompah, oompah, oompah.
> Oompah, oompah, oompah, oompah.

On the banks of the Humber,
Lived Cunning John, New Labour brave,
And he loved an English maiden,
Tracey Temple was her name.
They stole kisses in the office,
In a cupboard, when they could,
In his apartment in Westminster,
And his house in Dorneywood.

Cunning John loved Little Tracey,
Little Tracey, she too was keen.
But on the banks of the Humber,
Lived his darling wife Pauline.

Then one morning in the papers,
Was a photo of the pair.
Tracey hoisted on John's shoulders,
With her knickers in the air.
Little Tracey sold her story,
For two hundred thousand quid.
And from then on, John's new nickname,
Was the Chipolata Kid.

(SCENE FIVE. Two Jags leaning on a picket fence,
    humming 'The Ballad of High Noon'.)

Do not forsake me, O my Tony,
Please don't do anything you'd regret,
I know the deal you made with Gordon,
And that's not something I'd forget.

20 | Who Wants To Be Prime Minister?

There was one priceless moment early on in Labour's first term when the full stupidity of allowing Two Jags to be Blair's deputy became only too apparent.

Prime Minister's Question Time is supposed to be the one occasion in the week when the PM is called to account by the House of Commons. The reality is, of course, just another slice of meaningless stage management. The PM has prior notice of most of the questions and his civil servants and spin doctors supply him with a list of pat, prepared answers.

In the event of a tricky one slipping through the net, he falls back on the tried and trusted technique of ignoring the question completely and attacking the opposition. Half an hour later everyone retires to the nearest bar, none the wiser.

Sometimes, though, just sometimes, it all seems worthwhile.

That's when – as happened on Wednesday, 14 April, 1999 – the prime minister was otherwise disposed and Two Jags stepped into the breach.

It shouldn't be that difficult. The party managers have it all planned in advance. He can expect a couple of gentle lobs from his own backbenches and although the Tories can be relied upon to bait him, all his answers have been written out for him in big letters. All Two Jags has to do is read them out.

That, of course, failed to take account of the legendary stupidity and incompetence of our esteemed deputy prime minister. He didn't disappoint.

The fun started when Two Jags turned over two pages by mistake and found himself answering a question which hadn't actually been asked yet. It was like that marvellous sketch David Renwick wrote for *The Two Ronnies*, when the *Mastermind* contestant keeps answering the previous question. Two Jags lost the plot completely when asked to comment on a new European banking tax which threatened to devastate the City of London.

It soon became apparent that he had absolutely no idea what the questioner was talking about. So no change there, then. But that was hardly his fault. He's not in government because of his detailed knowledge of the international futures market. However, instead of owning up to his ignorance, he tried to bluster his way out of it, burbling on about the poll tax.

The Tory benches were convulsed with laughter. There wasn't a dry seat in the House. His supporters on the Labour side tried to excuse their deputy leader's gaffe by claiming he was dyslexic.

This all went out live on the cable news channels, but was worthy of prime-time television. This kind of inept performance deserved a wider audience – and I decided to give it one by putting Two Jags in Chris Tarrant's hot seat.

'Ladies and gentlemen, welcome to *Who Wants To Be Prime Minister?* Our first contestant is John Prescott, a scuba-diver from Hull. Good evening, John. What would you do if you became prime minister tonight?'

'I'd renationalise the railways and buy meself another Jag.'

'Right, John, first question. Who won the last election?
Was it a) New Labour b) Old Labour c) Hard Labour or d) the *Sun*?'

'Can I go fifty-fifty, Chris?'

'Computer, take away two wrong answers.
OK, John, which is it: a) New Labour or d) the *Sun*?'

'Can I ask the audience, Chris?'

'Certainly, John. Audience, press your buttons now. Well, would you believe it? They've split fifty-fifty too. What's it to be, John?'

'Er, dunno. Can I call a friend?'

'Of course you can, John, but this is your last chance. Who do you want to call?'

'My friend Tony.'

(*Ring, ring.*)

'Hello, is that Tony?'

> *'Yeah, hi.'*

'This is Chris Tarrant, from *Who Wants To Be Prime Minister?*

> *'Great to talk to you, Chris. Love the show, it's my favourite, especially Mr Blobby. Love you, too.'*

'Thanks, Tone. I've got a friend of yours here. He needs your help. The next voice you hear will be his. It's over to you, John. You've got thirty seconds, starting now.'

> 'Ay oop, Tony.'

> *'Who's that?'*

> 'John.'

> *'John who?'*

> 'John Prescott.'

> *'I'm sorry, doesn't ring a bell.'*

> 'You know me, Tone, deputy prime minister and minister for the environment, transport, the regions and Mauritius.'

> *'No, never heard of you. You must have the wrong number. Bye.'*

'Well, John. I'm sorry to have to press you, but it seems you don't have any friends. You'll have to make your own mind up. Who won the last election, was it a) New Labour or d) the *Sun*?'

> 'Er, um.'

'I can't help you, John.'

> 'Er, were it New Labour?'

'Are you sure?'

> 'Er, no, it were the *Sun* wot won it.'

'And that's your final answer, is it, John?'

'Yes, Chris, it is.'

'John, I have to tell you, John, it's the wrong answer. You've won absolutely nothing.'

'What do you mean it's the wrong answer? I'll bloody have you. Just because I didn't go to university. Sodding Campbell put you up to this, didn't he?'

'Join us after the break, when one of these ten people get the chance to play *Who Wants To Be Prime Minister?*'

21 | The Day I Discovered I Was Gay

I know this must come of something of a shock to you. To be honest, it came as news to me. But I've discovered I'm gay.

And, chaps, even if you're married, I've got a bigger surprise. You're all gay, too. You just don't know it.

I hadn't the faintest idea, either. For years, I've lived in blissful ignorance of my true sexuality. If it wasn't for the National Lottery Board, I probably still wouldn't be any the wiser. Nor would you.

We must all thank the lottery trustees for financing the pioneering work of a group called Mesmac, which stands for Men who have Sex with Men, Action in the Community. Mesmac operates in Yorkshire and receives a £74,000 grant from the lottery. Among its many valuable services, it buys and distributes condoms to rent boys and advises male prostitutes how to milk the welfare system, with the help of a further £800,000 from health authorities.

But Mesmac is always looking to expand into new territories. That's where we married men come into the equation.

A highly trained Mesmac outreach worker observed 'a noticeable number of married men' at a men-only sauna. His bosses were horrified.

'These men were not accessing health promotion information and at Mesmac it's part of our remit to work with men who don't identify as gay,' said the organisation's publicity material. Mesmac is determined to break through to this 'difficult-to-reach population of men'.

Consequently, it launched a campaign to contact married men and invite them to counselling sessions. Adverts were placed in local newspapers and places where men gather, though I haven't noticed many in the gents in the West Stand at White Hart Lane.

All this is based on the fact that one vigilant Mesmac employee saw a 'noticeable number of married men' at a men-only sauna.

Most married men, I would imagine, have at some time in their lives used a men-only sauna. That's because most saunas for men are located in men's changing rooms at swimming pools and health clubs. Women aren't allowed. They have their own women-only saunas in the ladies' changing rooms.

As far as I am concerned that has always been a blessing in disguise. Men tend not to look their most impressive in saunas. Especially if they've just got out of the swimming pool. The vast majority of British men treat a sauna as a hangover cure, somewhere to sweat out fifteen pints of lager and a particularly unpleasant chicken tikka masala. Little did we realise that the true reason we use saunas is because we are all latent homosexuals. That is until Mesmac came along to enlighten us. Where would we be without them?

But, you know, on second thoughts, I'm not convinced. If there's anything absolutely guaranteed to put you off homosexuality for life it's a men-only sauna – though a quick peek round the door would probably send any discerning heterosexual woman fleeing into the arms of the nearest lesbian.

Perhaps they've got it wrong. Maybe we don't 'identify as gay' because, er, we're not gay. Call me controversial, but the conclusions of one AIDS worker at one men-only sauna are not exactly scientific.

My grandad was convinced that any man who wore suede shoes was a brown-hatter, but in those days you couldn't get a grant for it. Today he'd have his own office block and a team of staff going round trying to convince anyone found wearing Hush Puppies to check in for counselling.

I don't suppose it has occurred to Mesmac that maybe, just maybe, the reason we married men are not accessing safe sex information is because we don't need it. And the reason they find us 'difficult to reach' is because a smack in the mouth may cause offence.

Still, mustn't let any of this get in the way of putting a few more homosexuals on the public payroll, which is what all this is really about. You don't have to be gay to work here, but it helps. What is the lottery for, if not for buying condoms for rent boys, helping male prostitutes fiddle their social security and persuading married men they're gay? Soon we'll have gay men going round door to door, like Jehovah's Witnesses, trying to convince us to convert.

The good news is that it means we can access services denied to mere heterosexuals. For instance, the last time I looked, lucky gay residents of Haringey, in North London, were being offered

'FREE CONDOMS AND LUBRICANT
IN THE COMFORT OF YOUR OWN HOME'.

That was the heading on an advert in the local council magazine, which promised: 'Free condoms and lubricant through the post for gay, bisexual and other men who have sex with men living in the London Borough of Haringey.' All you had to do was fill in a form and send it Freepost to Rubberstuffers – a charity funded by the area health authority. You didn't even have to buy a stamp. Hey presto, all you need for a little light buggery – direct to your front door.

When I lived in Haringey, it was difficult enough getting a pizza delivered.

What puzzled me at the time was who were these other men who had sex with men, who weren't actually gay or bisexual? Were they Cybermen? Mr Men? They couldn't be Michelin Men, or they wouldn't need rubber johnnies.

That was before I discovered Mesmac and saw the light.

I had visions of little mopeds with boxes on the back bearing the Rubberstuffers logo whizzing round North London dispensing packets of three and tubes of KY jelly to men who couldn't be arsed to find an all-night chemist.

Now, I couldn't care less what people get up to in the comfort of their own homes of an evening. But I fail to see why it is any business of the state to facilitate sexual activities between men at the expense of the taxpayer.

And before some of you start bouncing up and down about

'homophobia' let me stress that the same applies to sex between men and women, or women and women, for that matter.

For the record, gays have among the highest disposable incomes in the country. They can afford to buy their own condoms. Every supermarket, pub toilet and all-night garage has a wide selection. Not just in North London, either.

I was in a pub in darkest Lincolnshire a while back and there was a machine dispensing condoms in a tantalising array of exotic flavours from soup to nuts, including ice cream.

In some parts of rural Lincolnshire, you can't even get real ice cream.

Make mine a Mivvi.

22 | Nice Work If You Can Get It

One of the most memorable adverts of the 1980s starred Maureen Lipman as Jewish grandmother Beattie. It was part of a series to promote the newly privatised British Telecom (BT – geddit?) and featured Beattie on the phone to her grandson.

He tells her he's just flunked his exams. 'What all of them?' she asks, horrified.

No, he replies, he did manage to pass sociology.

'You got an ology?' she exclaims proudly, her mood brightening considerably as she plants the candles on the celebratory cake she has baked for him.

'You get an ology, you're a scientist!'

It was a classic, an entire sitcom condensed into about thirty seconds. What we didn't realise then was that twenty years later it would go on to form the foundation not only of Labour's education, education, education policy but its Soviet-style programme of investment in public services, which has added 800,000 people to the public payroll and made one in four of the workforce directly dependent on the state for their wages.

These days you get an ology and you're laughing all the way to your index-linked pension. And it doesn't matter what your ology's in, they'll find you a job. Ipswich Council advertised for a 'Garbology Officer, salary £20,370 to £23,313. Are you looking for an opportunity to be involved with an exciting new initiative between the archaeology and waste management service?'

Never really thought about it, to be honest. When I left school, the careers master would try to steer you in the direction of accountancy, medicine, teaching and the law if you were academically inclined – or plumbing, bricklaying and journalism if you weren't.

I had no idea there was an exciting future to be forged at the cutting edge of archaeology and waste management. No one had ever heard of garbology, which the advert informs us is the archaeology of rubbish. The successful candidate would, amongst other things, 'show children in school how to explore their heritage through the study of waste' and 'use techniques of archaeology to involve communities in an understanding of changing waste patterns' and 'work with older people using retrieved objects as a focus for reminiscence' and organise training programmes and workshops for people from a diverse range of backgrounds. 'Does this sound like you?'

If it does, I suggest you should try to get out more.

Until now, we all thought those winos you see sifting through skips and pushing supermarket trolleys full of rubbish through the local shopping streets were life's flotsam and jetsam, to be pitied and handed the odd pound coin for a can of Special Brew.

Now it appears they're not tramps at all, they're Garbology Officers on a mission. What we have here is a marvellous illustration of the reality of the way Labour governs Britain. Step one is to encourage people to go to 'universities' which are little more than jumped-up polytechnics to meet targets set by Whitehall. Because so few are actually equipped to tackle nuclear physics or the classics, meaningless courses have to be invented to keep them occupied.

Step two comes when they leave after three years with degrees in everything from media studies to diversity management which aren't worth the paper they're printed on. Then, instead of dumping them on the dole where they'd swell the unemployment statistics, jobs have to be created so that they'll be forever grateful and vote Labour come election time.

Which is how you end up with Garbology Officers and Transgender Policy Units, cluttering up town halls, government departments and the NHS.

Hundreds of thousands of meaningless jobs have been created since 1997. Public spending has doubled. Council tax rose more than seventy per cent in eight years to pay for all this 'investment'. But if you ever wondered where the money goes, all you have to do is borrow a copy of the *Guardian* any Wednesday. Don't buy one, it only encourages them. Turn to the Society section and study the classified ads. There you find more than 120 pages of public sector jobs – all paid for by the British taxpayer. Check out some of these from a single issue.

Bedfordshire wanted to spend £100,000 a year on a Deputy Chief Executive/Strategic Director of Resources. Basically, a glorified assistant town clerk. The people of Bedfordshire won't notice the slightest bit of difference – except the increase in their council tax.

London was getting a Public Champion for Public Space – whatever that is – on £60,000 a year.

Sheffield was urgently seeking a Divisional Manager for Delivery and Quality – to enable teenagers 'to make the best possible transition to adulthood'. Why? That's another £70,000.

Lewisham, which was in the middle of a dustmen's strike, was urgently seeking three policy officers on £37,400 and a Diversity and Engagement Manager on £40,000-plus. How many dustmen could you get for that?

Elsewhere, the Royal Borough of Kingston was anxious to engage a squad of 'Floating Support Workers, under a Senior Floating Support Worker', who 'will have responsibility for supervision, appraisal and development of the floating support team'. Salaries between £23,000 and £25,000 a year.

Float on.

Among the things Derbyshire found itself short of were four Detached Youth Workers, on £25,000 each. Do they have Semi-Detached Youth Workers, too?

Transport for London, responsible for bringing traffic in our capital to a complete standstill, was looking for an assortment of co-ordinators and administrators, including someone to 'provide service for the flagship consultants'. 'World Class Streets for a World Class City', the ads boasted. That'll be something to do with narrowing the roads, changing all the traffic lights to red, building humps and congestion charging, then. Salaries up to £31,000.

There were a dozen pages of health service vacancies. More co-ordinators – they like their co-ordinating in the public sector –

customer relationship managers, patient pathway supervisors, a few extra floaters, a handful of Sure Start managers, some strategists, liaison officers, bilingual advocates, a team of assertive outreach managers and a healthy – no pun intended – compliment of facilitators. Wages? Anything up to £35,000.

I could only find a few adverts for nurses. None for doctors, porters or cleaners.

Is it any wonder that the extra billions shovelled into the NHS has produced less than a two per cent increase in operations?

The London Borough of Sutton was desperately seeking, amongst others, a 'Person Centred Planning Co-ordinator and a Traverse Co-ordinator. £29,000 plus car allowance.'

Greenwich needed an 'Adult Protection Co-ordinator. £30,000 a year.' Could be a job for Mad Frankie Fraser, but I doubt he could afford the cut in wages.

My personal favourite among the 600 or so jobs going begging that week was the £29,244 vacancy for a co-ordinator at the Hopscotch Asian Women's Centre, in Camden. That's more than a junior doctor gets.

It would be funny, if it wasn't so serious. Most of these are brand-new posts. However did we manage without them?

None of these jobs contributes anything to the economy and they cost all of us a small fortune. Take West Yorkshire, where an exciting vacancy arose for 'A Get-Away Boys Development Worker' on £24,265 a year. The lucky applicant was wanted to work with the Teenage Pregnancy Team, Young People's Services, Youth Offending Team, Young Families Plus, Guidance Services, Social Services, training and lifestyle skills providers, colleges, Begin, Connexions, West Yorkshire Local Education Authority, other youth and community organisations and our old friends at Mesmac (men who have sex with men).

The successful candidate is now, amongst other things, organising and delivering 'get-away boys' activities for young men and their workers to explore their sexuality.

We've got a word for that, haven't we children?

Meanwhile, Manchester City Council was looking for a Lesbian

Development Worker on £20,000 a year. The post was 'established to facilitate the formulation and development of sustainable networks and self-organised groups among the Lesbian Communities of Manchester [their capitals] and to co-ordinate volunteer involvement within the Project'.

Why? I wasn't aware lesbianism was a disability. Quite the opposite, judging by the number of councils desperate to recruit them.

Couldn't they just give them jobs as 'five a day' co-ordinators? However did we manage without them? Councils all over the country, at the government's behest, have hired thousands of these individuals to lecture us on healthy eating. The 'five a day' bit relates to the number of portions of fruit and vegetables we are expected to consume. They've even produced a handy guide explaining what kind of produce is good for us. Egg-shaped new potatoes, for instance. What shape potatoes did they think we might be eating? Eiffel Tower-shaped? Hovercraft-shaped? Aren't all potatoes egg-shaped? Or egg-ish?

A small fortune has been shelled out employing these people at up to £30,000 a year, index-linked pensions, comfy offices, company car and one for yourself.

They churn out leaflets and newspaper adverts extolling the benefits of broccoli and suchlike. What effect they have, who knows?

A friend of mine says if God had meant us to eat broccoli he'd have given it hooves and made it go 'moo'.

Do you think when they dreamed up the welfare state they thought they'd end up hiring madwomen in sensible shoes to go round ordering people to eat broccoli?

Me, neither.

But they're out there. And still you wonder where your council tax goes.

I don't have anything personally against five-a-day co-ordinators. I'm sure some of them are very nice people. They think they're doing good work. And, in the scheme of things, they're probably doing more good than harm. It's just that I don't think it's any business of the government to employ busybodies to tell us to eat our greens. The five-a-day brigade are simply part of the hidden unemployment. The government likes to boast that the jobless figures are at an all-time low. But that's only because they keep hiring people to do pointless jobs.

There's a whole world out there which has absolutely nothing of value to do, at vast expense. In a previous life they'd be taking in washing or selling the *Big Issue*.

Yet at the same time one bit of the government is flooding the country with garbology officers and five-a-day co-ordinators, another bit is hiring lawyers to sue supermarkets for telling us fruit and veg is good for us.

Yes, you did read that right. The trading standards people took Tesco to court for running a campaign to persuade people to eat vegetables. In association with Cancer Research UK, Tesco printed labels on millions of grocery items proclaiming: 'Eat at least five different portions of fruit and veg a day to prevent cancer.'

Isn't that exactly what the government is hiring five-a-day co-ordinators to do? Shouldn't they be rejoicing in the town halls that their message is getting across?

Er, no.

No one is saying that the ads aren't true. It just that some pedantic *Guardian* reader in trading standards – what we used to call weights and measures – has spotted that the labels breached something called the 1939 Cancer Act. Like me, you probably had no idea there was such a thing. Most of us assumed that in 1939 the government had bigger things to worry about. Such as the Second World War, for instance.

Apparently not.

The labels were also in breach of some other law passed in 1996 to stop shops selling quack cures.

Fair enough. But isn't the official line that eating five brussels sprouts and a mango every day will stop you getting cancer? Which is why we've got all these five-a-day co-ordinators in the first place.

So why was Tesco being dragged before West Mercia magistrates, and Asda hauled before the bench in Swindon for the same 'offence'? Because common sense and proportion have no place in the governance of Britain any more. Rules is rules. Government exists for the purpose of giving people in government something to do, however fatuous – even if all it amounts to is hiring one lot of people to tell you to eat your greens and another lot to take them to court for doing exactly that.

The salaries of those jobs advertised in the *Guardian* that Wednesday amounted to roughly £18 million, not counting gold-plated, index-linked pensions, perks, secretaries, cars, office space, health insurance, cheap mortgages and one for yourself.

That adds up to over £900 million a year. The true cost is anyone's guess. And that's just one day's ads in one newspaper.

When I first did this exercise about ten years ago, there were thirty-seven pages of jobs and the annual total was £395 million. Now it's three times that. Trebles all round. That's inflation for you. The 'floaters' certainly keep the *Guardian* afloat. It's one of the last great nationalised industries, sustained by bucketloads of taxpayers' money in the form of subsidy by advertising.

It not just the *Guardian* jobs pages either. One week I decided to look, at random, at a typical English town, Luton. There I found an exciting and varied selection of jobs with Luton Council on offer in the local paper.

> Wanted: Lesbian, Gay, Bisexual and Transgender Policy Officer, up to £28,179, to help members of the LGBT community access council services.
>
> Consultant Learning Mentor, £22,635, to work under the direction of the Aimhigher/Learning Monitor.
>
> Peripatetic Learning Support Assistant, £9,598 (part-time) to support people of Traveller heritage (Irish Travellers, Gipsy Travellers, Circus and Fairground families).
>
> Parenting Skills Co-ordinator, £28,179, a new post responsible for undertaking parenting assessments and co-ordinating the systemic family therapy scheme.
>
> If none of those take your fancy, how about becoming a Referral Order Co-ordinator, on £28,179?

One paper, one council, one week.

Not many teachers, policemen, dentists or even roadsweepers there. Go to any local rag, any week of the year and it's the same. This is what Labour calls 'investing' in public services. Why do the gay, lesbian, bisexual and transgender residents of Luton need someone on £28,179 a year to help them 'access' council services. Don't they want the same services as everyone else – clean streets, even pavements, working lamp posts, meals on wheels, tidy parks?

How difficult can it be to 'access' the refuse service? Try leaving your dustbin out before the binmen come round. There, that didn't hurt, did it?

Why should the taxpayers of Luton – or anywhere else, for that matter – provide support for 'travellers' who have never paid a penny in tax in their lives?

What the hell is a Parenting Skills Co-ordinator? And why should Luton Council want to pay one £28,179 a year?

While British industry slims down and produces ever more with fewer people, the public sector produces less with ever more people, while sucking the lifeblood out of the rest of us. You want roadsweepers, dustmen, bobbies on the beat. You get Floating Support Workers, Facilitators and Diversity Managers.

In Scotland, it's even worse. There fifty-two per cent of all the money spent north of the border comes out of our taxes, largely English taxes. It's been a recurring theme of my column over the years. Here's just one example.

In the Forth Valley, Stirling Council, in conjunction with Falkirk and Clackmannanshire councils and the Scottish Environmental Protection Agency, advertised for a

'Nappy Outreach Worker, £17,877. An enthusiastic individual to raise levels of awareness of and use of real nappies across the Forth Valley and so reduce the amount of disposables sent to landfill. You will promote the use of real nappies to target audiences in a variety of ways, including a programme of real nappy information sessions and taking display materials into local communities. You will also build partnerships with key stakeholders within the area and help to develop a long term real nappy project for the Forth Valley area. You will be a self-motivated individual with an interest in improving our environment and experience of and enthusiasm for real nappies. This post will involve working closely with members of the public and partner organisations, therefore the ability to communicate with people from a wide range of backgrounds is essential. Previous experience in a health or environmental field would be an advantage. A full driving licence is essential.'

Of course it is. No doubt they threw in a Mondeo, too.

The thick end of £18,000 is not a shabby wage in the Forth Valley. I'm sure redundant car workers, miners, fishermen and oil refinery technicians are queueing round the block to get their applications in.

I remember when my dad came home from work at the factory and never went back. Instead, he got a job as Nappy Outreach Worker, working alongside the Five-A-Day Co-ordinator and the Lesbian, Gay and Transgender Policy Officer.

We were promised a New Jerusalem. We got Nappy Valley.

Shortly after I drew attention to this ludicrous appointment, I discovered that in the Forth Valley the government had closed a local maternity ward, which used to deliver 1,400 babies a year.

In a land of milk and honey, maybe there would be the money to pay someone to encourage you to use real nappies or rummage through your dustbin and help dewy-eyed OAPs reminisce about the war through fondling old Ovaltine tins.

But we live in a country which is having to import nurses, doctors, dentists, plumbers, brickies and carpenters from all four corners of the world because instead of training our own people to do something useful we are encouraging them to take ologies in rubbish.

Gordon Brown would have us believe all this 'investment' has been pumped into building 'world class' schools'n'ospitals and recruiting millions of nurses, doctors, teachers and coppers. But the vast majority of those being hired as a result of Gordon's Soviet-style spending spree never get anywhere near a hospital ward or a classroom. They simply join the legions of time-wasters and meddlers in those hundreds of thousands of non-jobs which have been created to keep the *Guardian*-reading classes in the style to which they believe they are entitled.

For instance, Strathclyde Hospital advertised for a Condom Distributions Schemes Co-ordinator.

> 'This newly created post provides an exciting opportunity to work closely with a range of partners to consolidate and promote the further development of innovative condom distribution schemes across Lanarkshire. A key responsibility will be to provide support, training and advice to potential and current service deliverers. The post-holder will also play a central role in liaising with product suppliers, in contributing to social marketing campaigns, and in developing and maintaining a database for monitoring and evaluation purposes. The ability to use initiative in responding constructively to day-to-day enquiries is important. Good interpersonal, negotiation and liaison skills are therefore essential, together with a non-judgemental attitude to safer sex issues. Candidates should also have an understanding of sexual health issues and services, health service structures, health promotion principles, and a project-management approach. He or she will work closely with the Condoms Distribution Schemes Project Manager, and will be a member of the BBV and Sexual Health Team. Salary £16,625–£20,224 per annum.'

BBV? Answers on a postcard, please. Never mind your hip operation. In Strathclyde, they've got their priorities right. Who needs nurses when you can hire a Something For The Weekend Co-ordinator?

After it was revealed that the government wastes £50 billion in taxes every year, this was another small reminder of where our money goes. Councils all over Britain embarked on hiring legions of Breastfeeding Co-ordinators, on salaries of around £27,000 a year. It makes you wonder how women ever managed in the past. One reader who sent me an advert from North Shields, Tyneside, asked: 'Can men apply?'

Only if they agree to vote Labour.

Peter Mandelson's grandad, Herbert Morrison, once said he intended to build the Tories out of London by carpeting the capital with council houses.

Fifty years later, Gordon Brown decided to employ the Tories out of Britain. He has taken a small fortune out of the productive sector of the economy with ever higher taxes and used it to bribe people to vote Labour by putting them on the payroll.

In Brown's Britain, you get an 'ology, you've got it made.

23 | The Old Woman Who Lived In A Shoe

Ever wondered how social services would have handled the Old Woman Who Lived In A Shoe?

If you remember your nursery rhymes, you'll recall that she had so many children she didn't know what to do. So she gave them some broth without any bread, whipped them and sent them to bed. That would make an interesting case study down at the town hall. Is it a job for the housing department, the social exclusion unit, the child protection team or the five-a-day co-ordinator?

Imagine the hastily convened case conference.

*

Clearly, this woman is a single parent, as there appears to be no Old Man Who Lived In A Shoe on the scene. Neighbours say a procession of Uncles Who Lived In A Shoe have come and gone over the years, usually after the pubs turn out, but none of them have stuck around for long.

The number of children living in the shoe would seem to indicate that the woman had slipped the attentions of the family planning clinic.

Social workers expressed concern that the children appeared to subsist exclusively on broth, despite government guidelines which recommend five portions of fruit and vegetables every day. They also feel that these children should be placed on the 'at risk' register, since there is evidence that they are regularly whipped by their mother. However, they are sensitive to the fact that physical chastisement is part of the Old Woman's culture and consequently are reluctant to intervene.

Apparently, the woman came to be living in a shoe after rejecting an offer of a council maisonette on the grounds that it only had three bedrooms and was a fifteen-minute walk from the bingo hall. Although her living conditions are far from ideal, officials are reluctant to break up the family and place any of the children in care. It was recommended that social services would work with the woman to find a solution in the hope that that a pair of wellington boots would become available shortly.

*

In case you're wondering where I'm going with all this, what set me off was a story about a thirty-two-year-old mother of nine, who was demanding that Leeds Council provide her with an eight-bedroom home for her growing brood.

Tracy Fulthorpe first became pregnant when she was seventeen. She subsequently married the father and they had one more child, but sadly he died of cancer aged twenty-five. The relationship was already on the rocks, she insisted. Since then she'd had seven children by three different fathers, none of whom contributed anything by way of upkeep – presumably because they, too, live on state handouts. Miss Fulthorpe would only name two of them. The other she refused to identify, saying the baby was 'unplanned'. Does she even know who the father is?

She wasn't working – when would she find the time? – and was receiving benefits equivalent to a salary of £25,000 a year – paying no rent or council tax for her four-bed house.

At the time of writing she was pregnant yet again and was demanding somewhere twice the size. She believed she was entitled to this because by looking after her own children she was 'doing [her] job for the government'.

I wasn't aware that it was part of Gordon Brown's New Deal careers policy to pay women to have children by absentee fathers. But I can see how it must appear that way to the likes of Tracy Fulthorpe. It's an inevitable consequence of the dependency culture.

Her children are, of course, entirely blameless. It's not their fault they are the offspring of a feckless woman and a parade of irresponsible men, who think it is their divine right to go on breeding and present the rest of us with the bill.

The only unusual aspect of this case is the large number of children involved. All over Britain there are thousands of 'families' like the Fulthorpes, sired by vanishing 'babyfathers' and wholly dependent on handouts. It's not fair on the kids and it's not fair on hard-working, responsible taxpayers who are forced to stump up billions for this selfishness. Things will never get better until a government is prepared to grasp the welfare nettle, slash benefits and explain to people that the world doesn't owe them a living.

Some days, I'm convinced there's a case for bringing back the workhouse. A couple of years ago, most of the newspapers featured the case of a family I christened the Asbos. Their real name is immaterial.

The three sisters sat there, without a care in the world, staring bovinely at the camera, displaying their bastard offspring whom they conceived at twelve, fourteen and sixteen respectively. Their crone of a mother, who looked at least twenty years older than her claimed thirty-eight years, had the cheek to blame their school for them getting themselves up the duff. Twice-divorced Mrs Asbo declared that the girls might not have got pregnant if they had received better sex education.

Of course.

And if they'd had better instruction in maths, the eldest girl would now be running the Treasury.

What utter claptrap. Kids can't move for sex education these days, for all the good it does.

Was Mrs Asbo really pretending that her little darlings had no idea where babies come from? Her sixteen-year-old had already had two miscarriages and an abortion, so she must have had some tenuous grasp of the link between cause and effect.

This happy little commune was costing the rest of us £31,000 a year in benefits. And mum still found time to complain that it was a struggle getting by.

It never occurred to her to start buying the kids' shoes from Matalan, then, not splashing out a small fortune on designer Nike trainers which the child will grow out of in about ten minutes. It's hard not to feel sorry for the children of these, I was going to say teenage mums but one of them was only twelve when she had her baby. Sorry, but the last time I looked, the age of consent was sixteen. Didn't Mrs Asbo explain that to her daughters?

And where, again, were the fathers? You guessed. They wanted nothing to do with these unfortunate toddlers they so casually sired. One of them was only fourteen himself, so there was little point in prosecuting him or setting the Child Support Agency on his tail.

So it fell to the rest of us to pay for the Swiss Family Asbo to luxuriate in their chosen lifestyle.

Most people have to strive hard to support their own families and bring up their children to the best of their abilities. Why the hell should we be expected to pick up the bill for the offspring of the feckless and promiscuous?

I wasn't joking about the workhouse, either. The best thing that could have happened to these hapless children would have been to be taken into some kind of protective custody while the youngest two mothers were sent back to school until they were old enough to get a job. Otherwise in another ten years – or less – these toddlers will be single parents of their own.

As it is, I wouldn't give them much chance. One of them was called T-Jay. What kind of name is T-Jay? It makes the poor kid sound like some kind of disinfectant. Another revelled in the name Amani – probably a spelling error or copied from a cheap designer label knock-off.

What hope have they got?

The welfare state was a good idea in principle but it has ended up subsidising the terminally selfish, stupid and lazy.

Incidentally, The Old Woman Who Lived In A Shoe is said to have been based on a notorious eighteenth-century drunk and prostitute, called Mary Buttwhistle, who is reported to have had twenty children fathered by her clients. She was supposed to be a warning to all young women about the dangers of drink and promiscuity.

Not a role model.

24 | Madness is all in the MIND

I've been lucky enough to win a couple of awards in my career, but my chest really swelled with pride when I was short-listed for the title of Bigot of the Year by the mental health charity, MIND.

What, you might ask, did I do to qualify for this singular honour? It was in recognition of a column I wrote about events at the Rampton top security hospital for the criminally insane, based on a report about a love affair taking place within its walls between the notorious child-killer Beverley Allitt and another mental patient nicknamed The Vampire because of his penchant for drinking the blood of his victims.

Apparently, they met at a disco organised by the prison author-ities at which staff handed out free condoms to inmates. A poster for Rampton's 'Couples Night' promised

'Fun and games with your partner.
Feeling fruity! Hobnobbing! Sexy Sundae!
Sign your name and your partners [sic] name on the list on your ward.'

It also transpired that Rampton employed an Afro-Caribbean hairstylist, offered cut-price leg-waxing and was considering arrang-ing a gay disco for homosexual offenders.

You might think this is not a way to run a secure institution for deranged criminals. And you would be absolutely right. Obviously MIND disagreed, although quite how raising the question amounts to bigotry is beyond me, though. It only goes to show yet again how the 'caring' classes consistently elevate the rights of their 'clients' above all else. I wonder what the relatives of those mur-dered by Beverley Allitt and her Count Dracula boyfriend made of it all. They have a right to expect that the killers are punished, not sent to an institutionalised Club 18–30 holiday camp. This is just another example of how much of the charity sector has been hijacked by full-time political activists recruited from the jobs pages of the *Guardian*.

The reaction of MIND to a legitimate matter of public concern is merely further confirmation. Certainly you won't find me putting a shilling in their tin next flag day. I have no intention of supporting any organisation which appropriates for political posturing and cheap publicity stunts public donations intended to help the less fortunate.

Having said that, I consider being accused of bigotry by a bunch of left-wing lunatics a badge of honour. The knowledge that something I wrote made them miserable was well worth it.

By the way, it's Mr Bigot.

25 | Nae Pooves, Nae Dugs

A gay couple were turned away from a Scottish hotel because the landlord refused to let them share a double bed. Tom Forrest, of the Cromasaig guest house, wrote: 'I have no hatred or fear of poofs, etc. I just do not approve of unnatural acts being performed in my home.'

Stephen Nock and his partner rightly complained that if they'd been black, Mr Forrest wouldn't have been able to discriminate against them.

The metropolitan liberal (in the literal sense of the word) in me agrees with them. To those of us who inhabit the media/political village, Mr Forrest's views can sound prehistoric.

But sometimes we forget that attitudes which are perfectly acceptable to many of us who live in London don't always find an echo further afield. What applies in Soho doesn't always travel to Solihull, let alone the Scottish Highlands. I'd imagine that Mr Forrest's neighbours would find nothing controversial in what he said. Nor would millions of others.

That's not to condone it, simply to try and explain it. We should remember that tolerance is a two-way street and the London-based media and political classes shouldn't always try to impose their own moral code and prejudices on the rest of the world. Yet this case convinced the government it was time to amend the discrimination laws to include private guest houses.

What's curious here, though, is that Mr Forrest was prepared to let Stephen and his partner have a twin room. What did he think they could get up to in a double bed that they couldn't do in twins? They could always have pushed them together. Perhaps he has the same code as 1950s Hollywood, which always insisted married couples were shown in twin beds and one of them had to keep one foot on the floor at all times.

Having said all that, it's not just gays that some Scottish

landlords object to. We were once turned away from a hotel in the Western Highlands because we had a dog with us.

The owner explained: 'It's nae personal. You either dae dugs or you dinnae dae dugs and we dinnae dae dugs.'

26 | Stayin' Alive

Publican Donald Cameron commited suicide when the brewery decided to turn his Birmingham pub into a 1970s theme bar.

He went to his car and gassed himself after being reprimanded when he refused to dress up in flares and a Bee Gees wig and insisted on wearing his usual suit and tie. He couldn't face becoming the object of public ridicule.

Drastic, maybe. Sad, most certainly. But let's hope it makes the breweries pause for thought.

If there is one group of people with even less regard for our history than New Labour and British Airways, it is those who run the big breweries. Over the past twenty years, few boozers have escaped unscathed. Old oak beams and real horse brasses have been ripped out and replaced first with Formica and chrome and then with fake oak beams and plastic horse brasses. Perfectly good pub names like the Dog and Duck or the Railway Tavern which date back centuries have been rebranded the Hungry Horse or Looney O'Mooney's. The karaoke has replaced the old joanna. Hundreds of delightful establishments have been turned into hideous theme pubs. The theme changes about once a year, from pastiche old Oirish post office to American sports bar.

If Bass wanted a genuine recreation of a 1970s pub, it would have asked Mr Cameron to wear an Arthur Scargill wig and a Bri-Nylon shirt with dark brown perspiration stains under the arms. The publican himself would not be serving. He would be sitting at the end of the bar, talking to his cronies, with an Embassy hanging from his lips. He would pause only to refill his glass from the Bell's bottle and cough theatrically into a soggy bar towel.

The ashtrays would be filled to overflowing, there would be uncollected glasses and empty crisp packets on every table. In one corner, two old ladies would be making a bottle of milk stout last all lunchtime. In the other, there would be a fight taking place between a man who looked like Harold Steptoe and an overweight peroxide blonde on large gin and limes.

The bar would only be open three days a week and drinkers would be plunged into darkness at regular intervals because of the power cuts. There would be no bar food because of the bread strike and the Cod War.

You would have to cross a picket line to get into the snug because the staff were in dispute over new flexible rostering arrangements. There would be bottled Mackeson only because the draymen had come out in sympathy with the barmen.

If you called a minicab, you would wait an hour for a rusty Morris Marina to arrive. It would probably only have two doors and would break down before you got home. The driver would be drunk, which was a blessing in disguise because the Scotch fumes would mask the stench of his halitosis.

Sounds positively ghastly, doesn't it? But it might just work. Following the success of the BBC's flashback cop show *Life On Mars*, there's something of a 1970s revival going on. Brut after-shave, Mateus Rosé, Blue Nun, spam, Cinzano, Babycham, Nimble bread and Cadbury's Smash are all making a comeback as marketing men tap into our taste for nostalgia.

All I can say is that anyone who is nostalgic for the Decade Taste Forgot wasn't there. It always amuses me when you see celebrities on naff TV shows waxing lyrical about Spacehoppers or loon pants. Even those who were born in the 1970s couldn't have been more than about two at the time.

Those of us who lived through it remember the strikes, queues, bare shelves, petrol rationing, power cuts, waiting lists for mort-gage rates in double digits, three-channel TV which started at lunchtime and ended before midnight, six months to get a phone installed. 'Crisis? What crisis?'

That's to say nothing of the ghastly fashions. I still can't believe I got married in a brown suit.

Have the New Nostalgics actually smelt Brut? Or ever drunk Mateus Rosé? It takes the enamel off your teeth. I lived on Smash for a while. Trust me, it's not a way to behave. Still, there's no accounting for taste.

It's a bit late for poor Donald Cameron, but the time might just be ripe for a 1970s theme pub, with the jukebox blaring out the Bee Gees' smash hit 'Stayin' Alive'.

Pass the Blue Nun.

27 | The Yellow Brick Road to Basra

After the first wave of fighting in Iraq was over, the British government decided Basra had a future as a tourist trap. Ministers hired consultants to develop the southern Iraqi town as a top cultural destination. Never mind the small matter of restoring order and installing democracy first, but why not?

One advertising man said: 'The most important thing for any brand is name awareness. And everyone knows the name of this place. 'Instead of hearing what Basra is like, why not see what Basra is like? It's quite zeitgeisty.'

I'm sure it is. But I can't see planeloads of thrill-seekers heading there just yet. Unless, of course, they turn it into an interactive theme park.

Roll up, roll up! Experience for yourself the thrill of becoming a suicide bomber for a day. No refunds.

The government also spent £152,000 sending two Whitehall 'gender and diversity' equality advisers to Baghdad.

In the immediate aftermath of the invasion, Iraq faced any number of problems. Electricity and water supplies had been disrupted, schools and universities were closed down, hospitals were desperate for staff and supplies. Oh, and don't let's forget the ever-present threat of terrorism.

Into the middle of this chaos, ministers thought it was appropriate to parachute in a pair of busybodies plucked from the jobs pages of the *Guardian*.

I suppose there might have been some merit in this madness had they been able to turn their hand to repairing power lines or dressing wounds.

Leave aside the staggering waste of British taxpayers' money, which could have been better spent elsewhere. What exactly are they supposed to contribute to the rebuilding of Iraq? Nothing could be more calculated to get up the noses of Muslims than being lectured on gender, diversity and equality by some hatchet-faced harridan from Islington. Who thought this was a good plan? I'd love to have been at the meeting which decided to send them.

> 'Now then, we've got millions without power in Baghdad, raw sewage running through the streets, hospitals without medicines and equipment, widespread looting and someone has just driven a truckload of explosives into a roadblock near Basra. Ideas, anyone?'
>
> 'Why don't we send out a couple of gender and diversity advisers?'
>
> 'Brilliant, Simpkins. Any other business?'

There couldn't be a better insight into the lunatic New Labour mindset. These people exist inside their own little bubble, where the trivial takes on exaggerated significance. Theirs is a world of five-a-day co-ordinators, healthy-walking advisers, lesbian-empowerment officers, smoking cessation enforcers and the thousands of other meaningless jobs. Now, not content with trying to force us to comply with their bizarre guidelines, they're attempting to impose their world view on the hapless Iraqis. As if they haven't suffered enough.

Meanwhile in Afghanistan, tribesmen were offered counselling to help them get in touch with their feminine side. The Foreign Office announced a plan to send in psychologists to help Afghan men confront 'gender issues'. Forget terrorism, land mines, poverty and heroin smuggling, what matters is sorting out their 'emotional problems'.

A report said: 'The patriarchal Afghan society does not encourage men to acknowledge or talk through difficult issues. This can mean they repress their problems and deal with them in inappropriate or antisocial ways.' This would explain why they push walls on top of women suspected of adultery. So Britain sponsored something called 'Inclusive Government: Main-streaming Gender Into Foreign Policy.'

Pity the poor Afghans and Iraqis. And don't be surprised if after being lectured by po-faced Islington diversity co-ordinators and inclusion facilitators, they figure they're better off under the Taliban and Saddam.

28 | Mind How You Go

When I started out in this game, the police went round in pairs and rarely appeared in the papers.

There'd be stories appealing for witnesses to a crime, an identikit photo of a suspect would be issued, and an inspector would occasionally read out a short statement outside court following a successful conviction. And that was about it. These days, the Old Bill are in the news pages more often than the Beckhams. But it rarely has anything to do with nicking villains, or tackling crime as most of us understand it.

I could fill this book with hundreds of examples of the lunacy, perversity and incompetence of the thick blue line, their obsession with minor motoring offences and so-called 'hate crimes'.

This isn't the fault of the handful of bobbies left on the beat, while the rest are sitting behind locked doors in police stations closed to the public – filling in forms, attending diversity seminars and suing each other for racial and sexual harassment.

It's down to the Guardianistas who have been determined for years to turn the police into an arm of social services and an instrument of social and political engineering. And it has been achieved with the craven compliance of the Association of Chief Police Officers (ACPO). If the police are now the provisional wing of New Labour, ACPO is the army council.

Virtually no organisation presents a graver threat to individual liberty in Britain today. ACPO has no constitutional authority. It is merely a collection of senior officers, yet it behaves like a central command.

It is not the job of the police to start rounding up free citizens for alleged thought crimes. No one should be treated like a criminal for speaking their mind, no matter how much their views may offend against fashionable, left-wing orthodoxy. If someone incites violence against an individual or a section of the community there are adequate laws already which can be used to bring them to book. Disapproving of aspects of someone else's lifestyle should not be an indictable offence in a country with the pretence of being a free society. Yet that is how senior officers have chosen to interpret their role. Here's an example.

All forty-three forces in Britain were issued with a 114-page document called *Hate Crime: Delivering A Quality Service*. This insists that all complaints about 'hate crimes' be rigorously followed up, whether or not they have any merit. Failure to do so, it warns, could leave the police open to allegations of 'secondary victimisation' if a complainant feels officers are indifferent to their grievance. So all manner of nutters and malcontents are indulged and perfectly innocent people are subjected to a nasty ordeal at the hands of the police purely to satisfy intolerant ideologues with an axe to grind.

Most of these purse-lipped lunatics ought to be given short shrift and shown the door. Some of them should be charged with wasting police time. Instead, the red carpet is rolled out and they are treated like valued customers.

This doctrine applies only to 'hate crimes'. No one cares if victims of burglary, car crime or street robbery suffer from 'secondary victimisation' when they're fobbed off with a note for the insurance. And things will get ten times worse if and when the government's ill-conceived anti-religious hatred bill hits the statute books.

The politicisation of the police is all but complete. We now live in a country in which rural constabularies boast not about the number of crimes they solve but how many homosexuals they employ, and feel the collars of anyone who utters mild reservations about the advisability of gay adoption.

In pandering to political extremists who wish to smother free speech and crush anyone who dares to dissent from their own warped agenda, the police risk alienating the vast majority of law-abiding people. Under New Labour, Britain has been turned ruthlessly into a police state.

No one wants to go back to the rough-and-tumble days of 1970s Regan and Carter policing currently getting an airing on

BBC1's *Life On Mars*. (Oh, I dunno.) But, as former chief constable
Keith Hellawell points out, at least back then the Old Bill solved
more real crimes and nicked more villains.

These days they don't even look for escaped prisoners. Have
you ever wondered: whatever happened to manhunts? I'm old
enough to remember when any murderer who went over the
wall of Wormwood Scrubs immediately became Public Enemy
Number One.

The jailbreak would be lead item on *News At Ten* and the papers
would all carry front-page photofits of the absconder, under the
headline 'Have You Seen This Man?' Incident rooms and hotlines
would be set up, with five-figure rewards offered for any sighting
of the fugitive or information leading to his recapture. Mobile
canteens would dispense hundreds of gallons of tea and thousands
of bacon sandwiches to the phalanx of coppers walking in wide for-
mation through Epping Forest, methodically poking the under-
growth in search of clues.

There'd be roadblocks, sniffer dogs, house-to-house inquiries and
posters of Britain's Most Wanted on every bus shelter and lamp post.

Questions would be asked in the House, prison officers would
take every breakout personally and the police vowed to get their
man, however long it took.

If there was any suggestion that the escapee had slipped
through the All Ports alert to a foreign jurisdiction, detectives in
worsted suits and trilbys would pack their toothbrushes and head
for the Costa del Crime with a posse of Fleet Street's finest in
hot pursuit. Even if they returned empty-handed, they at least
exhausted their options.

In the days when Britain took the administration of justice
seriously, escaped prisoners such as Buster Edwards and Ronnie
Biggs became household names, such was their notoriety. The
grandaddy of TV cop shows wasn't called *No Hiding Place* for
nothing.

A prison break was a big event. David Bowie even wrote a song
called 'Over the Wall We Go!' poking fun at the police after a
couple of high-profile escapes.

Fast-forward to 'tough on crime' Tony Blair's Britain. Since Labour came to power, more than 1,000 murderers, rapists and robbers have escaped from open prisons. They didn't have to go over the wall, they simply walked out of the front door. Nearly 400 have had it away on their toes from a single nick, Leyhill in Gloucestershire, since 1997. Twenty-five are still out there somewhere, including one murderer who has been on the run for eight years.

Well, I say 'on the run'. I shouldn't think anyone is even bothering to look for him. And that's just one prison. The Home Office either won't, or can't, give accurate figures for other jails.

When was the last time you turned on the news or opened a paper to learn of a full-scale manhunt for an escaped prisoner? How many of Britain's Most Wanted can you name? Me neither.

A few years ago, one absconder was headline news. Now hundreds vanish into thin air and the authorities shrug. The police stick a description on a website and hope that they'll turn up.

It's not just home-grown villains, either. We've learned about hundreds of foreign criminals at large on our streets after fleeing jail. No one seems to know where they are. Have they vanished back into the 'community' or have they left the country? Your guess is as good as mine. Not only has the government no idea of who enters Britain any more, they don't bother checking up on who leaves, either.

Most of these escaped criminals are only caught when they reoffend, as so many of them do, often with tragic, fatal consequences.

We might ask why murderers and sex offenders are being housed in open prisons in the first place. But then again, we might also wonder why they take the trouble to abscond, given that under Labour's lenient sentencing and parole guidelines they'll all be out in five minutes anyway. The safety of the public and the security of our borders are two over-riding responsibilities of any government. On both counts, Labour has been found wanting miserably.

Not so much failure, perhaps, as deliberate dereliction of duty. Occasionally, when rumbled, they throw a human sacrifice such as

Charles Clarke to the pack and hope that the rumpus will all go away – which it generally does when the next crisis or three lumbers over the horizon. They reserve their real wrath not for the outrageous incompetence and indifference of the system but for those who have the audacity to draw attention to it.

This hasn't happened by accident, it has happened by design. This is the Britain they always wanted – a country where the 'rights' of criminals over-ride the right of the rest of us to sleep soundly in our beds; where Public Enemy Number One is not the escaped murderer or sex offender but the law-abiding, tax-paying citizen who wants merely to defend his own family and property.

So what are the Old Bill doing if they're not out looking for escaped convicts, or arresting burglars and muggers? What happened to all the 'tough on crime' rhetoric Blair fed us? Well, there's still plenty of crime out there – just not the kind of 'crime' most of us recognise. As I said, I could fill this book with examples of police madness. But that wouldn't leave room for much else. So I'll bring you a handful of cases to give you a true flavour of modern policing.

Every year, in my column, I hand out the annual Mind How You Go awards, for stupidity and bloody-mindedness beyond the call of duty.

In no particular order, these are a few from my Mind How You Go Hall of Fame.

In Oxford, a student was arrested for joking that a police horse was 'gay'. Who approved that? It must have passed across the desk of at least one senior officer. Did the stupidity of it all not occur to anyone at Oxford nick? Probably not. ACPO guidelines is ACPO guidelines.

Under the 'hate crimes' edict, the author Lynette Burrows was interviewed under caution for having the temerity to question the wisdom of allowing gay couples to adopt young children.

An elderly couple in Fleetwood, Lancashire, were questioned

for eighty minutes and warned about their future behaviour simply because they wanted to distribute some Christian literature alongside gay rights pamphlets at the local town hall.

🚓 The Metropolitan Police decided to spend £70,000 sending officers on 'Shakespeare awareness' courses. The programme was designed to instil 'inspirational leadership' by drawing on *Henry V* and *Julius Caesar*. Wherefore art thou, Romeo Bravo Echo?

🚓 In Lincolnshire, an amateur cricketer was dragged before the courts three times charged with nicking a scarecrow for a prank – even though he took it back.

🚓 In Aberdeen, the ever vigilant McPlod launched a campaign against a growing menace to society. They warned bus drivers that they will be charged with careless driving under Section 3 of the 1988 Road Traffic Act if they splash pedestrians by driving through puddles.

🚓 In Herefordshire, police hauled a shopkeeper away from his Sunday lunch and threatened him with prosecution for selling golliwogs. This wasn't an isolated piece of lunacy, either. The Golliwog Squad was also making itself busy in Worthing, Sussex. Police said they were treating as a matter of 'priority' a complaint about gollies being displayed in a local store. Owner John Scadgell faced charges under Section 2 of the Public Order Act, which makes it an offence to exhibit anything which could be considered threatening, abusive or insulting.

The Old Bill said Mr Scadgell was committing a racially aggravated offence. The complaint was made by a thirty-six-year-old graphic designer called Gerald Glover, who is quoted as saying: 'I just thought it was disgusting. When I saw them, I thought "Oh my God," and I was just stunned. I don't know what message it sends out to children today.' For heaven's sake. Children don't look at gollies and go out and join the BNP. I've never met any black person who looks even remotely like a golliwog. I thought we'd grown out of all this 1980s nonsense.

The Home Office even says that displaying golliwogs is not an offence. That didn't stop the zealots at Worthing nick. As far as they were concerned, this was a 'hate crime' and must be given top priority. We have now reached the stage where crime is an intangible thing. It may not technically be against the law, but it becomes a crime if someone says it is. Mr Glover should have been told politely to go away and get a life. If he persisted, he should have been sectioned. You've got to be pretty sick to see evil in a harmless cuddly toy. And whichever police officer sanctioned the investigation should be demoted. The reality is he'll probably be put on the fast track to promotion to chief constable.

Police in Hackney, East London, offered muggers, robbers and drug addicts £10 Marks & Spencer and Boots shopping vouchers to take part in a crime survey.

Merseyside Police hired an American to teach coppers how to ride a bike. A spokesman said: 'They'll learn how to get on and off and generally cycle along.' They'll also be taught to mend a puncture.

I don't know about you, but I could do all that when I was about seven. One minute my dad was holding the saddle, the next he was gone. Er, that was all there was to it.

Go to any playground and you'll see kids as young as four pedalling away merrily. What about the cops who can't manage a two-wheeler? Will they get a trike, or one with stabilisers?

West Yorkshire Police scrambled a £3.3 million 180mph helicopter, complete with satellite navigation and thermal imaging equipment – to chase two boys suspected of taking a pedalo in a boating lake, without paying. The desperados were duly rounded up and charged – but whether with nicking the pedalo or pedaloing above the speed limit wasn't clear.

Patrick Hamilton is a former paratrooper, a Falklands veteran who served seven tours of duty in Northern Ireland. He spent twenty-five years in the army ready and willing to lay down his life for freedom and justice. He must wonder why he bothered.

When Mr Hamilton, fifty-two, saw his sixteen-year-old daughter Catherine being menaced by a gang of hooligans, he rushed to her defence. She was being threatened by a gang of teenage boys and girls who followed her back from her part-time job at McDonald's, in North Shields, Tyneside. Mr Hamilton gave chase, grabbed hold of one of the gang and tried to make a citizen's arrest.

When police arrived, he called out: 'I've got one, I've got one.' But the police weren't interested in nicking the trouble-maker or going after the gang. Instead, they arrested Mr Hamilton, handcuffed him and drove him away in a police car. He was held at the local police station for an hour before being released without charge.

Mr Hamilton, who now works as a college lecturer teaching youngsters who want to join the police or armed forces, was livid. And rightly so. He said: 'I can't believe the police treated me and my family like this. It's disgusting. I can't believe the police protected these scum.'

I can.

The police have gone from being on the side of the law-abiding, through being neutral, to actively siding with vermin.

Mr Hamilton's arrest is par for the course. The Old Bill can't be bothered to go after thugs, either because they're frightened of getting a kicking, or because they're scared of the left wing, legally-aided lawyers who infest our so-called justice system. So they take the easy option and nick the good guys. While brave men like Patrick Hamilton fight for freedom in Iraq and Afghanistan, this is the kind of 'justice' they can expect back home.

Well done, North Shields Police.

In Kent, a court heard that a WPC who formerly worked as a topless model was considering her future in the force after being kidnapped at knifepoint by her lesbian lover and taken on a terrifying hundred-mile drive.

Following the hearing, she left the court hand in hand with her new girlfriend, who worked at the same bus depot as the woman who kidnapped her.

In North Yorkshire, Sergeant Christopher Lamb, with twenty-six years service, returned to work dressed as a woman and announced that he was having a sex change and in future wanted to be known as Nicola.

Chris/Nicola appeared at a press conference, wearing pink lipstick, a bottle-green blouse and a knee-length grey skirt. The chief constable of North Yorkshire, David Kenworthy, said he was delighted at the sergeant's decision and pledged his full support. 'We celebrate diversity in the North Yorkshire Police,' he said.

On Merseyside, a police press officer demanded £100,000 compensation for the stress involved in dealing with reporters over the James Bulger case eight years earlier.

In Hertfordshire a man was breathalysed while riding a skateboard through a shopping precinct.

In an Essex shopping precinct, a disabled pensioner was breathalysed after one zealous young policeman spotted her drinking a can of lemonade shandy. She was sitting on her invalid electric shopping trolley at the time.

The *Herts. Advertiser* led its front page with a story about a trainee chef who was arrested for drink-driving in Wheathampstead. Ian Bromwich was stopped at 11.20pm. He was riding on the pavement on a child's scooter, powered by an engine from a garden strimmer.

We are not told how fast he was going, but it is safe to assume that we are not talking Emerson Fittipaldi here. How fast can an 18cc engine designed to trim grass possibly propel a grown man on a child's scooter?

If he was a danger to anyone other than himself I should be amazed. Wheathampstead is hardly a walk on the wild side, especially at 11.20pm.

Now you might have thought that any policeman with half a brain would simply have told him to get off and walk home safely. You might also have thought that a senior officer at St Albans nick would have halted the prosecution and had a quiet word in the arresting officer's ear.

When the case came to court, even the prosecuting solicitor expressed some amazement. At that stage, the magistrates should have thrown it out.

But no. Instead of laughing the whole business out of court and ticking off the police for wasting everybody's time, the presiding magistrate announced that it was an 'extremely serious case'.

Mr Bromwich was fined £300 and ordered to pay £45 costs. To a trainee chef, £345 is a hell of a lot of money. He was also banned from driving for two years. He doesn't even have a driving licence.

You couldn't make it up.

Is it any wonder that the police and the justice system are viewed with such cynicism by so many decent, law-abiding people? Perhaps the chief constable of Hertfordshire would like to explain if he thinks this was an effective use of police time. Hertfordshire Police were in the middle of a summer offensive against drink-driving. It would be instructive to learn whether officers were put under pressure to achieve a certain number of arrests.

Perhaps the Home Secretary might explain how a woman with absolutely no sense of proportion managed to become a presiding magistrate.

You might also be interested in the two stories either side of the report of Mr Bromwich's court case on the front page of the *Herts. Advertiser*. One was about a robbery at a local computer firm. Equipment worth £8,000, containing valuable files and information, was stolen. At the time the newspaper went to press the robbers had not been apprehended.

The other was a sad tale of how a burglar broke into a house and stole a video recorder used by a two-year-old boy suffering from cystic fibrosis to watch his *Teletubbies* tapes. Police are appealing for witnesses.

If the burglar had also stolen the child's scooter and stopped off for a pint on the way home he would almost certainly have been caught.

Not to be outdone, Mansfield Police seized the record for nicking the youngest ever drink-driver. A sixteen-year-old boy was banned for being over the limit and driving without a licence or insurance. So, was he screaming around in a stolen XR3? Doing 110mph through a shopping precinct?

No, he was riding a Go-Ped – a kiddies' scooter with a tiny engine.

Shortly afterwards, in Staffordshire, the war on motorists took another exciting new twist. Following the skateboard, strimmer-powered scooter and shopping trolley incidents, other forces began to compete to see who could stretch the definition of 'motor vehicle' to breaking point in their zeal to nick as many otherwise law-abiding citizens as possible.

So, congratulations to WPC Donna Gibbs and her boss, Inspector Nick Baker. WPC Gibbs, Staffordshire's answer to Juliet Bravo, was driving her panda car through the village of Codsall when she spotted three boys riding a home-made go-kart.

It sounds like a scene straight out of *Just William* and recalls a more innocent age before PlayStations when youngsters made their own amusements in the fresh air, instead of sitting in their bedrooms glued to computer screens, downloading pornography from the Internet.

That's not how Juliet Bravo saw it. She stopped her car, pulled the boys up and said they were breaking the law because they hadn't got a tax disc or insurance. After lecturing them, she took their names and addresses. A few days later their parents received a letter from Inspector Baker informing them that their sons were guilty of antisocial behaviour.

Needless to say, the parents were livid – not with the boys but with the petty-minded police. One of the boys' mothers, Karen Cross, said: 'When I was young, my sister and I built our own go-kart. It is part of growing up.'

Precisely. When I was a boy, building your own kart out of planks half-inched from the nearby building site and pram wheels recovered from the local scrapyard was a rite of passage. With no brakes and rudimentary steering made from string likely to snap at any time, we were a downright menace, both to ourselves and anyone unfortunate enough to get in the way. It was like the chariot race from *Ben Hur*. The only way of stopping was either to hit a wall head-on or slam your shoes down onto the pavement. Frankly, you were better off hitting the wall, especially as most of us only had one pair of shoes in those days. There was always someone limping to school with the soles and heels hanging off their Start-rites, sporting a clip round the ear from their mum or dad.

Mrs Cross was prepared to concede the possibility that Juliet Bravo was concerned for the safety of the boys and other pedestrians and road-users. She admitted: 'I know that young lads can cause problems sometimes. If the police officer was concerned about the vehicle or their safety, she could have told them: "Come on lads, you are causing a problem. You could hurt yourselves or cause an accident, let's have you home and off the streets."'

That is, of course, what any sensible copper would have done. Moreover, not so long ago, if a silly slip of a WPC did go back to the station and tell her inspector she had taken the names of three young boys riding a go-kart, she'd have spent the rest of the week cleaning out the cells after the winos.

But that's not how it works any more. A bit of fun now constitutes 'antisocial behaviour'.

In the scheme of things, riding a go-kart without road tax or insurance comes a long way down the anti-social pecking order. It's not even an offence. You'd have thought the police would be pleased that three teenage boys were getting rid of their energy in such an innocent, harmless fashion and not shoplifting, robbing people of their mobile phones, spraying graffiti all over the place or kicking in bus shelters.

It's not as if the Old Bill haven't got anything else to do. In Staffordshire that same year, burglaries went up seven per cent and violent crime increased sixteen per cent.

The Staffordshire Plod seem to specialise in this kind of nonsense. Sergeant Peter Davies threatened to prosecute villagers in Eccleshall for giving away bottles of sherry on tombola stalls at the village fete without a licence, contrary to Section 160 of the Licensing Act 1964.

While Eccleshall, like most of rural Britain, is plagued by burglary, car crime, drugs and vandalism, Davies decided to go after the tombola barons of the WI, the Young Farmers and the Ladies' Bell-ringing Circle. The stallholders were forced to pack up and local charities were considerably poorer as a result.

Greater Manchester Police came up with a novel plan for combating crime over the festive season – by sending Christmas cards to known offenders asking them to behave themselves.

Kent Police went one better. They sent a Valentine's card, with a big wet kiss on the front, to a burglar with seventeen convictions. His girlfriend thought it was from another woman and threw an ashtray at him. He then sued the police for compensation – on legal aid, naturally.

Keighley Police in Yorkshire announced a major crackdown on

crime. Detective Chief Superintendent Roger Gasson said: 'The festive season is a busy time for us. We are determined to do what we can to stop offenders causing Christmas misery.' So when Mrs Susan Drummond, a cleaner, found herself being pelted with bricks by a gang of about twenty-five youths outside the nursery where she works, she retreated inside and dialled Keighley Police. When she eventually got through, she was informed that there was no one available to respond because the officers were 'mealing'.

That's cop speak for having their tea.

Essex Police introduced speedboat patrols to intercept a possible al-Qaeda attack on Walton-on-the-Naze.

The Old Bill are fighting a constant battle against a chronic lack of resources. That's the excuse they always give for not turning out. So you can imagine the amazement of shopkeeper Gary Haggas, from Middlesbrough, when he saw four police cars racing past his shop and a police helicopter hovering overhead. What crime could warrant such an impressive turnout – an armed robbery, an al-Qaeda attack, a murder?

Er, no. A policeman had just had his bike pinched behind his back while he was carrying out a spot check on a man outside the shop.

Speaking of bikes, for the past forty-seven years butcher Roger Papworth had parked his old-fashioned delivery bike against a lamp post outside his shop in Woodhall Spa, Lincs.

As he was working flat out to meet the Christmas rush, PC Andrew Pogson marched in to the shop and told Mr Papworth it was causing an obstruction. 'He threatened to arrest me and two members of my staff if it wasn't moved immediately,' said Mr Papworth.

A police spokesman said he was committing an offence under the 1980 Highways Act.

Then why wait so long to nick him?

Mr Papworth complained: 'Don't they have anything better to do?' Yes, but they can't be bothered.

🚓 Cambridgeshire is plagued with illegal Gipsy campsites. But rather than do anything about that, Old Bill decided the real victims here are not the taxpaying, law-abiding locals but the non-taxpaying, lawbreaking invaders. The police spent £10,000 on a special CD advising 'travellers' of their, er, 'rights'.

Chief Superintendent Simon Edens believes the 'travellers' are victims of racism, who suffer 'disgusting and offensive' abuse every day. On which planet did he complete his diversity training? It obviously wasn't anywhere near Cambridgeshire, which is home to a massive illegal settlement at Smithy Fen, where locals have been subjected to constant antisocial behaviour and the murder of their postman since the 800 'travellers' moved in.

Otherwise he wouldn't have had the 2,000 CDs produced in Romany. Only a handful of 'travellers' speak proper Gipsy.

Most of them are Irish. He'd have been better off getting Terry Wogan to voice it.

When I first heard there was a special CD for travellers, I thought it was a Greatest Hits compilation – including 'Tarmacking Across The Universe' and 'I've Got A Brand New Combine Harvester (or at least I did have until that lot moved onto the village green)'. Soon to be available in car boot sales near you.

🚓 Police in Oldham threw into jail a couple who were accused of stealing a motel-room sheet which they had actually put out for the laundry.

🚓 A driving inspector from Blackburn drove through a puddle, splashing a copper standing on the pavement. Although he apologised, he was taken to court at a cost of £20,000. Magistrates threw out the case.

🚔 A homosexual cop sued Hertfordshire Police for compensation because he wasn't allowed to wear his earrings on duty.

🚔 Scotland Yard employed a convicted burglar as a policeman in Belgravia for three years.

🚔 Two coppers on crowd-control duty in Soho were discovered having sex in the back of a van with two porn stars. They let the women play with their handcuffs and fondle their helmets. The whole episode was caught on film.

🚔 In Plymouth, police threatened to tip off insurance companies if burglary victims had left a window open or a door unlocked. Insurers can then punish householders by refusing to pay out on claims and raising premiums.

This was the Plymouth Plods' response to a record thirty-four per cent year-on-year increase in burglaries in the city. It was bad enough when they couldn't be bothered to do anything more than give you a note for the insurance. Now they seem determined that you shouldn't even be entitled to proper compensation for your stolen property.

The city's police commander, Chief Superintendent Morris Watts, said: 'It is part of a number of measures to raise awareness of the issue and to hammer the message home that you must take better care of your property.'

Brilliant.

Only in Blair's Britain could a senior police officer have come up with a plan to persecute victims in order to combat a crime wave. If Chief Supergrass Watts and his force had been doing their job properly, the people of Plymouth would be able to leave their doors and windows unlocked without fear of being burgled, as they could within living memory. But he seems to think burglary is a force of nature, a phenomenon against which society can do nothing except batten down the hatches and hope for the best. Anyone who doesn't turn his house into Fort Knox is clearing gagging for it.

I wonder if Supergrass also believes women in skimpy clothes deserve to be raped. I shouldn't have thought so, otherwise he'd have been back wearing a pointy hat and directing traffic, while being forced to attend gender sensitivity realignment courses.

Someone should have had a word in his shell-like and told him that the job of the police is to patrol the streets, arrest criminals and protect property – not to act as a nark for the Man from the Pru.

They might also suggest that presiding over a thirty-four per cent annual rise in burglaries should be a resignation matter, not the occasion for a sanctimonious, patronising and threatening lecture to the law-abiding people who pay his wages.

Superintendent Supergrass' attitude is sadly typical of so much of our modern police force – sorry 'service'. They're all far too busy to actually do anything about crime. They've much more important things to attend to.

Take Welwyn Garden City's finest. We are not talking *NYPD Blue* here. A thief robbed the local Wine Rack, making off with customer's purse containing £100. Two days later, manager Andy Smith spotted chummy going into a nearby fish and chip shop. He called the police but the thief made good his escape. The Old Bill said they couldn't find the chip shop.

Two weeks later, the thief actually walked back into Wine Rack. And, as luck would have it, there were five police officers standing in the street only yards away.

Andy ran out to tip them off and ask them to arrest the man. Unfortunately, the cops couldn't help. They were engaged on a top-priority mission, vital to national security – putting out traffic cones. Nicking villains could wait.

Hertfordshire Constabulary defended the officers' dereliction of duty. A spokesman said they were properly engaged tackling 'serious traffic disruption'.

The people of Welwyn Garden City can sleep easy in their beds, knowing that although they've got a police force which couldn't organise a fish supper in a chip shop, it is a world-beater when it comes to cones and contraflow systems.

Lifeguard Neil Prendergast unleashed the full fury of the police when he was pulled over for driving through Oldham with a small St George's cross on his number plate. He was given a £30 fixed penalty notice for displaying a notice 'not fixed in accordance' with road traffic regulations. The fact that the flag was perfectly legal didn't stop the officer giving him the ticket. It all counts towards the collar quota, I suppose.

Greater Manchester Police said: 'We will have to consider the exact wording of the law on this.'

What's to consider? It's not an offence.

When they're not ignoring crimes or persecuting innocent victims and law-abiding motorists, there's nothing the Old Bill like more than suing each other. Which is why Police Federation rep PC Des Keanoy found himself under investigation for slapping the bottom, or putting his hand round the waist – depending who you believe – of a female inspector at a conference in Blackpool.

Quite apart from the fact that that is precisely what conferences in Blackpool are for, how did this woman rise to the rank of inspector without being able to handle this kind of nonsense? Couldn't she just have slapped his face or kicked him in the lunchbox? If she can't cope with an overfamiliar subordinate how would she react to an armed robber with a sawn-off Purdey?

A motorist in Stirling was banged up for two days for revving his car in a 'racist' manner next to a pair of Libyan immigrants.

We're always being told that the purpose of speed cameras is not to nick motorists or raise money, it is to promote road safety and save lives.

How many times have we heard that nonsense trotted out?

Perhaps someone can explain it to seventy-one-year-old Stuart Harding, from Aldershot, Hampshire. He's just been banned from driving and ordered to pay £364 costs.

His crime? To put up a notice on the A325 warning drivers: 'Speed Trap – 300 yards'. There had been eighteen accidents on that stretch of road in a year and Mr Harding was trying to get motorists to slow down before a busy spot where people were crossing to a Sunday morning car boot sale.

You might have expected the police to be grateful. Far from it. They nicked him. Magistrates used new powers intended to combat antisocial behaviour to punish him by taking his driving licence away.

Mr Harding doesn't understand how he's done anything wrong by encouraging people to obey the law.

Me neither. Perhaps the clue is that police regularly catch drivers exceeding the limit on that stretch. On one morning alone, they issued 200 tickets. At £60 a time, that's £12,000. Not a bad morning's work. Easier than catching burglars.

So when will they stop lying to us? They don't want people to slow down. The purpose of speed cameras is not road safety. It's about nicking people and raising money.

Scotland Yard ordered officers to stop referring to young offenders as 'yobs'. This emerged after a meeting of the Metropolitan Police Authority. The deputy chairman, one Cindy Butts, objected to a report which said the force was 'proactively tackling gangs and yobs across London'.

Mizz Butts complained to Met chief Ian Blair that the term was 'alienating'. She said: 'I have a problem with the language of "yobs". It sort of sets up and defines too much as "self" and "other".'

How does someone like Cindy Butts end up on a police committee? There's no accounting for madwomen, but why did the Old Bill give in to her? Where's it all going to end?

'Put your trousers on, chummy, you're bleedin' nicked.'

No chance.

'Would you mind awfully slipping into your trousers, my dear chap, and accompanying us to the station?'

That's more like it.

And finally, Esther, Younis Nabi was arrested and put in a cell for four hours for displaying an 'offensive' poster in the window of his mobile-phone shop in Northampton. Encouraging people to get a hands-free kit, it read: 'Don't be a Tango Whisky Alpha Tango'.

Work it out for yourselves.

Five, yes five, Old Bill turned up to nick him, even though he was only trying to get people to obey the law.

What a bunch of Whisky Alpha November Kilo Echo Romeo Sierras.

Mind how you go.

29 | Blair Force Too

The Metropolitan Police Authority was pleased to announce the latest appointment to its ranks. Kirsten Hearn is a fat, blind lesbian who used to work for Haringey Council.

She once made a video on the rates entitled: *How to Become a Lesbian in Thirty-five minutes*. Miss Hearn's interests include dancing naked in front of her gas fire and on her website she describes how she likes to lie in bed alone so she can 'eat Mars bars, fart and masturbate'.

Not all at the same time, I trust.

As the official press release put it:

> Kirsten's background has been in public service, training, community action and creative arts. She currently leads an Empowerment Coaching and Training Consultancy supporting individuals and organisations to develop their services, people and products to meet the challenges of a new era. Previously she worked for sixteen years in local government where she led corporate, strategic organisation and staff development initiatives, specialising in equality and diversity.
>
> Kirsten is a non-executive board member of Transport for London where, amongst other roles, she works on social inclusion transport issues, health and safety strategic issues, best value scrutiny and community consultation.
>
> Kirsten has been a freelance equality trainer since 1983 and has been active in voluntary organisations since 1980. She is the Lesbian, Gay, Bisexual and Transgender Community Liaison Executive Committee member of Regard, the national organisation of disabled lesbians, gay men and bisexuals, and is a member of the board of the Consortium of Lesbian, Gay and Bisexual Voluntary Organisations Council.

That was back in June 2002. Last time anyone looked, she was still there, drawing her exes and helping guide the direction of policing in this great capital city of ours.

What else do you need to know?

I could write a book on what's gone wrong with the police, but a cursory examination of Miss Hearn's CV probably says it all. It's a snapshot of the kind of qualifications you need to get on in the cut-and-thrust world of Labour's 'world class' public services.

If her influence were limited to making videos on the rates about how to become a lesbian in thirty-five minutes, it would be outrageous enough. That she is considered a fit and proper figure to lord it over Scotland Yard is beyond parody. It does, however, explain how a police force which was once the envy of the world is now a national disgrace and an international laughing stock.

Instead of serving the paying public, who are only interested in the prevention of crime and the capture of criminals, the police 'service' is dedicated to pandering to the political prejudices of full-time political activists – laughably described by Labour as 'independent' members of police authorities.

The Old Bill had pretty much fallen to the Guardianistas by the time Tony Blair arrived in Downing Street, but over the past decade it's gone from bad to horrific.

Chief constables no longer get promoted on their ability as thief-takers, or because they have earned the respect of the men under their command through sterling service on the front line. They are political appointees who have to tick all the right boxes with the left wing criminal justice Establishment, which infests the Home Office.

It was a trend I spotted a few years ago, in September 1999, in the shape of an article in *The Times* by the chief constable of Surrey. It was based on a speech he had made to something called The Social Market Foundation on 'The Future of Law and the Politics of Order'. At first glance I thought: at last, a senior police officer is grasping the nettle. I thought wrong. This is what I wrote at the time:

The chief constable equates the police with 'one of those sleeping industrial giants which do not notice a change in the marketplace'.

Britain is now a 'multicultural and modern nation' and the police must adapt, he says. The article is obsessed with gay and lesbian rights, ethnic minorities, the role of women officers and the 'old-fashioned' culture of the police, which must be 'modernised'. He talks about the isolation of police officers from the 'community'. There's a great deal of 'post-Macpherson' angst, peppered with fashionable management gobbledygook about 'downsizing' and New Labour drivel about 'stakeholders'.

The only thing the chief constable doesn't mention is crime.

It is the kind of speech which could have been delivered by the head of Camden Council Equal Opportunities Unit after six months on a McKinsey management course. It may ingratiate him with his *Guardian*-reading bosses at the Home Office but it has no relevance to policing Surrey, one of the wealthiest and whitest counties in Britain. Only 2.8 per cent of the population of Surrey comes from the ethnic minorities, and that includes Chilean General Pinochet, [then] under house arrest and police guard in Wentworth.

There are no race riots in Dorking. Gay and lesbian militancy was not on the march in Virginia Water the last time I looked – although, curiously, buggery was up seventy per cent according to official figures.

If police are isolated from the 'community' it is because they rarely come into contact with members of it unless they are stopping them for speeding or random breath tests. The 'market place' hasn't changed. The police have. Police stations have been closed, officers withdrawn from the beat. What the 'community' wants is more 'old-fashioned' policing, not less of it. More attention to the 15,000 burglaries and car crimes in Surrey last year, for instance. If the chief constable is right about the future of law and the politics of policing, things can only get worse.

The following year, when I was writing my novel *To Hell In A Handcart*, I returned to that text. I was trying to write a speech for one of my characters, Roberta Peel, tipped to be the first woman commissioner of the Metropolitan Police.

I sat for hours trying to improve upon the speech delivered by the chief constable of Surrey, but after a while I gave up. It simply couldn't be bettered as an example of politically correct drivel. So apart from a few flourishes around the edges, I just cut and pasted chunks of it into Roberta's mouth.

The chief constable of Surrey grew up to be Sir Ian Blair, commissioner of the Metropolitan Police – not so much a copper, more a social worker with scrambled egg on his hat.

Before I go on, I want to absolutely correct any impression that I am anti-police. My late father used to be a policeman. I was brought up to respect the boys in blue and the rule of law. The British police force contains some of the kindest, bravest, most decent people in the world. Even though I wasn't thrilled about Blair's appointment, he was what we had to live with.

On the couple of occasions I'd met him, I found him personable, although the least police-like policeman I'd ever come across. He was more like a New Labour apparatchik. Although I was one of Ian Blair's most vociferous critics when he was scaling the greasy pole, I was prepared to give him the benefit of the doubt when he took over. Judge him on what he does, not on his job application, was my reasoning.

Blair had a tough act to follow. His predecessor Sir John (now Lord) Stevens – aka Captain Beaujolais – was an old-fashioned copper, popular with police and public alike. Stevens cut a reassuring dash at a time of heightened anxiety over terrorism. He was an impresario who got the best out of those under his command and raised morale in the ranks. Though thoroughly modern in his methods, there was a whiff of Dixon of Dock Green about Beaujolais, which comforted and reassured people.

Ian Blair is a different kind of cop. Not for nothing was he described as New Labour's favourite policeman. You don't get to become the most senior copper in Britain without the wholehearted approval of Number 10 and the Guardianista Establishment in the Home Office.

I'd been critical repeatedly in print over Blair's apparent obsession with diversity, multiculturalism and poovery. But that was his job application. What mattered was how he did the job. He made a promising start. First up he pledged to put more bobbies on the streets. Then he supported publicly moves to give householders the right to use everything except 'grossly disproportionate' force against burglars – until he was slapped down by the government. He called for the establishment of a special squad to protect Britain's borders against criminals who enter the country illegally.

So far, so good, then. But there was always going to be something, wasn't there?

OK, in the scheme of things, you may think it harsh to quibble over Blair's decision to change the Met's logo. It used to read: 'Working for a safer London.' Blair changed it to: 'Working together for a safer London.' And instead of being written in joined-up italics, it's presented in plain type – so it doesn't discriminate against the short-sighted. It was claimed the old typeface fell foul of the Disability Discrimination Act.

If you wanted to be picky, you could argue that the new logo still discriminates against the blind, the dyslexic and anyone who can't read English.

It wasn't just the £4,500 spent on changing the sign outside Scotland Yard or the tens of thousands more it cost printing new stationery and repainting vehicles. The real question was why on earth does the police force need a mission statement in the first place? What was wrong with a blue lamp with 'POLICE' on it?

And what's with all this 'working together' business? You don't get a lot of that on *The Sweeney*. Imagine Jack Regan bursting in on a blagger and shouting: 'Put your trousers on, chummy, we're bleedin' working together for a safer London.'

Since then, I'm afraid, the jury is not so much out as sitting in the Magpie and Stump with a pork pie and a White Shield Worthington having returned a swift guilty verdict.

Beaujolais was a lucky general. There never was a major terrorist attack on his watch. Ian Blair must have trodden on a black cat whilst walking under a ladder. Calamity has been his constant companion, often self-inflicted.

He lost the dressing room early on when he insisted on disciplinary action against three white officers accused of racism – even though there was overwhelming evidence that the charges against them were trumped up. They were eventually cleared after an internal inquiry chaired by Scotland Yard's most senior Asian officer.

Blair hasn't missed an opportunity to ingratiate himself with the diversity commissars. He even came up with a plan to scrap the Met's traditional cap badge after a stroppy Asian traffic warden complained that it was 'offensive' to minorities, has written to all his officers demanding to know if they were homosexual, so he could meet his target for sexual minorities, and is obsessed with fashionable 'hate crimes' rather than old-fashioned crimes like burglary and mugging. Despite that, he's managed to fall out with the Black Police Association, the Muslim Police Association and the most senior gay officer in the Met.

Blair is no one's idea of a lucky general. It's not his fault that Islamist bombers chose to attack London on his watch. But perhaps it wasn't wise of him to boast on the wireless on the morning of 7 July, 2005 that the Met's anti-terrorist operations were the envy of the world and his officers were 'playing their socks off'. Less than an hour later, four homicide bombers blew themselves up on the London transport network, killing fifty-two people and injuring hundreds more.

A few weeks later, his officers shot dead a Brazilian electrician, Jean Charles de Menezes, at Stockwell Tube station, wrongly suspected of being a terrorist bomber. My sympathies at the time were with Blair and the officers involved. They were damned if they did and damned if they didn't. The death of Menezes was tragic, but he was in the wrong place at the wrong time and was a casualty of a war not of our choosing.

But Blair's decision to go missing in the immediate aftermath of the shooting destroyed whatever credibility he had and cost him any chance of getting the benefit of the doubt.

The abortive raid on a suspected terrorist safe house, thought to be harbouring chemical weapons, in Forest Gate, East London, cost Blair any remaining respect he had so assiduously courted among Muslims – even though the Independent Police Complaints Commission decided the raid was entirely justified.

Blair then forfeited any support he might have had from the press with an intemperate attack on newspapers, accusing them of 'racism' for concentrating on crimes like the appalling murder of two little white girls in Soham, Cambridgeshire, while ignoring crimes against members of the ethnic minorities.

This went down particularly badly at the *Daily Mail*, which had campaigned bravely for the prosecution of a gang of white South London thugs for the murder of black student Stephen Lawrence.

I'll leave someone else to write the biography of Ian Blair, but I'm prepared to bet he doesn't stay in his job until he retires. Last year he made a fatal mistake, when it was revealed that he was secretly taping his telephone conversations with the Attorney General. The whole thing smacked of Nixon-style paranoia. It's likely that these aren't the only calls he records.

So it was no great surprise when an audio cassette dropped through my letter box in a plain brown Jiffy bag, shortly after the shooting of Jean Charles de Menezes.

It was from an anonymous source at Scotland Yard. Here are the edited highlights.

'Commissioner speaking.'

'Morning, guv. This is George.'

'Hello, George, what's occurring?'

'There's been a bit of a cock-up on the anti-terrorism front, I'm afraid.'

'Not another bombing?'

'No, guv. Worse than that.'

'What could be worse than another bomb?'

'We've shot a suspect.'

'Where?'

'On the Tube, at Stockwell.'

'Well done. Medals all round on this one. I could be looking at a peerage.'

'Er, it's not that simple, guv.'

'What do you mean?'

'I think we've made a ghastly mistake. We may have shot the wrong man.'

'He's not gay is he?'

'Not that we know of, guv.'

'Let's hope not, for your sake, George. You know my zero tolerance of homophobia. If the victim turns out to be a member of the gay community, you'll be back at Elstree directing traffic and wearing a pointed hat. Did you check his sexuality before you shot him?'

'There wasn't time, guv.'

'Wasn't time?'

'No, guv.'

'Couldn't you tell?'

'Tell what, guv?'

'If he was gay.'

'How were we supposed to do that?'

'You're a trained observer, George. Did he walk like a homosexual?'

'How do homosexuals walk, guv?'

'You know, swinging his hips in a suggestive fashion. Not that I'm stereotyping any member of a vulnerable minority, you understand.'

'Perish the thought, guv.'

'Was he wearing an Aids ribbon?'

'Can't say I noticed, guv.'

'Did he talk with a lisp?'

'I've no idea, guv. He didn't have time to say much before we blew his head off.'

'So you're absolutely sure he wasn't gay?'

'Guv, what does it matter? We shot an innocent man. Isn't that bad enough?'

'Christ, he wasn't black was he?'

'Not as such.'

'What's that mean, then?'

'Well, he might have been.'

'Might have been?'

'Difficult to tell, guv. There's not much left of him. The lads found a Brazilian passport in his backpack.'

'There you go. I knew he was black.'

'Not all Brazilians are black, guv.'

'Haven't you ever heard of Pele? This is disastrous. What was a Brazilian doing trying to blow up the Northern Line?'

'That's my point, guv.'

'What point?'

'He wasn't a suicide bomber.'

'Then why did you shoot him?'

'He looked like a suicide bomber and you told us that if in doubt we were to shoot first and ask questions later.'

'I said that?'

'Yes, guv. Shoot-to-kill, remember?'

'You're not pinning this one on me, George.'

'Guv?'

'I've got my reputation to think of. I've been on the wireless this morning talking about how we're playing out of our socks in tackling terrorism.'

'Unfortunate piece of timing, guv.'

'And now you tell me that we've – you've – just gunned down a member of a visible ethnic minority, who wasn't a suicide bomber and may or may not belong to the GLBT community.'

'GLBT, guv?'

'Gay, lesbian, bisexual, transgender, you cretin. Didn't you attend the last diversity seminar?'

'No, guv. I was raiding a ricin factory in Wood Green at the time.'

'That's no excuse. Here we are working together for a safer London and you're going round upsetting the vast majority of the peace-loving Muslim community looking for weapons of mass destruction. Doesn't the name Macpherson mean anything to you?'

'Guv?'

'This is typical of the institutionalised racism I'm confronted with daily. The press are going to have a field day. Look at the ridiculous fuss they made over those two girls in Soham.'

'Guv, we're going to have to put out a statement.'

'Can't we say he was a member of the BNP who was shot while in the process of committing a hate crime?'

'Don't think so, guv.'

'Where did he stand on gay adoption?'

'Dunno.'

'Did he make disparaging homophobic remarks to a police horse?'

'Eh?'

'He wasn't reading out the names of the soldiers who have died in Iraq?'

'No, guv.'

'Did anyone see him depositing junk mail in a litter bin?'

'Not that they mentioned, guv.'

'Was he a fox-hunter?'

'Search me.'

'Was he resisting arrest for parking on a double-yellow line?'

'No.'

'You sure he's not a middle class, dinner party cocaine user?'

'Pretty positive, guv.'

'No chance he was rude about the Welsh, I suppose?'

''Fraid not, sir.'

'Doing 35mph in a built-up area?'

'Nope.'

'That's it, then. We're screwed. I've got to go, the Attorney General is on the other line. And by the way, George.'

'Yes, guv.'

'This conversation never happened.'

30 | The Mad Mullah of the Traffic Taliban

It used to be that the madness which now possesses modern policing was confined to London and the larger metropolitan areas. I suppose I first began to notice that all was not well elsewhere back in the early 1990s when the then chief constable of Warwickshire announced somewhat alarmingly, and with a straight face, that he had lost control of the streets of Leamington Spa.

I can remember thinking at the time: Leamington Spa? It's hardly a walk on the wild side, is it? If they couldn't keep order in Leamington Spa, what hope was there for the rest of us? But then, keeping public order long ago ceased to be a police priority. Similarly burglary, car crime, in fact anything involving the defence of the private citizen or the protection of private property. There were much more exciting avenues to be explored, such as hounding motorists, attending diversity courses, filling in forms, investigating 'hate crimes' and carpeting the country with speed cameras.

Coincidentally, Peter Joslin, the chief constable of Warwickshire who was having such difficulty with the lawless residents of Leamington Spa, was also chairman of the ACPO traffic committee when the first speed camera in Britain was introduced along a stretch of road near Chiswick Bridge, in West London.

At the time, I was presenting the morning show on LBC Radio and invited him on air to talk about it. I can remember putting it to him that the police wouldn't be satisfied until there was a camera on every road in Britain.

Not at all, he insisted. They would only be sited at accident black spots and were not there simply to raise money. Over 5,500 cameras later, the dreaded Gatsos are raking in more than £250 million a year, even though the government now admits that speed is a factor in just one in twenty accidents.

No one has been more zealous in pursuit of motorists than one Richard Brunstrom, chief constable of North Wales, who succeeded Joslin as chairman of the ACPO traffic committee. This was the policing equivalent of handing Pete Doherty the freedom of Medellín.

Shortly after being appointed, Chief Constable Brunstrom announced that he was 'going large' on drivers who strayed over the legal limit.

'Going large'. Curious language for a senior police officer.

Soon, North Wales had more speed traps than sheep. Brunstrom boasted of catching 4,000 motorists a month – more than any force in the country – and described people who drive at 32mph in a 30mph zone as no better than 'yobs' who terrorise communities. At one stage, North Wales nicked 32,333 speeding motorists in five months.

Brunstrom has declared a jihad on motorists. He is obsessed with speeding to the point of insanity and has called for all cars to be fitted with limiters to prevent them travelling over 70mph in any circumstances. It was this which led me to dub him the Mad Mullah of the Traffic Taliban.

One of his first acts in his ACPO role was to write to police forces instructing them to refuse to co-operate with any requests for information about speed cameras. Brunstrom, who styled himself 'Chair of the Association of Chief Police Officers Roads Policing Business Area', said under no circumstances must those operating cameras co-operate with road safety expert Paul Smith, who set up a website to expose the truth about so-called 'safety partnerships'.

The only reason this deranged, jumped-up traffic warden got the job at ACPO is that proper coppers from bigger forces have better things to do.

While he was busy 'going large' on ordinary motorists, he turned a blind eye to the 102 drivers of North Wales police vehicles caught speeding that year. The Mad Mullah even bought himself a 140mph E-class Merc. Or rather, those who paid council tax in North Wales did. At least twenty other top cops and police administrators were also given high performance company cars.

I don't mind chief constables having a motor appropriate to their status. But given that Brunstrom wants anyone who drives at over 31mph hanged, drawn and quartered and their entrails strewn along the prom at Llandudno, couldn't he have set an example and settled for a milk float?

But then, cops like Brunstrom don't think the usual rules apply to them. And they don't like criticism, either, especially when it comes from the people who pay their wages.

The Mad Mullah even called a press conference to monster a pensioner who had the audacity to query a speeding ticket. Then his junior jihadists accused a fifty-seven-year-old prospective Tory candidate of racism and threatened her with a 'swift police response'. Her crime was to protest at a public meeting about Brunstrom's fatwa on motorists. Businesswoman Felicity Elphick complained that the police should not put most people in the same category as some of those they had to deal with in Caia Park – a notorious, troubled, multiracial housing estate near Wrexham. In 2003 it was the scene of riots between locals and asylum seekers, which resulted in eighty arrests.

Mrs Elphick insisted she was merely pointing out that the people at the meeting were upright, upstanding citizens, not boy racers, joyriders or hooligans.

She subsequently received a letter from Assistant Chief Constable Geraint Anwyl warning her that what she had said had 'serious racial undertones. In the event of further inflammatory conduct you can be assured of a swift police response.'

It beggars belief.

Under Brunstrom, the North Wales Constabulary has become like one of those weird cults you find holed up in the mountains of the Appalachians, armed to the teeth and addled by self-righteousness, paranoia and conspiracy theories. The Mad Mullah runs his Taliban like a private army. He embarked on insane investigations into 'racism' by Tony Blair and *The Weakest Link* host Anne Robinson over harmless remarks they made about the Welsh.

One of his sidekicks even threatened Lord Mackenzie, the distinguished former head of the Police Superintendents'

Association, over some mild criticism he made of policing in North Wales.

All this while prosecuting a relentless 'zero tolerance' war against motorists. Brunstrom still found time to advocate legalising heroin and giving free needles to addicts and also distributed free suntan lotion to his officers to protect them from skin cancer in an area which has one of the highest levels of rainfall in the British Isles.

His obsession with diversity has seen him photographed dressed up as a druid and his lunacy has spread throughout the ranks. I happened to remark in my column that it was probably only a matter of time before the Mad Mullah sent his officers out onto the streets wearing burkas so as not to offend any Muslims there might be living in Llandudno.

How many more times? I should have known better. A couple of weeks later Brunstrom's deputy, Clive Wolfendale, turned up at the inaugural meeting of the North Wales Black Police Association and performed a rap song.

Wolfendale, I should point out, is a middle-aged white man with silver hair. Perhaps he misread the invitation and thought he was addressing NWA (Niggas With Attitude), not the NWBPA.

When I read the story I thought I might have some fun and write my own Welsh cop rap. But I couldn't do any better than Wolfendale himself. It is impossible to parody. Ali G couldn't improve on it.

Here's the rap in full. It helps if you picture the scene, a man dressed as Mr Brownlow is on stage in front of a room full of police officers drawn from the ethnic minorities. In Wales.

I'm just a white boy called the Deputy CC
They said I'd never make it as a bitchin' MC
You got it all wrong, 'cos now here I am
Giving it for real in the North Wales BPA jam.

They call me Roxy, or Ms Dynamo on stage
Unlike my brother here, I never look my age
I'm goin' to spill it all about the boys in blue
Show you what it's like within the not-so-solid crew

So listen!
Watcha doin' here today
Checkin' what the Heddlu Gogledd Cymru gotta say
Put away your cameras and your notepads for a spell
I got a story that I really need to tell.

Bein' in the Dibble is no cakewalk when you're black
If you don't get fitted, then you'll prob'ly get the sack
You're better chillin', lie down and just be passive
No place for us just yet in the Colwyn Bay Massive.

The Beeb Man stuffed us with the Secret Policeman
It's no good moanin' 'cos he found the Ku Klux Klan
Job ain't what it used to be
It's full of blacks and gays
It was just us white homies in the
Really good ol' days.

So what we bothrin' with this stinkin' institution
No love, no heart, no sense, no proper constitution
No one loves the coppers 'cos we're rotten to the core
Cross between the devil and a governmental whore.

What is the purpose of a black association?
It's just another stupid race relations job creation
We got our meetings and our various sub-committees
Packed with some do-gooders and a lot more Walter Mittys.

Forget all of that bullshit an' I'll tell u why we're here
Things are sometimes better than they usually appear
The New World Order means the streets are gettin' hot
Trust in one another is really all we got.

The BPA is sayin' that we're all in the same boat
Black or white in blue, we're all wearin' the same coat
If this don't happen then the lot of us are screwed
Caught up in the mis'ry of the international feud.

So Roger, Nick and Larbi will you give us one more chance
Danny and Silvana, I'd really like to dance
To Essi and to Imdad I want to give a hand
Let's hear it for Ms Dynamo and all her backin' band.

There's no time for jam tomorrow, we need the jam today
That's why we launchin' our association in this way
Thank you all for coming and remember what we say
Support your local sheriff and the North Wales BPA.

Stop it, stop it! Checkin' what the Heddlu Gogledd Cymru gotta say? The Colwyn Bay Massive? God knows how long it took him to write it. I'm astonished the Rubber Heels didn't charge him with wasting police time.

When you've stopped laughing, consider the implications of this patronising drivel. I've no idea how many black police officers there are in North Wales but I'm sure they come from a range of backgrounds and have a diverse spread of interests, from opera to stamp collecting. Why should Wolfendale have assumed the only way he could communicate with them is by making a complete berk of himself aping a home boy from South Central Los Angeles? We can only give thanks that he didn't limbo on stage in a grass skirt and start playing a calypso on an oil drum.

Wolfendale had clearly taken complete leave of his senses. He obviously thought this is the way to get on in the Old Bill. And frighteningly, he may be right. He'd already risen to deputy chief constable and must be in line for the top job when the men in white coats come for Brunstrom. That's always assuming another of the Mad Mullah's acolytes doesn't beat him to it.

Meet Inspector Gary Ashton, Brunstrom's Ayatollah in Colwyn Bay. A couple of years ago he wrote to every taxi firm in the seaside town. The letter warrants quoting at length:

One of the priorities of the North Wales Police is to tackle anti-social behaviour which takes many forms and can broadly be described as any action that adversely impacts on the quality of life of an individual.

As a result of recent consultation . . . it is apparent the practice of taxi drivers arriving at addresses to collect a fare and signalling their arrival by use of their audible warning instrument is prevalent and has the cumulative effect of impacting upon the afore mentioned [sic] quality of life . . .

I therefore seek your support to bring about an immediate and permanent end to this practice and would ask that you instruct all your drivers to stop using their audible warning instruments to alert fares with immediate effect.

If the practice continues, in addition to reporting drivers for this offence, which is contrary to Regulation 99(1) of the Road Vehicles (Construction and Use) Regulations 1986, Section 42 of the Road Traffic Act 1988 and Schedule 2 to the Road Traffic Offenders Act 1988, their details will be recorded and if found to have committed the offence on more than one occasion I will seek to exercise powers under the Crime and Disorder Act 1988 (as amended by the Police Reform Act 2002 and the Antisocial Behaviour Act 2003) to have an Antisocial Behaviour Order (ASBO) issued against that person.

An ASBO prohibits the person subject to it from engaging in specified behaviour, such as use of audible warning instrument whilst stationary. Breaching an ASBO is an arrestable offence.

Just pause for breath a moment, while I nip into the kitchen to pour myself a large one.

What sort of clown calls a horn an 'audible warning instrument'? Is that an audible warning instrument in your pocket or are you just pleased to see me?

Have you ever read a more pompous, more ridiculous letter? Talk about nuts and sledgehammers.

Let's agree that it's not much fun being woken at 3am by a cabbie picking up a neighbour for the early easyJet to Malaga. But during the day, how else are we supposed to know the cab's arrived? It's no good ringing the taxi firm. They'll tell you he's two minutes away, just turning into your road. That's what they always say, even when he's sitting in a caff eating a cheese roll and reading Dear Deidre.

A quick toot on the horn doesn't do much harm in the scheme of things.

Yet in the course of his letter, Ayatollah Ashton cites not one but SIX different Acts under which sounding your 'audible warning instrument' is a criminal offence.

This is three strikes and you're out, North Wales-style.

Strike one – you get your name taken.

Strike two – you get an ASBO.

Strike three – you get arrested.

What happens if you get caught a fourth time – a ritual beheading, posted on the North Wales Constabulary website?

'Charlie One, this is control, please state your position.'
'Roger, control, This is Charlie One. POB, Acacia Avenue, surrounded by armed police.'

Is this really a crime worthy of an ASBO? If Ayatollah Ashton belonged to the NYPD, every cabbie in Manhattan would be serving fifteen-to-life on Rikers Island.

It's not as if they haven't got anything better to do. Last time anyone looked, North Wales was awash with heroin and the burglary clear-up rate was the worst in the country – falling to six per cent at one stage. And what's the best they can come up with? Toot your horn (sorry, audible warning instrument) and win an ASBO.

If that wasn't daft enough, the Mad Mullah issued an edict that all police dogs must be muzzled in case they bite suspects. Isn't that the whole point of police dogs? But the MM published a training manual warning that the use of dogs 'has the potential to breach human rights'. The plan is that instead of biting, the dog launches itself like a missile at the suspect. Sergeant Ian Massie explained: 'It is one of the additional options open to us to muzzle our dogs and get them to use a headbutt. We believe it is a safer option for an offender to be headbutted.'

I am sure the persecuted motorists of North Wales will be thrilled to learn that some of the money they pay in speeding fines is being used to teach Alsatians how to give suspects a Glasgow Kiss.

What the hell did they ever do to deserve the Mad Mullah and his men? At one stage the *Daily Mail* asked: Is this the worst copper in Britain?

I think we can take that as a yes.

31 | Remake *The Sweeney*

Without any shadow of a doubt, the finest British television programme ever made was *The Sweeney*. Originally broadcast in the mid-1970s, it has won over a whole new audience through reruns on satellite and cable. It proved so popular that plans were announced to make a brand-new series, bringing Regan and Carter bang up to date, in line with modern policing.

This is a serious mistake, if the draft script which landed on my desk was anything to go by.

(DS Carter is sitting at his desk reading the Guardian. Enter DI Regan, unshaven and hungover.)

'Morning, guvnor.'

'Shut it, George.'

'Get out of the wrong side of bed, did we?'

'Wrong bed, more like, George.'

'Who's been a naughty inspector, then?'

'Seemed like a good idea at the time.'

'Not Lovely Rita, meter maid?'

''Fraid so, George. Right old boiler.'

'I'd keep your voice down if I were you.'

'Why?'

'Haven't you read the noticeboard?'

'Leave it out.'

'Any officer overhead making sexist remarks will be considered to be guilty of sexual harassment and subject to disciplinary action, by order of the commissioner.'

'Harassment? I was lucky to escape with my life. Haven't they seen Lovely Rita? It was like going ten rounds with Giant Haystacks. Give us a fag, George.'

'Sorry, guv.'

'Don't be a tight-fisted git.'

'It's not that, guv. The squad room has been declared a no-smoking zone.'

'Bloody hell. Where's my Scotch? I've got a mouth like a Chinese wrestler's jockstrap.'

'You won't find it in there, Jack.'

'If you've drunk it, I'll have you back directing traffic.'

'Hold on. It wasn't me. It was the new chief inspector.'

'Thieving bastard. I'll kill him.'

'Her, guv.'

'Who?'

'Her. The DCI. She started this morning. The first thing she did was confiscate all alcohol on the premises.'

'Bloody cheek. Where's Haskins?'

'Gone, guv.'

'Gone where?'

'Early retirement on grounds of ill-health.'

'There was nothing wrong with Frank.'

'You know that and I know that, guv. It was that complaint what did for him.'

'What complaint?'

'That Yardie who alleged Mr Haskins had made racist remarks towards him.'

'I don't believe it. That geezer is the biggest pimp and drugs pusher in London. When we nicked him he was waving a machete and had just sliced some bloke's ear off.'

'According to community liaison, guv, he is a respected member of the community and should be handled with kid gloves. After all, we don't want another riot, do we?'

'Anyway, what's this DCI bird like? Would you?'

'Not many.'

'I might give it a tug then.'

'Don't do it guv. She's not worth it.'

'S'pose not. Tell Taffy to bring the motor round the front.'

'He's not here.'

'Where the bloody hell is he, off with that old scrubber he was pouring gin down in the Feathers last night?'

'No, guv, he's in court.'

'Oh, yeah. I forgot. The Acton security job.'

'No, guv, Stratford industrial tribunal.'

'Eh?'

'He's suing the Met for £100,000 compensation.'

'Why?'

'Because you called him a pugnacious Welsh troll, that's why.'

'He is a pugnacious Welsh troll.'

'That's as maybe, guv, but it's still discrimination under the new code of conduct. There's a fair few bob to be made these days. I was reading in The Job that some bird up north got half a million out of the force because the lads in the canteen kept complimenting her on the size of her Bristols.'

'You'd think she'd be grateful. Where's Bill?'

'Cottaging, guv.'

'About bloody time, too. You can't go into a toilet in London without some iron blowing you a kiss. Let's hope he feels a few collars before they feel him.'

'Er, that's not what I meant, guv.'

'What did you mean?'

'I mean, he's gone cottaging, guv.'

'Yeah?'

'He's come out, Jack.'

'Bill's not ginger.'

'I know, guv. But he thought it was the only way he was ever going to get promotion. They've just introduced a fast-track system for gay and lesbian officers. Bill said if they think he's a brown-hatter he could make inspector in six months.'

'Christ, George. Fancy a pint?'

'Love to, guv, except it's my counselling session in ten minutes.'

'Counselling?'

'They reckon I've got pre-menstrual syndrome, or something.'

'Don't you mean post-traumatic?'

'Traumatic stress, toxic shock. All the same, innit?'

'What's brought this on?'

'It's because that blagger we nicked last week was carrying a shooter.'

'That's what blaggers do, George, carry shooters.'

'I know, Jack. But the new DCI says I may be suffering from delayed wossname and I'll feel better if I talk about it.'

'Well you can tell me about it over a pint.'

'I could do, Jack, but then I wouldn't get two weeks off sick on full pay thrown in.'

'Hell's bells. Lend us a needle and thread. That nympho traffic warden ripped my flies open last night. I'd better stitch them up.'

(Regan removes his trousers just as a young woman enters the squad room.)

''Ere, love, do us a favour, would you? And when you've finished, if you wouldn't mind sewing up me strides for me. Ha, ha'.

'I beg your pardon, Inspector?'

'Don't get your pinny in a twist, love. Wrong week, is it?'

(George Carter intervenes.)

'Er, guv, this is the new DCI.'

'That's right, Mr Regan. Put your trousers on, you're bleedin' nicked.'

32 | 999

Scotland Yard decided to join the call-centre culture and contract out 999 calls to a private answering service. Police chiefs said it would improve efficiency, as well as making substantial savings on the £100 million it costs to answer around 2 million emergency calls each year.

Genuine emergencies would be relayed immediately to police stations. In the case of non-urgent calls, operators are on hand to offer advice.

Shortly after the scheme was introduced I dialled 999 out of curiosity.

(Ring, ring. Ring, ring.)

'Thank you for calling the Metropolitan Police Emergency Service. If you have a touch-tone telephone, please press star now.'

(Press star button.)

'Please hold while your call is transferred.' Beep. 'Transferring.'

'Hello?'

'Sorree, all our operators are busy. You are being held in a queue. The Metropolitan Police values your call. Thank you for dialling 999.' (Cue irritating muzak version of the theme from The Bill.) 'Thank you for holding. Transferring.'

'Hello?'

'Thank you for calling the Metropolitan Police. We are committed to serving our customers, regardless of race, religion, disability or sexual orientation. If you have a touch-tone phone, please press hash now.'

(Press hash button.)

'You have reached the Metropolitan Police Emergency Service. If you have a touch-tone phone please listen carefully to the following instructions. If you wish to report a burglary, please press 1. If you wish to report a motor vehicle crime, please press 2. If you have any other query, please press 3.

(Press 3.)

'Thank you for calling . . .'

Yes, yes, get on with it.

'. . . the Metropolitan Police Emergency Service. All our operators are busy. You are being held in a queue. If you have a touch-tone phone, please press 1 now.'

(Press 1.)

'Transferring.' (Irritating musak version of the theme from Dixon Of Dock Green.) 'Thank you for dialling 999 . . .'

'Hello? I wish to report—'

'Your call is important to us. If you have a touch tone-phone, please listen carefully. If you wish to make a complaint about racial harassment, please press 4. If you suspect one of your neighbours of being drunk in charge of a skateboard, press 5. If you wish to speak to the dedicated gay and lesbian advice line, please press 69.'

(Press all buttons repeatedly in frustration.)

'Thank you for calling the Metropolitan Police. PC 149 Hollis speaking. How may I be of assistance?'

'At last, thank goodness. Look, I want to report—'

'Where is he?'

'Who?'

'Your neighbour on the skateboard.'

'Sorry, but I've been hanging on for ages and I just pressed any button in the hope I might get through to a human being.'

'But you've come straight through to the skateboard drink-drive hotline.'

'Never mind drunks on skateboards, I wish to report—'

'So you haven't seen anyone drunk in charge of a skateboard?'

'Er, no.'

'Lawnmower?'

'No.'

'You do realise that wasting police time is a criminal offence, punishable by up to five years in prison?'

'Look, I'm sorry, but I just wanted to report—'

'Transferring.' (Irritating muzak version of theme from *Z-Cars*.)

'Thank you for calling the Metropolitan Police Emergency Service. If you have a touch-tone phone, please press 1.'

(Throw phone out of window.)

'All our officers are on sick leave. Please try later. Evening all.'

(Calls charged at 38p a minute off-peak, 50p peak.)

33 | The Tears of a Clown

In October 2006, David Blunkett eventually got round to publishing his own version of his political downfall. The Blunkett Tapes were serialised in the *Daily Mail* and the *Guardian* and made compulsive reading.

To recap and cut a long story short, Blunkett embarked on a three-year affair with Kimberly Quinn, the still-married publisher of the *Spectator* magazine. He fathered a child, William, by her. In 2004, she got pregnant again. She wasn't convinced, but Blunkett embarked on an obsessive paternity suit.

Eventually, just before Christmas that year, he was forced from office when it was revealed he had fast-tracked a visa application for William's nanny, even though he claimed at the time he had no recollection of the matter. This is what I wrote at the time.

You leave government with your integrity intact, Tony Blair told the departing David Blunkett.

No he doesn't. He leaves with his integrity in tatters.

Heaven knows we've had to wade through some old toffee since the Blunkett affair burst in August. But some of the stuff we've been asked to swallow since even he realised the game was up has really taken the Jaffa Cake.

Did he offer to resign or did the prime minister ask for his resignation? Neither, apparently. With tears rolling down his cheeks, Blunkett told how he and Tony hugged and they just knew.

I'm sorry. That's how they do things in *The Sopranos*. A last hug from Tony before Paulie takes them into the car park and puts a bullet in their head.

Call me a heartless bastard. But I had tears rolling down my cheeks when I watched Blunkett being interviewed. In between shouting at the telly, I couldn't stop laughing.

He just doesn't get it, does he? Blunkett said he sacrificed his career for his 'little lad'.

No, he didn't. (Whatever he thought.) He went because he got caught abusing his office. At least, that's the official explanation. In the end, as so often these days, it was an email which did for him. This proved that, despite his denials, he had fast-tracked a visa for his girlfriend's nanny.

Blunkett, curiously, had no recollection of any of this until it came to light this week. Strange, that. How many times have we been told that Blunkett has the best grasp of a brief of anyone in cabinet and that he can remember the minutest detail? Here is a man who has total recall when it comes to Paragraph 5, Subsection 3, Clause 16, of the Cycling Without Lights (Capital Punishment) Bill. But he can't recollect a single thing about fixing a visa for his bird's Filipina au pair. Given that he was obsessed with Kimberly Quinn to the point of Broadmoor, you might have thought that is one detail he would remember.

Not that he admits fast-tracking anything, perish the thought. He told his officials: 'No favours, but slightly quicker.' Perhaps he's getting confused with his reply when Kimberly first told him she'd always wondered what it would be like to sleep with a blind man.

No favours, but slightly quicker.

It suits Blunkett's purpose to believe that it was the email wot dun him in. If that's what gets him through the night, fine. The truth is more complicated than that and it tells us much about the society in which we now live. The new rules forbid us from asking how a blind man can do such a demanding job as Home Secretary in the first place. We can't criticise the fact that he got another man's wife up the duff, not once but twice. Mustn't be 'judgemental'. Goodness me, no. So we fixate on whether a nanny's visa application was accelerated.

OK, so it was against the rules. But in the scheme of things it's a fairly minor misdemeanour. If Blunkett had put his hands up to it from the off, he might have survived. Coming on top of revelations that he'd laid on official cars for Kimberly and sent her government rail warrants for dirty weekends at his country cottage, the email was enough to finish him.

It also turns out that he fixed a second visa for Kimberly's nanny.

Oh, and I haven't mentioned the woman he was knocking off at the Department of Education, whose boyfriend got mysteriously promoted.

He was clearly in no fit mental state to continue to hold one of the highest offices in the land. And then there was that book (by the journalist Stephen Pollard) in which Blunkett – for reasons best known to himself – decided to tip the bucket over the heads of his cabinet colleagues.

Dumb move. In Blair's Britain, a minister can be caught with his trousers round his ankles in the company of a choirboy on Hampstead Heath and still get away with it. He can impregnate every single one of the Dagenham Girl Pipers and it will be waved away as a 'private matter'. But tell the world that Jack Straw's a complete waste of space and Two Jags is a thin-skinned tosser and you're toast, old son – even if the world had already worked that out for itself.

By the time Michael Howard chucked Blunkett's biography across the Commons, Andy was already waving bye-bye.

Blunkett had long since lost the backbenches and his officials at the Home Office had grassed him up to the Budd Inquiry into the visa application. You can't put Tony Blair on offer in public and expect to last the day. A quick hug and you're steered towards the back door of the Bada Bing. You needn't take the dog, David.

And still he thinks he's done nothing wrong. He found time on Wednesday night to take a swipe at the media, even though he's enjoyed the most sympathetic coverage a man up to his neck in mire could possibly hope for.

Missing you already.

He still insists he's resigned for the sake of his 'little lad'. I don't buy it. If he thought he'd be cleared over the visa application, he'd have clung on to office.

Even then it was only a matter of time before it all kicked off again. Come the birth of the second baby in February, the circus would be back in town with its tents pitched outside Blunkett's front door. And it would prove as difficult to shift as a convoy of Gipsy caravans on a piece of Green Belt. Just what Tony needed in the weeks before a general election.

As Blunkett heads off to spend more time with his lawyers and continues to pursue Kimberly Quinn with the kind of zeal which would probably get him served with an ASBO in other circumstances, it would be comforting to think that it would eventually dawn on him precisely how he has brought about his own downfall.

He was unlucky to fall in love with a woman I described a couple of weeks ago as a CORGI-registered bunny-boiler. But if he hadn't gone bonkers when she gave him the elbow and become consumed with lunacy he might still be Home Secretary.

Blunkett hasn't been brought down by the woman he loved. He has brought his own world crashing down.

He's only guilty of loving too much, we're told. That didn't stop them hanging Ruth Ellis.

The tears David Blunkett cried on TV were for no one but himself.

That should have been the end of the matter. And of Blunkett. But it just kept on coming. It was the best Christmas panto for years. It turned out that Kimberly had been entertaining a number of other lovers at the same time she was seeing Blunkett.

Tucked away in the coverage of the affair the following week-end was also mention of the fact that before she came to England she had a job at Disneyland, playing Snow White.

Given what we know now, I shouldn't be surprised if she didn't treat the Seven Dwarfs to regular roasting sessions in Goofy's Bounce House.

It's a small world.

Some day her prince will come. But in the meantime she's certainly been whistling while she works.

Who's been sleeping in my bed?

Well, for a start there's Michael, Stephen, David and now Simon. So don't bet against Doc, Grumpy, Happy, Sleepy, Bashful, Sneezy and Dopey getting a piece of the action. Or Dave Dee, Dozy, Beaky, Mick and Tich, either.

Following the outing of *Guardian* journalist Simon Hoggart as another one of Kimberly's lovers, Fleet Street and Westminster are buzzing with semi-reliable rumours of a couple of other prominent notches on her bedpost. The odds are some other sucker is about to have his Christmas spoiled. I told you this wasn't going away in a hurry.

Blunkett is behaving like a suicide bomber. If he can't have her, neither can anyone else. If he's going down, everyone else is going up in smoke.

The former Home Secretary almost certainly put Hoggart in the frame. The Funny People would have had Kimberly under surveillance and would have updated Blunkett on her active extra-curricular sex life. This year's Special Branch Christmas video compilation should be a scream.

Some reports suggest that Blunkett confronted Kimberly over her relationship with Hoggart. But, predictably, she denied it and he carried on sleeping with her regardless.

A 'friend' said: 'One day she'd be with Hoggart, then with Blunkett on another. Hoggart was aware of Kimberly's dalliance with Blunkett but didn't seem to mind.'

And where does her husband fit into all this, not to mention any other lover who may pop out of the woodwork in the next few days? Following the body fluids doesn't bear thinking about.

Hoggart denies that he is the father of the baby Kimberly is expecting in February. Or the other child. Blunkett thinks he's the daddy and so, according to those ever-helpful 'friends' does Stephen Quinn.

I'm reminded of a classic episode of *Only Fools and Horses*, involving Trigger's birth certificate. Under 'Father's Name' it read: 'Some soldiers'.

Whose name goes on the certificate in February? Some politician? Some journalist?

I can't help wondering where Kimberly ever found time to do her job at the *Spectator*. Not so much a publisher, more the office bike.

As well as writing for the *Guardian* and presenting *The News Quiz* on Radio 4, Hoggart is also the *Spectator*'s wine correspondent. In an unconventional arrangement, it's said that he gets paid in wine, not by cheque. Perhaps poking the publisher is another one of the perks.

It's a while since I wrote anything for the *Speccy*, so I wouldn't know. But it sounds like I escaped with my life, judging by some of the stories coming out of Doughty Street.

In the normal course of events, bloke from the *Guardian* knocking off a bird from the *Spectator* wouldn't register on the radar, save for a couple of paragraphs in *Private Eye*. And that would have been a matter for Mrs Hoggart and her rolling pin. Not the nine o'clock news.

It's the involvement of Blunkett which has catapulted Hoggart onto the front pages. You can't go round screwing the Home Secretary's mistress, especially when she's already married to someone else, and expect to get away with it. Especially when said Home Secretary has clearly gone tonto and is hell-bent on revenge, regardless of the consequences to himself or anyone else who gets caught in the crossfire. Blunkett has managed to convince himself that he's the victim here. There was some unbelievable drivel in one of the Sunday papers, which had him complaining that an American heiress had brought down a poor, underprivileged working-class boy.

As John Junor used to say, pass the sick bag. Has Blunkett forgotten he was the third most powerful politician in the country when he started sleeping with another man's wife? And then tried to destroy her marriage.

As the Budd Inquiry is discovering, Blunkett abused his office to fast-track a visa for Kimberly's nanny. That's on top of the bent rail warrants and the misuse of his official limo . . . There's more chance now of him ending up in the Priory rather than the Treasury. And he's brought it all on himself.

The real tragedy here is that there are two young children involved. One is almost certainly David Blunkett's, but he'll grow up in the shadow of a vicious battle between his mother and his natural father.

As for the unborn child, who knows who's the father? By the end of the week, you can probably perm any one from five.

And that's before the Seven Dwarfs have sold their story to the Sunday papers.

One thing we do know for certain about Kimberly Quinn.

Snow White, she ain't.

HI-HO!

And still it went on. A few weeks later it was revealed that the father of Mrs Quinn's second baby wasn't Blunkett at all. No one was quite sure who it was and she wasn't saying. Bookies started laying odds. We were back to Trigger and 'Some soldiers'. Among the front-runners was a mysterious Asian gentleman. Meanwhile there was already talk that Blair was planning a speedy return to the cabinet for Blunkett. This was my take.

She's a game girl, isn't she? I wonder if Kimberly has any idea for certain who's the daddy.

What odds could you have got before the results of the DNA tests were revealed?

Apparently, bookies were offering Blunkett at 2–1, Simon Hoggart 11–4, Boris Johnson 33–1 and 40–1 the field, including the band of the Royal Horse Guards.

The husband, Stephen Quinn, didn't make the starting line-up. Yet he has steadfastly stood behind his errant wife, bitterly accusing Blunkett of leaking the DNA evidence.

Mr Quinn did, however, stop short of confirming that he was the father of Kimberly's second son, Lorcan.

That was always unlikely, unless his reverse vasectomy operation was a medical miracle right up there with Ernest Saunders' recovery from Alzheimer's.

But, presumably, if the tests prove Blunkett isn't the daddy, they must also prove who is.

For now, no one's saying, and Mr Quinn is determined to bring both children up as his own – even though the eldest boy, William, is beyond doubt Blunkett's.

Mr Quinn said at the weekend that it wasn't a choice between 'Persil and Daz'. I assumed that Daz must be the mystery Asian suspect . . .

So the plot thickens.

Rewind to the summer and it is obvious that she was already pregnant with Lorcan when she went on a family holiday with Blunkett and William. She must have had an inkling then that there was a possibility Blunkett wasn't the father of the one in the oven. Yet she strung him along until she tired of him.

So who is the father? It plainly isn't Stephen Quinn, even though he's on both birth certificates in the 'Some soldiers' box.

Isn't it an offence to make a false declaration on an official document? Do we care? Not really. We've all had a good laugh.

But where does this leave Blunkett? He has been taken for a prize mug by Kimberly Quinn but deserves no sympathy.

This is a mess of his own making.

I've never bought into the lonely-old-man-who-hadn't-had-his-leg-over-for-thirty-years theory.

At the Department of Education Blunkett was knocking off a junior member of staff. By all accounts, Blunkett didn't go short when he was running Sheffield Council, either.

That's his business, you might argue. But when the Home Secretary gets another man's wife pregnant and then becomes embroiled in a vicious paternity battle we are entitled to ask if this is a proper way for the third most powerful politician in the country to behave.

In the end it cost him his job, but only because he was using government limos and rail tickets to ferry his lover to their assignations.

And mainly because he used his position to fix up a visa for the woman who is always described as Kimberly Quinn's nanny.

Blunkett has claimed all along to have no recollection of fast-tracking the visa. But, hang on, this woman was looking after William – Blunkett's son. Are we really expected to believe that Blunkett can't recall anything about a matter which affected his own child?

This was his son's nanny. You'd have thought he might remember something.

And still the scandal continues. Blunkett had to be sacked because he became an embarrassment to Blair. But he remains in the grace and favour Belgravia mansion which went with his old job – even though he owns another flat in London. He still enjoys the chauffeur-driven limo. And, if we believe what we're told, he's lined up for an early return to government if and when Labour wins the next election.

The arrogance of these people is breathtaking. They think they can get away with anything. Even when caught, it's five minutes in the ducking stool and then it's time to 'move on'.

But is Blunkett in a fit state to return to high office? The Kimberly Quinn affair seems to have unhinged him. The news that Lorcan isn't his son was utterly humiliating and now he faces an acrimonious battle over access to William. But Blair seems determined to bring him back. We shall see.

Whatever happens in May, Blunkett shouldn't be allowed anywhere near another red box for a very long time.

Not that that will stop them.

Nor did it. The day after Labour's historic third general election victory, in a comeback of Mandelsonian proportions, there was Blunkett strolling out of Number 10 having been reinstated to the cabinet as work and pensions secretary.

If Captain Oates had been a member of New Labour, he wouldn't have said: 'I am going outside and I may be some time.' He'd have stood up and declared: 'I'm just popping outside. I won't be long.'

That's if he left the tent at all. Even if he did, he'd have been back in five minutes, announcing that it was time to 'move on'.

Six months later, with grim but hugely satisfying inevitability,

Blunkett was back in Captain Oates mode. This time he had to go because he failed to declare his shareholding in a company, DNA Bioscience, which was bidding for government contracts. Blunkett had taken up the offer of a directorship with the firm during his brief hiatus between the Home Office and the Department of Work and Pensions.

At least this time we were spared the self-pitying squealing about only doing what he had to do for the 'little lad'. But even though Blunkett walked the plank he still refused to accept that he'd done anything wrong. Maybe the Viagra went his head. It was that he couldn't survive. All the usual New Labour guff about this being just an unfortunate lapse in judgement, time to move on, draw a line, blah, blah, wouldn't wash. Yes folks, it's 'personal tragedy' time again, ten months after Blunkett last left the cabinet 'without a stain on his character'.

This wasn't about breaches of ministerial codes of conduct. It was about greed and hubris. And we all know what follows hubris. Had it been purely a matter of Blunkett using his political position to fill his boots financially, he might well have survived. Blair is in no position to condemn any of his colleagues for abusing their office for profit, given that the prime minister and his wife behave like truffle hounds whenever there's a whiff of a freebie or a fat cheque.

New Labour has never thought the usual rules apply to them and Blunkett is no exception. Codes of conduct are made to be broken.

Blunkett might have clung on had he not alienated so many of his colleagues. Even old mates like Peter Kilfoyle were queuing up to put the boot in by the end. To say Blunkett lost the dressing room is an understatement. And when you've already lost the boardroom, as Blunkett managed to achieve so spectacularly when he comprehensively trashed just about every single one of his cabinet colleagues to Stephen Pollard, your chances of staying in the Premier League are less than zero. Only the patronage of Tony Blair kept Blunkett alive politically.

Blunkett then made the classic mistake of holding out against

Blair's welfare reforms, which he was specifically sent to the Department of Work and Pensions to force through.

Blunkett took a Stanley knife to his own throat. He may have thought he was demonstrating his independence from the outgoing regime and repositioning himself for a high-flying role in a future Brown government. But if that was the plan, he was as deluded as he was when he convinced himself that he was the father of his lover's second child. One set of psychological flaws is enough for any cabinet table. Gordon Brown wouldn't want a flake on the strength, even though Blair seemed to see his administration as some kind of care-in-the-community programme. Look around the cabinet and ask yourself this: if you were running a business, how many of them would you employ? What is it they bring to the party that half a dozen of your closest friends couldn't do ten times better?

If they weren't in politics, Two Jags would be lucky to hold down a job as a bouncer at a working men's club and Blunkett would be playing the harmonica and selling matches outside Woolworths in Sheffield. Examine Blunkett's track record. The towering achievement of his municipal career was virtually bankrupting Sheffield. His time as education secretary coincided with record numbers of children leaving school barely able to read or write. At the Home Office, civil servants and judges ran rings round his crass populism and he left us with a crime epidemic, police morale lower than it was among the crew on the *Bounty* and an asylum and immigration system in utter chaos. You couldn't advertise for David Blunkett. If you employed a top firm of City headhunters to recruit the person best able to sort out Britain's pensions crisis, Blunkett wouldn't make the shortlist. And even if he did make it through the door, imagine the interview.

'Why did you leave your last job, Mr Blunkett?'

'I was sacked for doing a favour for the nanny of me illegitimate son by another fellow's wife.'

'Next!'

It is a measure of his self-delusion that Blunkett managed to convince himself he was not only a sex god but a brilliant business-man qualified to sit on the board of a biotechnics conglomerate, even though his experience of DNA testing was limited to finding out whether he was the father of his mistress's baby. When offered a seat on the board of DNA Bioscience, didn't Blunkett's legendary political antennae twitch ever so slightly? When he bought shares in the company, did it not occur to him that his best chance of making a killing would be if DNA Bioscience was to win a money-spinning contract from the government, which Blunkett knew perfectly well he would be rejoining after the general election?

So you might have thought he would have counted his blessings and kept his head down, not become embroiled in a share-dealing fiasco which was always destined to end in tears — and possibly in court. Even the City Slickers might have spotted that one. Who joins the board of a company for a fortnight in the confident belief that he's soon to be restored to the cabinet?

It's not as if he wasn't warned. Three times he was told officially that there was a serious potential for conflict of interest, not least because the contract for which DNA Bioscience was bidding was in the gift of the Child Support Agency, for which Blunkett himself was directly responsible.

The real lapse of judgement here was Blair's decision to hurry Blunkett back into government when he was clearly away with the fairies and had been since he embarked on his lunatic legal action which ran up the huge bills he subsequently said he had to take outside directorships to pay.

Then there were the diaries, for which he is reported to have received a substantial advance.

Tom Lehrer said satire died the day Henry Kissinger won the Nobel Peace Prize. What on earth would he make of the Blunkett Tapes?

Blunkett's unintentionally hilarious ramblings are a sumptuous catalogue of self-delusion and denial. And when the laughter sub-sides, they also provide a frightening reminder that at a time when foreign criminals were waltzing out of prisons, illegal immigrants arriving by the lorryload and jihadists plotting to blow up the

London Underground, the man in charge of the Home Office was howling at the moon.

If you ever wanted proof positive that politicians are from another planet, here it is in spades.

It's difficult to know where to start. Blunkett insists throughout that 'private is private' but he invaded his own privacy when he got another man's wife pregnant. It was his own barking paternity suit and his fast-tracking a visa application for his son's nanny which rendered him unfit for office.

Yet he can't even bring himself to mention Kimberly Quinn's name in his book, referring to her simply as 'my friend'.

Those of us who said at the time that Blunkett should be sectioned received confirmation from the horse's mouth. 'Even I am beginning to doubt myself. I think I am going mad.' Despite this, both Blunkett and the prime minister thought he could tough it out.

'Tony knew my emotional health was failing – his support was an act of friendship and defiance.'

No it wasn't, it was an act of sheer stupidity and recklessness. Blunkett belonged in a padded cell, not one of the great offices of state, charged with the defence of the realm. Blair kept him on as long as he could, not in the interests of good government but because he thought it would be seen as a sign of weakness to have to throw another body out of the back of the wagon.

(What was that I was saying about a care-in-the-community scheme?)

Though he regrets his 'lapse of comradeship' Blunkett blames Pollard for bringing forward the publication date of his book. Most of us would simply call Pollard's timing astute.

Blunkett has always insisted that we discount his disability, though it was difficult not to admire someone who had overcome his blindness to rise to high office.

However, this bluff Yorkshireman clearly has a skin of pure Rizla. In common with most politicians, he fixates on everything said or written about him, even down to knowing the exact number of words in an uncomplimentary newspaper article (3,700, since you ask).

Regrets, he's got a few. For instance, attacking 'the key person in my life as a bad mother' (copyright Isaac Hayes, 'Theme from *Shaft*', Stax Records, 1971.)

But the whole tone of the Blunkett Tapes is to portray himself as a victim, recalling his stomach-churning TV interview which ended with tears streaming down his face.

Frankly, I can't improve on this side-splitting piece of work ('Prince Charles told me he understands what I'm going through.' 'Thank God the *Sun* is totally with me.')

Priceless.

34 | The Secret Sex Diaries of David Blunkett

Speaking as someone who has difficulty remembering what day of the week it is, let alone what I was doing the Tuesday before last, I was amazed that the former Home Secretary David Blunkett managed to keep a detailed diary of his sex life.

Apparently, he recorded every time, date and place he slept with his married lover, Kimberly Quinn, during their three-year affair. And, no doubt, every position and the duration, too.

It was to be a further two years before Blunkett's diaries were published, so I had no option but to improvise.

12 October, 2001
Drinks at the *Spectator*. Four glasses Chateau Boris, two vol-au-vents. Heady atmosphere. Introduced to Kimberly. She is tall and blonde, just how I like them. Over a Scotch egg she tells me she has always wondered what it would be like to sleep with a blind man. This is her lucky day.

7 November, 2001
Haircut, feed dog, let another 3,000 asylum seekers stay in Britain permanently. Meet Kimberly for lunch. Two glasses Chablis, bottle claret, large Remy. Back to flat for afternoon rendezvous. Kimberly is gagging for it. It's been a long time for me, but it's like riding a bike. Time: 4.32pm. Duration: 47 secs.

23 January, 2002
Bring forward legislation to increase detention without trial. Gun crime figures up 200 per cent. Make note to announce crackdown. The papers always love a good crackdown. Kimberly phones. She is desperate to see me. She tells me she is married, but it's over. After

six weeks together she and her husband have grown apart. Meet at flat later, where Kimberly performs an act of oral love upon me. Time: 7.03pm. Duration: 1 min 7 secs.

12 March, 2002
Record immigration figures. Tories want tougher border controls. Accuse them of racism, announce plan for ID cards. Kimberly is coming to cottage. Should I buy bumper pack of condoms? Is she on the Pill? Perhaps I should ask.

14 March, 2002
Bacon and egg, down-the-line interview with David Frost, then back to bed with my tall, blonde bombshell for long lie-in. Have missionary position sex twice at 9.31am and 11.02am. Duration: 1 min 36 secs and 3 mins 11 secs respectively.

28 June, 2002
Announce new anti-terror laws. Take dog to vet's for worming. Lunch with Kimberly. Four glasses Sancerre, two bottles Bollinger, treble Armagnac. Repair to flat and bend Kimberly over kitchen table. Time: 3.59pm. Duration: 1 min 49 secs.

5 July, 2002
Kimberly tells me she is pregnant. The baby must be mine, since she assures me her marriage is over and, anyway, her husband has had a vasectomy. So I must be the father. Crack open a bottle of champagne and celebrate. Hand shandy on settee. Time: 8.04pm. Duration: 1 min 7 secs.

14 February, 2003
Announce new crackdown on asylum, the sixth since I got the job. Oh, joy, Kimberly has had a baby boy, William. Now I have a new family.

No sex for a few weeks. Curiously, Kimberly stays in the family home with her husband, even though she assures me the marriage is over and we will soon be together.

23 April, 2003

Together again at the cottage. I send the ministerial limo to pick up Kimberly. She tells me she is leaving her husband and says I am a very naughty boy who must be punished. Time: 11.46am. Duration: 2 mins 17 secs.

29 September, 2003

Labour Party conference. I make acclaimed speech announcing new crackdowns on terror, litter, speeding, asylum and cycling without lights, which in future will be punished by a £5,000 fine or two years in Belmarsh. After triumphant round of cocktail parties – four glasses champagne, bottle of South African Chardonnay, half a pint of Pimm's, six large Scotches, eight Pringles and a sausage roll, I return to my room, where my beautiful blonde Kimberly is waiting for me to make mad, passionate love to her. Trip over coffee table and pass out on bed. I awake to find a warm tongue caressing my ear. It is Sadie, my guide dog. Kimberly has left.

30 November, 2003

Kimberly brings William to the cottage. I have supplied her with two free rail tickets for ministerial spouses. Well, we are man and wife in all but name, aren't we? Or we will be when she leaves her husband. And if Mandelson can move his bloody Brazilian nancy boy into Hillsborough Castle, then I can give the woman I love a freebie ride on Virgin trains. Kimberly suggests we experiment with whipped cream and the handcuffs I got from Scotland Yard. Time: 9.41pm. Duration: 1 min 57 secs.

14 December, 2003

Announce new crackdown on fireworks, punishable by £10,000 fine and five years' hard labour. Burglary figures highest on record. I blame the Tories. Meet Kimberly for afternoon of passion at flat. She has something to confess. She isn't blonde. Is there anything else she is keeping from me? There is! Under her coat she isn't wearing any knickers. Time: 5.27pm. Duration: 17 secs. Whoops!

31 May, 2004

Fast-track visa for Kimberly's nanny, before we leave for romantic holiday in Corfu with Kimberly, William, two civil servants and four bodyguards. Dinner on the terrace. Eight lagers, four bottles retsina, one bottle seven-star Metaxa brandy. Walk hand in hand along the beach. Maybe it's the sun, the sea air or the pressure I've been under at work – thirty-five new crackdowns already this year. Despite Kimberly's tender coaxing, I can't rise to the occasion. Time: 11.56pm. Duration: 0 secs.

5 August, 2004

I announce that five-a-day co-ordinators will be given powers of arrest and stop-and-search. In a new crackdown on crime, another 200 police stations are to be closed. And to show my determination to crack down on illegal immigration, I decide that 300,000 asylum seekers already here can stay. Meet Kimberly at flat and have taken the precaution of swallowing a Viagra tablet with my afternoon bottle of Beaujolais.

She tells me she is pregnant again. Wonderful news. I say if it's a boy, we will call him David, after his father. Not so fast, she says. She thinks this child is her husband's. Our relationship is over and she's patching up her marriage.

11 August, 2004

Instruct solicitors to demand a DNA test. If I can prove the babies are mine she'll have to leave her husband and come back to me.

I can't believe I'll never stroke her blonde hair again – or whatever colour it is. Go to bed alone after *Newsnight* and think of all those times Kimberly and I have made love in so many different ways. I can't sleep. I think the Viagra has begun to work. Time: 11.43pm. Duration: 5 mins 32 secs.

35 | My Shared Lady!

Shortly after Blunkett's doomed affair with Kimberly Quinn cost him his job at the Home Office, plans were announced for a West End version of *Blunkett – The Musical*. It was also to feature the parallel affair between *Spectator* editor and Conservative MP Boris Johnson and journalist Petronella Wyatt, which added hugely to the gaiety of the nation.

Producer Martin Witt promised: 'It will be sensitive, not judgemental.'

Coincidentally, I'd already been working on my own version, which was both insensitive and judgemental.

Lay-deez and gen-ul-men, welcome to the Opening Night of *My Shared Lady!*

(SCENE ONE. A cocktail party at the *Spectator*. Kimberly Quinn is toying with a glass of champagne. Boris introduces her to bearded man with dog. 'Kimbers, old girl. Have you met Blunkers, the Home Sec?' Kimberly starts to sing.)

> All I wanted was to meet
> Someone who'd get me to Downing Street
> And with a cabinet seat
> Oh, wouldn't it be luvverly.
> You're the man that I wished to find,
> There is something upon my mind.
> To sleep with someone blind
> Oh, wouldn't it be luvverly?

(Blunkett joins in)

> There's an accent of which I'm fond
> A gentle lilt from across the pond
> I hear you're tall and blonde
> I'm told you're very luvverly.

(Kimberly again)

> Oh, so luvverly standing abso-lutely
> Six feet tall.
> I've been told that I could pass for
> Jerrr-ry Hall.
>
> Here's my number, call me soon
> I must go and work the room.
> Hey, isn't that Geoff Hoon?
> Oh wouldn't it be luvverly?
> Luvverly, luvverly, luvverly. [fade]

(SCENE TWO. Blunkett and his dog, walking through
        Covent Garden market. Cue Blunkett.)

> The gentle sex was made for man to marry
> But someone else is wed to Kimberl-ee
> She's been with Tom and Dick and Harry,
> But with a little bit of luck,
> With a little bit of luck,
> She'll forget them all and marry me.

(Scene Three. Across London, Petronella is confronting
　　　Boris over his refusal to leave his wife.)

Just you wait Boris Johnson,
Just you wait.
Have I got news for you, Boris
It's too late.
You've upset all the Scousers
You couldn't keep it in your trousers
Just you wait, Boris Johnson.
Just you wait.

(Scene Four. Kimberly breaks the news to Blunkett
　　　　　that she is pregnant.)

I haven't slept all night
I haven't slept all night
I don't know what to do.
I know I'm looking rough,
That's 'cos I'm up the duff.
The baby's father's you.
I don't know what to tell my husband.
He's bound to think that he's the dad.
I only wish t'were true
I'd never slept with you
I must be mad, mad, mad, mad, MAD.

(SCENE FIVE. Blunkett and his dog outside the Quinn's
  Mayfair pad after Kimberly has given him the elbow.)

I have often walked down this street before.
But you've never ever padlocked the front door before.
All I want to do is have a word with you
Knowing that you're inside with my kid.

(SCENE SIX. Blunkett is summoned to the prime minister's office,
where the PM is surveying the first editions of the following day's
        newspapers. After half an hour, Blunkett emerges.)

I'm getting fired in the morning
Just after PM's Question Time,
Blair is a coward
He's scared of Howard
I thought he was a friend of mine.

I'm getting fired in the morning
Ding, dong, Big Ben is going to chime
Just tried to please her
Fixed up the visa
Now get me to the court,
Get me to the court,
For gawd's sake get me to the court
On time!

36 | This Time Last Year We Were Millionaires

John Sullivan's brilliant creation Del Boy Trotter, in *Only Fools and Horses,* was a fabulous incarnation of Thatcher's Britain. I've borrowed Del Boy a few times over the years to make a point. So how did the Trotters – Del, Rodney and his Uncle Albert – fare under New Labour? I caught up with Del around the time of the foot-and-mouth crisis, as he arrived home from a fire sale at the Millennium Dome.

'Awight, Rodders, sorry I'm late. I had to pick up Damien from the London Oratory on my way home.'

'I still don't know how you managed to get him in there, Del. You don't even live in the catchment area.'

'Since when did that matter, bruv? You know my motto – education, education, education. It's not what you know but who you know.'

'Who do you know at the London Oratory?'

'The caretaker's a mate of Trigger.'

'Yeah?'

'Anyway, enough of that. We've got work to do. Give us a hand with this.'

'What the hell is that, Derek?'

'It's a gerbil, Rodney.'

'It looks more like a hamster to me, Del.'

'Hamster, gerbil, same difference.'

'It's six feet tall, Derek.'

'Well spotted, Rodders. I picked it up in the sale at the Dome.'

'What do we want with a six-foot-tall plastic gerbil?'

'Not us. I thought Mike at the Nag's Head might use it. Go nice in the beer garden.'

'Haven't you heard?'

'Heard what, Rodders?'

'The Nag's Head is closing. It's being turned into a tapas bar.'

'Fromage frais. Is nothing sacred?'

'How much did you pay for this giant rodent, Derek?'

'Three grand.'

'Three grand?'

'Yeah, that little French geezer, J-R, let me have it cheap.'

'You've been had, Del.'

'No, Rodney, this is a work of art. Don't worry, I'll knock it out to the Tate Modern. They'll buy any old rubbish. Trust me, this time next year we'll be millionaires.'

'This time last year we were millionaires, Del. We'd still be millionaires if you hadn't put all our money into the Internet.'

'That's not fair, Rodders. luvlyjubbly.com was valued at £300 million.'

'Yeah, for about ten minutes. I told you it was a mistake to let Mickey Pearce handle the marketing.'

'Easy come, easy go, Rodders. Onwards and upwards. I bumped into Boycey down the Dome.'

'Don't you mean Lord Boyce of Peckham?'

'I was forgetting myself. Still at least Marlene's a lady for the first time in her life.'

'I can't believe Boycey's a member of the House of Lords.'

'You know New Labour, Rodney. They love a dodgy businessman.'

'I hear his offer to buy the Dome has been successful.'

'Correct. He was the only bidder in the end. He's going to turn it into the biggest used-car lot in South London.'

'How did he pull that one off?'

'Best not to ask, Rodders. But put it this way – where do you think those two Jags came from?'

'Say no more, Derek.'

'Seen Trigger lately?'

'He was in the caff this morning. Bit shaken up, actually. He was pushing his cart across Clapham Common the other night and this Welsh bloke comes up to him and asks, well, you know.'

'Soixante-neuf, Rodney. That must have given him a nasty turn.'

'Yeah, he had to beat him off with his brush.'

'Some people would pay good money for that, Rodders.'

'I'll tell you what people will pay good money for, Del. Passports, that's what.'

'Passports?'

'Yeah, Denzil was telling me that the geezer who runs the Indian restaurant at the back of the Steve Biko leisure centre—'

'Mr Hinduwossname? Does a very cushty aloo vera.'

'That's him. Anyway, he was telling Denzil that there's this bloke in the Peckham Labour Club who knows someone in the Home Office who does a very nice line in passports in exchange for a no-questions-asked contribution to party funds.'

'They do like a drink, this lot. You know that bent brief on the Old Kent Road, defends all the Bermondsey blaggers?'

'What about him?'

'He only finds himself at a dinner in the West End the other night when this geezer claiming to be the Lord Chancellor sidles up to him and asks him for a monkey. Says he might be able to put a bit of work his way.'

'Reminds me, Del. Did you manage to shift those burglar alarms you bought from that Kurdish geezer?'

'Oh, our "Tough on crime, tough on the causes of crime" range. No, someone broke into the lock-up and nicked them.'

'What else did they get?'

'Not much. For some reason they didn't touch that rack of fox-hunting clobber I bought in the other day. That was a right bargain – coats, hats, saddles, the lot. I thought I might take a trip down to the country at the weekend.'

'Berkeley Hunt?'

'Watch it, Rodders. We could kill two birds with one stone. Knock out the old hunting pink at a car boot sale and pick up a few sheep and pigs at the same time.'

'Sheep and pigs, Del?'

'Yeah. I thought it might be a good time to go into the livestock business. There's this geezer, friend of Boycey's, got a farm the other side of Sevenoaks. Boycey reckons he's got some fire-damaged stock going cheap. We could do ourselves a right favour. Take it off his hands and then sell it on to the French. They can't get enough of it, by all accounts. Europe, that's the future, Rodders. It's time to go into the export business.'

'You can't be serious, Del.'

'Never more so, Rodney. We need to broaden our horizons. You know what they say – never look a gift sheep in the mouth. Mickey Pearce is taking the Transit over to Calais next week to fetch a load of cigarettes. We could go with him and load up with lambs on the way out. Boycey's got contacts across the Channel. Think of all those lovely euros.'

'I don't believe you, Derek.'

'Pity Uncle Albert's not still around. He'd have enjoyed a day trip to France.'

'With his track record on boats it's probably just as well.'

'Oi, Rodney. Have a bit of respect.'

'Sorry, Del. I do miss him.'

'Me too. He never got over losing to Ken Livingstone. Come on, I've got half the Body Zone strapped to the top of the van.'

'You should get rid of that van, Derek. It's a wreck.'

'Cordon sanitaire, Rodders. That's where you're wrong. Don't you read the papers? Reliant's shut down for good. And that makes this little van of ours a modern classic. It should be worth a small fortune. This time next year Rodney . . .'

37 | Brass Tax

It's a popular misconception that government raises taxes to pay for essential public services which can only be provided by the state.

Mrs Thatcher's wholesale privatisations of the 1980s gave the lie to that. The truth is that tax-raising has become an end in itself. There is now a whole industry devoted to the business of finding ever more ingenious and intrusive ways of picking our pockets.

The government spent £27,000 of our money sending council-tax inspectors to Disney World for a Mickey Mouse conference on how to use satellite surveillance to snoop on householders who carry out home improvements.

When you hear ministers talk about getting down to brass tacks, they're probably thinking about taxing your new brass taps.

Talk about brass neck.

This system, which will allow town-hall jobsworths to invade our homes to check for illicit double glazing and undeclared jacuzzis, upon which we will then have to pay penal levels of tax, is being nodded through without a peep.

Why hasn't there been more outrage at these disgraceful, totalitarian proposals? There were riots over the poll tax fifteen years ago. The government intends invading the privacy of millions of householders in pursuit of the last penny of tax to feed Labour's greed.

Council tax bills could treble, on top of the average seventy per cent rise under Labour since 1997. Ministers think we should pay more to reflect the rise in the value of our houses over the past ten years. What they ignore is that the only time you realise the value of your house is when you come to sell it. And then only if you buy a cheaper property or decide to cash in your chips and rent.

The vast majority of people plough their profits into another house – and get hammered with outrageous stamp-duty demands into the bargain. While property values have soared, wages haven't kept pace. So where the hell are people expected to find the money to meet a 300 per cent increase in their council tax, especially pensioners and those on fixed incomes?

What ministers should be doing is taking a scythe to council spending, not screwing every last penny out of already hard-pressed taxpayers to finance so-called 'services' which we didn't ask for and don't want. We don't look for much from local government. All we expect are decent local schools, properly maintained streets and public parks and the rubbish collected at least once a week.

How difficult can that be? Yet these straightforward tasks seem beyond the competence of most town halls. There's never any shortage of money to blow on fancy herringbone paving schemes, tacky street furniture and elaborate traffic humps. But try getting the council to fix a wonky pavement or fill in a pothole.

They've all got foreign policies, anti-discrimination directorates, transgender empowerment programmes and anti-nuclear strategies, but seem incapable of getting anyone to sweep the streets.

Local government has lost all sense of what it's there for in the first place. While some of us are facing a 300 per cent tax hike over the next few years, back at the town hall it's trebles all round and jobs for life. And to pay for all this excess, the government has been working on new council-tax bands to be introduced in 2009. Here are some typical examples and the estimated amount of tax each category can expect to pay.

BAND A: Central London. Cardboard box, single occupancy, dog on a string, bottle of Strongbow. Estimate: £0.

BAND B: Cottenham, Cambs. Caravan, family of nine, Nissan Patrol, Tarmac lorry, three dogs, up to six horses, cash business. Estimate: £0.

BAND C: Surbiton. Between-the-wars semi-detached. Pensioner on fixed income, single garage, two gnomes, votes Tory. Estimate: £5,000.

BAND D: West London. Luxury £250,000 accommodation provided by local authority. Afghan hijacker and family, living on benefits, one plasma television, two mobile phones, Vauxhall Astra. Estimate: £0.

BAND E: Birmingham. Three-bed detached, integral garage, one satellite dish, stone cladding. Self-employed plumber, married, two kids, own van, suspected of voting UKIP. Estimate: £7,500.

BAND F: Notting Hill. Minimalist flat, politician, same-sex relationship, Brazilian boyfriend, Labrador, additional home in Brussels. Estimate: £0 (after mortgage discount and stamp-duty relief).

BAND G: Norfolk. Bleak House, farmer living alone, two shotguns, six burglaries, nearest police station twenty-five miles away. Estimate: five years.

BAND H: Westminster, Clapham, Hull, Dorneywood (vacated 2006). Four homes, two Jags, one scuba suit, salary £130,000, plus generous expenses, living allowance and First Class air travel. Estimate: £0.

38 | Dances with Dwarfs

My television career could best be described as chequered. It's ranged from critically acclaimed, serious current affairs to what can only be described, literally, as a complete parcel of bollocks. The highs have included winning a Silver Rose of Montreux hosting one of the first reality shows for Channel 4, *Wanted*, to the train wreck which was *Littlejohn: Live and Unleashed*, named the thirty-second worst television show of all time in the *Radio Times* in August 2006. Admittedly, this was only in the opinion of one man, the TV critic John Naughton (I wonder what I did to upset him), but in fairness he probably wasn't too wide of the mark.

Live and Unleashed was commissioned by Sky One as part of a deal which took me back to News International in 1998. It was made by the same team which produced the successful *Littlejohn: Live and Uncut* for three series on London Weekend Television. Sky wanted something which would bring the verve and values of tabloid newspapers to television and we figured that on satellite – which was then nothing like the force it is today – there were fewer constraints and we would have more opportunity to experiment than on network terrestrial TV.

Hence, the parcel of bollocks.

The second programme in the series showcased the first – and, I believe, the only – live television performance by the Half Monty, a team of stripping dwarfs, touring the clubs cashing in on the success of the movie, *The Full Monty*, the story of how a group of redundant steel workers turned Chippendale.

All I can say, m'lud, is that it seemed like a good idea at the time.

The Half Monty replicated their act in the studio. I can still see the looks of horror on the faces of the audience as the five dwarfs ripped off their G-strings at the climax of 'You Can Keep Your Hat On'. And I can hear my mother-in-law Joyce, sitting in the third row, saying: 'They're not small all over, are they?'

I'll spare you the full, gory details of the after-show party in the green room. Suffice to say, what they lack in stature, dwarfs certainly make up for in thirst and sexual appetite. Say what you will, the show was certainly different. Emboldened by the impact of the Half Monty, my producer Brent Baker decided that dwarfism and nudity should become the leitmotifs of the series. Which is how we ended up with a dwarf on every programme; a pint-sized performance of *This Is Spinal Tap*; and one half of the long-disbanded pop duo the Allisons performing the British entry to the 1961 Eurovision Song Contest completely naked. His determination to defy all instructions to keep his guitar strategically placed over his wedding tackle tested our long-suffering director's skills to destruction. The series ended with Jeremy Beadle introducing me and a dwarf singing Wilson Pickett's 'In the Midnight Hour', while dressed as the Blues Brothers.

Littlejohn: Live and Unleashed was a bit like the 1960s. If you can remember it, you probably weren't there. Still, it didn't go unnoticed at the time.

Dawn Airey, then head of channel Five and now running Sky, noted the abundance of the vertically challenged on the programme and wrote in *Broadcast* magazine that she couldn't work out whether we had an enlightened policy of employing under-represented minorities or were having a laugh.

There were some concerns within Sky and elsewhere that we were exploiting vulnerable members of the restricted-growth community. Nothing could have been further from the truth. They were grateful for the work. After one show, the chief dwarf, who had appeared in every programme, came up to me in the bar and apologised that he wouldn't be available the following week, owing to a prior engagement in a dwarf-tossing tournament in Barnsley. He recommended his brother-in-law as a capable stand-in and we were more than happy to oblige.

So there you are. Now, the truth can be told. Dawn, we were having a laugh.

*

Live and Unleashed was a bit of harmless fun. It didn't claim to be art, it didn't claim to be improving, it didn't claim to be educational, and it went out on a niche channel.

If I'd have gone to Greg Dyke, when he ran LWT and I was presenting *Littlejohn: Live and Uncut* every Friday night, and proposed a show called *Celebrity Stools*, in which experts sort through other people's number twos, he'd not only have given me short shrift, he'd have called security.

But these days, no one bats an eyelid. This is precisely the kind of stuff which gets put out at prime time. Since when did colonic irrigation become a suitable subject for pre-watershed family viewing?

Channel surfing one evening, I came across a programme presented by a madwoman who invited willing members of the public to have a hosepipe stuck up their backside. It's like a motorway pile-up. You feel guilty watching, but you can't help yourself. I think it was called *You Are What You Eat*.

The night I stumbled across it, a woman from Scotland had agreed to submit herself to the scrutiny of a 'nutritionist' called Dr Gillian McKeith. While the patient lay under a blanket – how shall I put it? – moving her bowels into a transparent plastic tube, the good doctor sifted through the slurry like a prospector during the California gold rush and concluded that it was a bit runny.

How the hell did something like this find its way onto so-called public service television? No doubt they're already planning a similar series starring the food and wine expert, Jilly Goolden.

'An excellent nose, nice chunky texture, a hint of Guinness and chicken vindaloo and a thoroughly toxic aftertaste'.

Stand by for *Celebrity Stools* on a Saturday night, introduced by Ant and Dec and featuring a panel of celebrities such as Simon Cowell and a Spice Girl having to guess the identity of some B-lister from the contents of their khazi. Think of it as an ironic, postmodern take on *What's My Line?*

'Looks like prawn bhuna to me, Geri. I think I know who it is.'
'Is it Russell Grant?'
'No, it looks female to me. Is it Linda Barker?'

I know some people think television is going down the toilet, but I didn't realise they were speaking literally.

If you think I'm joking, let me also produce in evidence a programme called *The Farm* which aired on channel Five.

It purported to be a serious documentary aimed at illustrating everyday agricultural life by parachuting 'celebrities' onto a farm and setting them a series of tasks – a sort of *Big Brother* with farm animals.

Needless to say, it was nothing of the sort. The highlight of this programme was someone called Rebecca Loos, er, pleasuring a pig. Miss Loos, some of you may recall, became briefly notorious for either sleeping or not sleeping with David Beckham, depending on who you believe. Since then she's never been out of the limelight, boasting about her sordid sex life, as if anyone gives a damn. But in today's shallow world, Miss Loos is what passes for a celebrity. Which presumably is how she managed to get herself hired by channel Five.

I never cease to be amazed by the lengths to which people are prepared to degrade themselves just so they can appear on television. I'm no prude and there's always the off button. But this was beyond the pale.

Who thought it was a good idea to broadcast it? Is Roger Mellie (*Viz* magazine's scatological Man On The Telly) running channel Five these days?

I've been trying to imagine what would have happened if I'd pitched the idea to a TV company even a couple of years ago.

Hey, I've got a great plan for a programme. Let's get that scrubber who claims to have slept with David Beckham, stick her on a farm and film her giving a hand shandy to a pig.

Watch out for the next series of *One Man and His Dog*.

The only question after that was how much lower could they go? We didn't have to wait long for an answer. It was called *Celebrity Hell Camp* and once again it starred Rebecca Loos and the usual cast of saddos, sickos, has-beens, wannabes, neverwillbes and assorted mental cases and exhibitionists who will do anything to appear on television. This time Miss Loos stole the show with an imaginitive demonstration of weight lifting – with what are euphemistically described as her 'private parts'. I say 'euphemistically' because Miss Loos's parts are about as private as the main concourse at Euston railway station.

But I would just add that the show also featured other 'stars', including someone called Jo Guest – described as a 'glamour girl' – drinking their own urine. It doesn't get much more 'glamorous' than that.

Now if people want to sup a pint of pee that's entirely a matter for them. I've had worse in some pubs. Similarly, if Miss Loos wishes to perform cunning stunts with an Evian bottle, who am I to argue?

I don't even have an objection to it being filmed.

Some years ago, when I was working for London's *Evening Standard*, I returned from lunch at around 4.30pm to be greeted by a commotion coming from the direction of the night reporter's office, tucked away off a side corridor. As I approached, I could see people spilling out of the door and could hear raucous laughter, punctuated by loud cheers. In the interests of investigative journalism, you understand, I poked my head around the door.

My colleagues were gathered four deep in front of a small television which was playing a video of a woman firing ping-pong balls in the air from between her legs while an acrobatic gentlemen bouncing on a miniature trampoline caught them in his mouth. One of the lads had brought it back from an overseas assignment in Amsterdam. I hesitate even to share this with you, lest it gives someone at Channel 4 an idea for a series or a postmodern remake of *It's A Knockout*.

Look, I'm not one for banning things, even if I find them offensive. Everything has its place. And the place for a film of a woman performing unusual feats with her private parts is – well, not to put too fine a point on it – in private.

Or at a stretch – so to speak – on a late night subscription satellite and cable channel. It shouldn't be broadcast on an unscrambled, terrestrial network with a public service remit in a grubby, cynical chase for ratings.

This time the ludicrous excuse for *Celebrity Hell Camp* was that the programme was examining alternative health practices. Of course it was . . .

How do you follow that? I wish I hadn't asked.

In July 2006, Channel 4 commissioning editor Andrew Mackenzie announced plans for a 'Wank Week'. The line-up included a documentary about compulsive masturbators, who do it up to twenty times a day, and a mass masturbation for charity, given the working title 'Wank-a-thon'.

Who thought that was a good idea? Presumably the same people who decided live cosmetic surgery on television was a way to behave.

One night, flicking the remote after *Match of the Day*, I discovered Vanessa Feltz hosting a programme about something called 'anal bleaching'. She stood there in front of a giant plasma screen, onto which was being beamed live pictures of an intimate operation being performed in a surgery in America. The first shot reminded me of Bill the Butcher cutting up a side of beef in *Gangs of New York*, which I'd been watching earlier on DVD.

Then she moved on to a procedure called anal tightening, which Vanessa told us was increasingly popular among aficionados of anal sex. As Basil Fawlty once observed, it's all bottoms with these people. It didn't seem to occur to her to point out that if they weren't so fond of back-door action they wouldn't need their anuses tightened in the first place.

But then the camera panned back to the plasma screen.

They're not going to show it, surely? They bloody are, you know.

It certainly made mine tighten.

Call me old-fashioned, but it wasn't that long ago when anyone who attempted to put live anal tightening on mainstream network television would have been arrested.

Where the hell do they go from here? How much lower than anal tightening can it get?

Lower! LOWER!

39 | Don't Mention the C-Word

We wish you a merry, er, Winterval,
We wish you a merry, um, holiday,
We wish you a merry, erm, you know (Kwanzaa/Diwali/whatever),
And a happy new, ahem, thingy.

The war on Christmas was well under way before Blair landed in Downing Street. What changed after 1997 was that the Labour lunatics who had waged cultural war from their town hall Tora Bora strongholds in the 1980s and early 1990s stepped up a division and brought their hatred of tradition into central government.

Their perverse version of multiculturalism embraced every creed and religion – except Christianity. While ordering us to celebrate diversity, they ruthlessly set about dismantling Christian festivals. That didn't extend to the Jesuit tradition of 'give me the child and I'll give you the man', although their version owed more to Chinese and Eastern European communism than muscular Christianity. The brainwashing starts early in Blair's Britain. Every state school in the country has some kind of ceremony to mark Diwali and Ramadan. But nativity plays and Easter are dying out. In East London, schools were banned from serving hot cross buns, in case it offended Muslims.

This depressing trend received the official New Labour stamp of approval when Tessa Jowell's Department of Culture, Media and Sport started sending out cards without mentioning the dreaded C-word. Instead, Tessa wished everyone 'Seasons Greetings' so as to avoid upsetting religious minorities.

The cards themselves looked like the wall of a fourteen-year-old's bedroom – a mishmash of images glued together. The design was so crass, so dreadful that under other circumstances it would have been shortlisted for the Turner Prize. Graham Newsome, the ministry's head of communications, said that sending Christmas wishes to people of different faiths would be 'inappropriate'.

What a bloody ghastly, weasel word 'inappropriate' is. It should always be written in blue pencil, since its main use is to censor freedom of speech, thought and behaviour. Newsome went on: 'We did have conversations about which way we should go with the overall design of the card. We asked all sorts of questions: Do we do something new? Do we go down the Christmas route? Whichever way you go the balance is difficult.'

Have you ever read such drivel? If you're not going to 'go down the Christmas route' when designing a Christmas card, why bother in the first place?

It gets worse. While there was no mention of the C-word and no Christian imagery, the card did feature a drawing of the minarets from a mosque and a pair of Hindu dancers.

Why? What possible justification is there for including religious imagery from other faiths on what is in all but name a Christmas card? If Tessa was terrified about causing offence, why send out cards at all? She certainly doesn't give a stuff about offending devout Christians by sending them Muslim and Hindu symbols on a card to mark a holiday celebrating the birth of Christ. You don't have to be a born-again Godbotherer to find that 'inappropriate'.

Would she send out a Ramadan card with a cross on the front and 'Seasons Greetings' inside? No, she'd probably turn up at her local mosque in a burka as a mark of respect, just as the Wicked Witch gets herself togged up like Mrs Gandhi whenever Blair goes rattling the collection tin around the wealthy Asian business community.

Like it or not, the only reason we have a holiday at Christmas is because it is a Christian religious festival. But the fascist left are engaged in a relentless assault on traditional Western, Judaeo-Christian values and morality. They want to control our every word, thought and deed, to rob us of our identity. They promote 'tolerance' but are themselves ruthlessly intolerant of anyone and anything outside their proscriptive, vindictive agenda.

Patronising the ethnic minorities by taking offence on their behalf is merely one weapon in their armoury. They must be resisted and ridiculed at every turn, but it's a losing battle.

I was browsing through the cards sent to me last Christmas. There was a marked increase in the number which contain no mention of the C-word. It's the corporate cards which tend to steer clear of any reference to to Christmas or the New Year.

Can't blame them, I suppose, given that every large organisation contains a fair share of professional malcontents, bristling with self-righteous indignation and primed with a hair trigger to take offence at any slight, real or, usually, imagined.

It can only be a matter of time before one of them turns up before an industrial tribunal demanding trebles-all-round compen-say-shun because their employer had the audacity to mention the C-word at the, er, Late December Party.

In anticipation of something like this, the Red Cross banned its 430 charity shops from putting up Christmas decorations on the grounds that it might be 'offensive' to non-Christians. A spokesman said: 'The Red Cross is a neutral organisation and we don't want to be aligned with any particular philosophy. We don't want to be seen as a Christian or Islamic or Jewish organisation because that might compromise our ability to work in conflict situations around the world.'

Cobblers. The Red Cross is a Christian organisation. Where do they think the cross comes from? Muslim countries have their own version, called the Red Crescent. Have they abolished Ramadan because it might be 'offensive' to Christians, or Jews, or Hindus?

What do you think?

In any event, I'd have thought it was pretty offensive to most Muslims – apart from Captain Hook and his hatemongers – to even suggest they might be offended by Christmas.

Let's get something straight. The modern Red Cross is decidedly not a neutral organisation. The leadership has fallen to the Guardianistas, like almost every other charity in Britain. They ruthlessly pursue an anti-British, anti-Christian, ultra-left agenda.

This is the same organisation, don't forget, which bankrolled the Sangatte departure lounge for 'asylum seekers' hoping to enter Britain and closed residential homes in Britain to concentrate on helping illegal immigrants.

There are thousands of decent, selfless people who volunteer for the Red Cross. But the leadership of this once proud organisation seems to hate this country and most of the people who live in it.

There appears to be no limit to the ingenious ways the killjoys try to ruin Christmas. Take the NSPCC. A couple of years ago it refused to accept second-hand toys for needy children, claiming such gifts breach European safety regulations. It said it would be too expensive to submit all the toys for inspection. The law the NSPCC quoted has been in existence since 1989. So why hasn't it been invoked before? Needless to say, the NSPCC refused to comment. The people in charge preferred to deprive children of a much-needed gift at Christmas rather than run the risk accusations of being 'bad Europeans'.

Anyone with a shred of common sense or humanity would simply have ignored the rules or challenged the Eurocrats to take them to court. Since 1989, how many children have been killed or injured by teddy bears, fluffy bunnies and cuddly toys donated to the NSPCC?

Precisely.

Once this kind of purse-lipped, self-righteous, censorious behaviour was confined to the barmier London boroughs. But under Labour, it's spread to the shires, too. While Tessa Jowell was sending out Christmas-free Christmas cards, the main library in High Wycombe, Buckinghamshire, banned posters for a church carol concert – in case, you guessed, it offended minorities. It was subsequently revealed that the same library played host to a party to celebrate the end of the Muslim festival of Ramadan. The councillor responsible, Margaret Dewer, said she was 'appalled at the attitude of so-called Christians making a fuss about this policy. We have a policy which aims to be inclusive and to respect the religious diversity of Buckinghamshire.'

Except, of course, Christians – 'so-called' or otherwise.

You expect this kind of nonsense from New Labour ministers like Tessa or hatchet-faced Labour councillors in Islington. But Margaret Dewer was a Conservative councillor – in High Wycombe, for heaven's sake. What better illustration could there be of the extent of the 'diversity' tyranny? When Middle England falls to the Guardianistas, the game is well and truly up.

(Incidentally, there was incredulity when some of those arrested on suspicion of plotting to blow up airplanes over the Atlantic turned out to be from High Wycombe, of all places. We should have paid more attention.)

I could fill a whole book with this kind of nonsense. In fact, in the USA a book called *The War on Christmas* hit the best-seller list. There are hundreds upon hundreds of examples of the lengths to which organisations will go to scupper the Christmas spirit.

Here's the Equal Opportunities Unit at Lancashire Constabulary (the force which brought you the Oldham riots), which issued a festive 'Checklist For Those Organising Events!' at C-time.

Note the exclamation mark! I bet they've got a notice in the office which reads: 'You Don't Have To Read the *Guardian* To Work Here – But It Helps!'

The eight-point 'checklist' naturally contains no mention of the C-word. I shan't bore you with all of it. (You could probably write it yourself after a couple of pints of egg nog.) But here are some of the highlights.

When sending out invitations, make sure to use 'inclusive language'. If you have colleagues who are disabled, take their needs into account. [eg, no basketball or dwarf-tossing contests.]

If you are booking a turn, make sure the entertainment is 'suitable' and the content isn't going to be offensive. [eg, no shirtlifting/Osama Bin Laden gags. And definitely no Jim Davidson/ Bernard Manning/Chubby Brown.]

Consider dietary requirements in catering arrangements. [No C-word pudding and only halal turkey.]

Finally, have you discussed with your colleagues how to challenge inappropriate behaviour? [I assume that means no cracks such as: 'Is that a truncheon in your pocket, or are you just pleased to see me?']

But who, exactly, is offended by the C-word?

Certainly not my Jewish friends, with whom we always exchange C-word cards. Karim, who runs Tandoori Nights, my local curry house, doesn't seem to have a problem with it. Neither does Mr Patel, our splendid newsagent. His shop is full of C-word cards, decorations, paper chains, fairy lights, seasonal selection boxes and tinsel angels. I've never known a Chinese restaurant turn away a party of New Year revellers on 31 December on the grounds that they're a couple of months early. A Muslim colleague of mine at one of my former newspapers used to look forward to C-word Eve. He'd mind the news desk while we went out and got slaughtered on Black Velvets at nine o'clock in the morning. For us, it meant a monumental hangover on C-word Day. For him, it was a double shift.

So what's the big deal?

Members of religious minorities, apart from the usual handful of mad mullahs who would be happier living in a cave in Afghanistan, accept C-word for what it is – a quasi-holy excuse for professional footballers to disgrace themselves in public; for secretaries to wake up next morning with their knickers on back to front and a photocopied picture of their aris on the office noticeboard; and for the rest of us to bury our differences for five minutes and split a dried-out turkey before *The Great Escape*.

The killjoys, as always, are the fascist left. If they had their way, Sinatra would be redubbed so he would be singing 'Have Yourself A Merry Little Holiday'. Noddy Holder would be screaming 'It's WinterVAAAALLL!'. And Roy Wood would be wishing it could be Diwali every day.

*

Every year it gets worse, as councils all over Britain have pulled the plug on Christmas trees, mangers, crosses and Santa Claus. In St Andrews, in Scotland, they even put on a play depicting the Virgin Mary as an alcoholic and Jesus as a homosexual.

I thought it was time for a revised and updated arrangement of

'Away In A Manger', for the twenty-first century. This is the extended twelve-inch version.

Feel free to sing along.

> Away with the fairies,
> No brains in their head,
> The little dictators
> Say Christmas is dead.
>
> The berks in the town halls
> Look down as we pray
> And rule that the manger
> Be taken away.
>
> In Birmingham's Bullring
> Poor Santa is banned
> His sleigh and his reindeer
> And elves have been canned.
>
> In Bury St Edmunds
> They've turned off the lights
> In Suffolk, Lord Jesus
> Offends human rights.
>
> They want our donations
> Down at the Red Cross
> But no celebrations
> They don't give a toss.
>
> And even St Tony
> Has tried really hard
> Not to mention the C-word
> In his Christmas cards.
>
> There's no carol service
> In High Wycombe, Bucks.
> The council's decided
> That 'Silent Night' sucks.

In Luton, Tower Hamlets
And old Camden Town
The Christmas decorations
Have all been torn down.

No turkey, no stuffing
And no Brussels sprouts
And mince pies and crackers
Are definitely out.

There'll be no King Herod
With crown on his bonce
And no Father Christmas
In case he's a nonce.

In Scotland, St Andrews
Where Mars bars they batter
Our Mary's a dipso
And Christ a brown-hatter.

Pray celebrate Diwali
And Ramadan praise
It's only Christianity
They want to erase.

There'll be no more mention
Of our Lord and Saviour
So God bless St Tony
Remember, Vote Labour!

40 | The Birth of Chris

To keep the PC brigade happy I thought it was about time we revised the nativity story for the twenty-first century.

And, lo, in a land far away a vision did appear to a woman called Mary. And it sayeth, thou will have a child and it will be called Chris, for that is non-gender-specific.

And Mary sayeth, I cannot be with child for I am a virgin who hath not layeth down with man, for I am also a lesbian.

And the vision sayeth, fear not that thou travellest on the other oxen cart, that is no bother we can fixeth it for thou to receive the insemination which is artificial.

And Mary was sore afraid and sayeth, but I am a poor peasant from a land far away and I have no money.

And the vision sayeth, worry thee not. All will be provideth. Thou will have to journey to the land of milk and honey which is called Ing-er-land.

And Mary sayeth, I have heard of this place, which welcometh people from a land far away, for it was on CNN. And she sayeth, but how do I get there?

And the vision sayeth, crosseth my palm with two hundred score and ten pieces of silver and my brother-in-law knoweth a man who will transport thou unto this land of milk and honey.

And so it came to pass that Mary joined others from the land far away and travelleth to Ing-er-land in a cart called a container lorry.

And having journeyed for many days across many lands, like a fish which is called a sardine, Mary reached a place teeming with a multitude of people from lands far away, some from even farther away than her own.

And she sayeth to a man who was called Dave, is this Ing-er-land?

And Dave sayeth unto her, no this is a place called San-gatte, but fear not for I am from the Red Cross and you can shelter herein until it is time for you to journey to Ing-er-land.

And so Mary dwelleth under the sign of the Red Cross for thirty days and thirty nights until her number cometh up.

And in the sky did appear a Eurostar, and Mary knew it was time. And as if by a miracle, the security fence was rent asunder and the people from all the lands far away poureth through.

And, lo, in five and forty minutes, Mary arriveth at a place called Ash-ford. And she sayeth to a man called Plod, is this Ing-er-land?

And the man called Plod sayeth, evenin' all, this is Ing-er-land, love, can I see thine papers?

And Mary sayeth, I have no papers, I seek asylum, just as the vision's brother-in-law had sayeth unto her.

And the man called Plod sayeth, then you want the place which is called Croy-don.

And Mary sayeth, is Croy-don where I get the milk and honey?

And Plod sayeth, yes, now off you go and if you reach the palace which is called Crys-tal you have gone too far.

And Mary came to Croy-don, where the multitude of people from lands far away gathereth. And she asketh the man who was called Jobs-worth was there room at the inn.

And the man who is called Jobs-worth said there was no room at Croy-don and told her to journey to the inn under the sign of the Elephant and Castle.

And when Mary reacheth the sign of the Elephant and Castle, there was no room because it teemeth with another multitude from the lands far away.

And a kind man who was called Del-Boy from the place called Peck-ham saw she was with child and sayeth unto her, you can sleepeth in my lock-up.

And it came to pass that Mary gave birth to a child which was called Chris, for that was non-gender-specific.

And above the lock-up, there appeared a sign which readeth Trotter's Independent Traders.

And three wise men saw the sign and thinkest to themselves, Del-Boy hath not the permission of the planning committee for that.

And so they journeyed to the lock-up, and when they got there they found Mary and the baby Chris swaddled in a three-quarter length sheepskin.

And they sayeth unto her, have thou no home to go to?

And Mary sayeth unto them, I am a seeker after asylum from a land far away.

And they sayeth unto her, haveth you a husband to look after you?

And she sayeth unto them, no I don't layeth down with man, I had the insemination which is artificial.

And they sayeth, you're a lesbian, and a seeker after asylum. You've come to the right place, for we are from the council which is called Lam-beth, and we come bearing gifts.

And there appeared three men from the sign of the Nag's Head, the one who was called Del-Boy, a man called Rod-ney and an older man with a beard who was called Al-bert.

And they all were bearing gifts. The wise men beareth keys to a council flat, and a benefits book.

And Del-Boy sayeth, now you have a bay-bee you will need a motor, leave it unto me, and I will have a word with Boy-cey, and the council will pay.

And the wise men from Lam-beth sayeth unto her, now you have a child called Chris, born in Peck-ham, the blind man who is called Blun-kett will givest thou a passport, no bother.

And Mary wept and rejoiceth, because now she knew Ing-er-land truly was a land of milk and honey, thanks be to Chris.

41 | Baghdad Broadcasting Corporation

Two items from a single BBC news bulletin. Item one: rail militants threaten transport chaos. Item two: al-Qaeda militants behead prisoner.

Spot the difference.

The first referred to plans by the RMT to call strikes on the railways and the London Underground. We were told the vote was swung by 'militant' members of the union's executive.

The second was about the cold-blooded slaughter in Saudi Arabia of an innocent South Korean contractor by a gang of desperados. Those responsible were described by the BBC as al-Qaeda 'militants'.

Now I can think of a number of ways of describing al-Qaeda. Terrorists, fanatics, murderers, barbarians, gangsters, all spring to mind.

But 'militants'? I don't think so.

Over the years, as an industrial correspondent, I must have written the word 'militant' hundreds, if not thousands, of times. I've come across militant train drivers, militant car workers, militant miners. I've seen some picket line violence in my time: bottles thrown, police horses punched. But to the best of my knowledge, even at the bitterest height of the miners' strike, I can't remember Arthur Scargill actually beheading anyone.

Bob Crow, the left-wing leader of the RMT, is everyone's favourite bogeyman these days. He's routinely described as a 'militant'. But in fairness to Bob, I've never heard him advocate decapitation as a legitimate way of pursuing a grievance. I can't ever recall any trades union 'militant' threatening to fly an airliner into a tower block unless their demands are met.

Unless I missed something, the Longbridge shop stewards

committee never sent anyone strapped with Semtex to blow up a Birmingham Corporation bus packed with passengers because the management wouldn't give them an extra five minutes on their tea breaks.

Yet the London bombers were also described as 'militants'. So perhaps the BBC can explain why they think 'militant' is the appropriate expression to describe a fanatical terrorist organisation hell-bent on the slaughter of innocent civilians and the downfall of Western civilisation.

How is it they can see no difference between an Islamist maniac chopping off the head of a helicopter engineer and an RMT official calling for a work-to-rule over a dispute about pension contributions?

The broadcasters are the main offenders, the BBC in particular. In TV land there's no right and wrong, only moral equivalence. Actually it's not even about equivalence, it's usually about present-ing terrorists in the best possible light. During the second Gulf War, I saw the BBC describe coalition soldiers in Iraq as 'gunmen'. Yet Hamas homicide bombers are always called 'activists'. Palestinian murderers act out of 'desperation'. When Israel acts in self-defence it is always 'perpetuating the cycle of violence'. In one breath they'll talk about a 'radical' new Tory plan to introduce education vouchers. In the next breath they'll describe the people responsible for blowing up a café full of civilians in Tel Aviv as Palestinian 'radicals'.

What has a Tory think tank seeking new ways to extend choice in schooling got in common with a terrorist organisation which routinely murders innocent men, women and children? But then the BBC has got plenty of previous. During the ideological struggles in the Soviet Union, hard-line communists were always described as 'conservatives'. Were they trying to tar the Tories with guilt by association? If only subconsciously, yep.

The problem with too many broadcast executives is that they are so convinced of their own moral and intellectual superiority that in their efforts to be 'non-judgemental' and 'impartial' they consistently present a warped version of the world to their viewers.

It's not just my view, either. They admit it themselves. In summer 2006, the BBC held a conference chaired by Sue Lawley, to examine their editorial standards. Andrew Marr, formerly the BBC's political editor and presenter of the Sunday morning slot formerly occupied by Sir David Frost, admitted the corporation was utterly unrepresentative of the majority of licence-payers:

> The BBC is not impartial or neutral. It's a publicly funded, urban organisation with an abnormally large number of young people, ethnic minorities and gay people. It has a liberal bias, not so much a party-political bias. It is better expressed as a cultural liberal bias.

Senior executives confessed that they openly promoted left-wing views, were anti-British, anti-Christian, anti-American, anti-countryside and pro-EU.

And terrified of upsetting Muslims. While they would cheerfully throw the Bible into the bin on air, they wouldn't dream of treating the Koran in the same cavalier fashion. While they would allow a Muslim woman newsreader to wear the veil, Fiona Bruce was told to stop wearing a crucifix on air.

My friend Jeff Randall, formerly the BBC's business editor, was once told not to wear Union Jack cufflinks because it was pandering to the BNP. The BNP, you notice, not the Royal Family, or the Church of England, or the British Legion, or the British Olympic Team. They wouldn't dream of banning the Irish tricolour on the grounds it was pandering to the IRA.

Jeff told them to get stuffed, but then he was the exception which proved the rule – the BBC is staffed to the gunwales with brain-dead, brainwashed Guardianistas.

It's in the coverage of multiculturalism and the Middle East where the institutionalised anti-Western, anti-Israel bias is most pronounced. In the wake of criticism levelled in the Hutton Inquiry into the Iraq dodgy dossier affair, the BBC decided to spend £50 million retraining journalists. Maybe as a basis for negotiation they should produce a new dictionary which begins: 'A is for al-Qaeda, a terrorist organisation which killed 3,000 people on 9/11 and hundreds more in Bali, Istanbul, Madrid, London and elsewhere – not a harmless bunch of cuddly idealists no different to the works committee at Acton bus garage.'

In October 2006, the BBC announced plans to launch two new channels in the next two years. One, in Arabic, will compete with al-Jazeera. The other, in Farsi, will be beamed into Iran. A spokesman said of the Persian-language venture: 'The new television service will be editorially independent of the UK government.' So why did Gordon Brown agree to subsidise it to the tune of £15 million? Wouldn't it be cheaper just to put out the BBC's domestic service on satellite? No one would notice the difference.

In the days before the announcement of the new channels, Radio 4 gave over a substantial chunk of the flagship *Today* programme to a party political broadcast by an Islamist maniac.

Those of us who live in the London area might just as well be watching the Baghdad Broadcasting Corporation when it comes to 'local' news. One night that week, the first five items on the World's Worst News Bulletin were all about Muslims. Coverage of the debate over the veil was conducted exclusively from an Islamic viewpoint, from what I could gather.

First, there was a live vox pop from a curry house opposite a mosque in Southall, where all those asked to comment had just turned out of Friday prayers. Back in the studio, the two invited guests were a 'moderate' Muslim and a bird in a burka. This is what the BBC calls 'balance'. We've even had the weatherman standing in the Edgware Road – the famous 'Arab Street' – giving us the forecast for Ramadan.

Why don't they just cut out the middleman and install a studio in Captain Hook's cell at Belmarsh?

'Something to look forward to on BBC1 this weekend, a brand-new series of *Fasting With Frost*. *Songs of Praise* comes from Regent's Park Mosque and this week's *What Not To Wear* features Jack Straw being given a complete makeover by the fashion editor of al-Mujaharoun. Over on BBC2, in *Top Gear*, Jeremy Clarkson tests the latest range of people carriers available free of charge to unemployed Muslim clerics. And don't forget to stay tuned for live beheading from Trafalgar Square, coming up after the latest national and international news, read by Abu Hamza.'

(Roll titles.)

'Good evening, infidel dogs. I spit on you. The mujahadeen are coming to murder you in your beds and the blood of your kafir children and your drunken whores will run through the streets of your decadent, godless cities. That's our top story tonight – and, of course, every other night.

'Some breaking news this evening – a plane has crashed into a skyscraper in New York. Unfortunately, only two people were killed.

'We also celebrate the fourth anniversary of the glorious Bali martyrdom operation, a shining day in history for all true believers.

'In an exclusive interview from Lebanon, the president of Iran tells our diplomatic editor, Sheikh Omar Bakri, of his plans to wipe the pariah, pigs-and-monkeys state of Izza-ray-el off the map in a nuclear holocaust, just as soon as he receives the plutonium from North Korea.

'Our crime correspondent, Abu Izadeen reports on the progress in the fatwa against the Danish cartoonists who insulted Islam.

'Later in the programme, in our consumer affairs slot, I'll be presenting a special report from West London on how you can become a property tycoon whilst living on benefits – and, indeed, while in prison.

'Our legal aid correspondent, Anjem Choudary, will be bringing you an update on the imposition of Sharia law in East Ham.

'There'll be the latest news on the campaign to have London Underground stations renamed after the four members of the 7 July martyrdom brigade.

'We've got exclusive footage from our brothers in Iraq, show-ing a Western aid worker slut having her head sawn off. If you can't wait for that, it is available right now on our website, where you'll also find easy to follow instructions on making ricin in your own kitchen.

'Sir Ian Blair apologises to all Muslims for something which hasn't actually happened yet.

'In sport, we ask if England goalkeeper Paul Robinson should have his right leg amputated to punish him for letting in that soft own goal in Croatia.

'And coming up after the break, a shocking report from the Great Satan on how, in their latest outrage against Islam, the rapacious, infidel running dogs of the illegitimate and immoral Bush regime have, er, banned online gambling . . .'

42 | EUTV

Whenever there's a coup in a Ruritanian country, the first thing the rebels do is seize the radio and TV stations, to control the flow of information and pump out their own revolutionary propaganda.

For the past thirty-five years, the European Commission has been conducting a coup by stealth. They didn't need to storm the TV stations since the broadcasters, particularly in Britain, and especially the BBC and Channel 4 News, have always been messianic about the federalist mission.

But after some countries voted against the European Constitution and public opinion in Britain put an effective block on joining the single currency, the commissioners in Brussels drew up plans for their own EUTV channel on satellite and cable to promote the interests of ever closer union. My mole in EU headquarters leaked me the proposed schedule.

EUTV1

6.00am GMTV

Daily breakfast show for farmers, produced by the European Agricultural Commission and dedicated to extolling the virtues of Genetically Modified crops.

9.30am Relocation, Relocation

Kirsty and Phil join Peter and Reinaldo as they swap their Notting Hill flat and Hartlepool terrace for a swanky townhouse in the ritzy rue des Jeunes Garcons, in Brussels.

10.15am Bargain Hunt

Today's programme follows French and German utility bosses as they buy up British water and electricity companies for a song.

12.00pm **Working Lunch**

A fly-on-the-wall documentary series which follows a group of MEPs as they trough their way through some of the finest Michelin-starred restaurants in Brussels and Strasbourg.

1.00pm **Tea With Mussolini** (2006)

Feature film about a young, heart-throb Conservative leader who is seduced by an Italian temptress with a dark family history. Stars Isabella Rossellini as Alessandra Mussolini and David Cameron as himself.

3.15pm **Britain's Best Back Gardens**

John Prescott at the wheel as thousands of back gardens in the South of England are bulldozed and replaced by hideous blocks of flats in line with EU planning directives.

4.15pm **Deal Or No Deal**

Popular family game show in which contestants compete to see who can negotiate away Britain's rebate to Brussels in exchange for nothing in return. Introduced by Tony Blair.

5.00pm **Ready, Steady, Cook**

Ainsley Harriot's kitchen is raided by health and safety inspectors enforcing new Brussels hygiene regulations, with hilarious consequences.

6.00pm **BBC News**

Another chance to see the special report on why opponents of the EU Constitution are all foam-flecked, racist, xenophobic, homophobic, BNP child molesters.

7.00pm **Wish You Were Here**

Judith Chalmers talks to visitors from all over the world who have taken advantage of Europe's open borders and are planning to settle in Britain. Live from Sangatte.

8.00pm **Rick Stein's Fruits of the Sea**

Rick's Padstow restaurant is forced into receivership as a result of the government's latest concessions under the Common Fisheries Policy. Rick and local fishermen get smashed on extra-strength scrumpy as the few remaining fishing boats in Padstow are put to the torch. Last in series.

9.00pm   **Two Metres Under**

Remake of the award-winning American series about a family firm of funeral directors. Tonight the brothers conduct a traditional open-air Hindu cremation ceremony on Hackney Marshes, following a successful legal challenge under Section 8 of the European Convention on Human Rights.

10.15pm   **What The Sicilians Did For Us**

Adam Hart-Davis cycles round Italy explaining how the Mafia have managed to defraud EU taxpayers out of hundreds of millions of euros through an elaborate subsidy swindle involving non-existent olive groves.

10.45pm   **They Flew To Bulgaria** (2005)

Made-for-EUTV update of the 1947 original, *They Flew To Bruges*, which starred David Niven as Second World War ace Wing Commander Binky Beaumont. In this new version, al-Qaeda suspects are spirited away to secret locations under a process known as extraordinary rendition, hotly pursued by legally-aided lawyers from the Hague. Stars Adolf Hitler as George W. Bush.

EUTV2

7.00am   **Cheese-Eating Surrender Monkeys**

Delightful French-made children's series about a group of spineless puppets who have discovered they have the power to turn food into oil. Your puppet-master is Saddam Hussein.

7.30am   **Teletubbies**

Tinky-Winky, Dipsy, Laa-Laa and Po and their genetically-modified rabbit wake up to find their hillside is covered with giant windmills under the EU's sustainable energy policy.

8.00am   **A Place In The Sun**

Jonnie and Jasmine fly to Greece where generous subsidies to local tobacco farmers are fuelling a booming market in second homes and Ferraris.

9.00am   **Pay Off Your Mortgage In Two Years**

Neil and Glenys Kinnock explain how anyone can quickly pay off their outstanding debts simply by getting their entire family on the payroll of the European Commission.

10.00am   Who Wants To Be A Millionaire

New daytime slot for the phenomenally successful game show, in which Chris Patten invites French peasant farmers to become rich beyond their wildest dreams, simply by phoning a friend in Brussels.

11.00am   An Inspector Calls (2005)

EU-funded feature film following a group of inspectors from Britain's office of the deputy prime minister as they raid suburban homes in search of jacuzzis, loft conversions, and mixer taps which have not been declared to the authorities. Stars John Prescott as Reinhard Heydrich.

1.15pm   Home and Away

How MEPs juggle a wife in Britain and a mistress in Brussels. Nigel Farage, of UKIP, has been having an affair with a half-German, half-Swedish blonde EU researcher called Liga. Worth watching for the nail-biting scene in which Mrs Farage discovers Liga's phone number on Nigel's mobile and decides to call her.

2.00pm   On The Fiddle

Undercover report into the millions of euros lost through creative expense accounting by MEPs.

3.30pm   You've Been Framed

John Reid introduces this exciting new show in which innocent British citizens are arrested and whisked off abroad to be sent to prison for life by publicity-seeking foreign magistrates under the new European Arrest Warrant.

4.30pm   The Weakest Link

Cruel game show in which Tony Blair is berated by a panel of EU politicians for his abject failure to con the British people into accepting the euro.

5.30pm   The Money Programme

An investigation into why the auditors have refused to sign off on the EU's accounts for the seventh year running (rpt).

6.30pm **Big Brother**

Davina McCall introduces the show from the headquarters of Galileo, the expensive new EU satellite system set up to spy on every single one of Europe's 456 million people.

7.30pm **Life On Mars**

New time-travel drama in which a traditional British politician falls asleep and wakes up in Brussels at the headquarters of the EU, where he is horrified by the bullying and corruption and the contempt his new colleagues have for the people who pay their wages.

9.00pm **Little England**

Award-winning comedy follow-up to Little Britain, from Matt Lucas and David Walliams. New characters include Maggie Handbag (catchphrase 'No, but, no, but, no') and gay Tory MP Sir Jasper Dandruff (the only Eurosceptic in the Valleys). Peter Mandelson guest stars as Sebastian.

10.00pm **What The Papers Say**

Exclusive video footage of a Danish newspaper editor being beheaded for publishing a cartoon of the Prophet Mohammed.

10.15pm **Closedown** (due to new European Working Time Directive).

43 | London Calling

In the wake of the 7 July bombings on London transport, I couldn't help wondering how the Second World War might have turned out if the modern diversity and human rights agenda had been in force back then and all reporting was subject to today's BBC producer guidelines.

*

London calling, London calling. This is the *Six O'Clock News* from the BBC, read by Lord Haw-Haw.

More than 20,000 people are believed to have been killed in a series of incidents in the East End of London. Militants loyal to the German führer, Adolf Hitler, have claimed responsibility. Our world affairs editor said this was an inevitable consequence of British aggression at Dunkirk. The prime minister, Winston Churchill, said today that those responsible were a tiny minority of criminals whose views did not represent the mainstream Nazi community, which is overwhelmingly peace-loving and law-abiding.

As the clear-up operation continued, Mr Churchill appealed for calm and said there must be no retaliation. Anyone caught fighting on beaches, landing grounds, fields, streets or hills would be arrested and prosecuted under the emergency hate-crimes legislation.

The commissioner of the Metropolitan Police, Sir Ian Blair, said he could see no connection between the word 'Nazi' and 'Blitz'. He said we must be vigilant against any increase in Naziphobia.

Sir Ian and his colleagues in the Association of Chief Police Officers are to sponsor a conference at Central Hall, Westminster, which is being addressed by the leading Nazi thinker, Dr Josef Goebbels.

Although Dr Goebbels advocates a policy of genocide aimed at eradicating the Jews from the face of the earth, the Mayor of London, Mr Ken Livingstone, described him as a man of peace and said he would be welcomed as an honoured guest.

In a statement from County Hall, Mr Livingstone also accused the American president, Franklin D. Roosevelt, of being a war criminal. He said the USA had completely over-reacted to an incident at Pearl Harbor carried out by a handful of Japanese insurgents. In Parliament, the Right Honourable George Galloway MP, thousands of whose constituents were killed in the incidents, refused to condemn the perpetrators. He said the wholesale bombing of civilians in London was a perfectly under-standable and justifiable reaction to the Treaty of Versailles.

In another development from Westminster, plans to intern thousands of foreign nationals on the Isle of Man for the duration of the conflict have been abandoned after they were ruled illegal under the Human Rights Act.

On the south coast of England there are reports of a number of men with German accents appearing in villages and attempting to buy a glass of beer at 9.30am, before the legal opening time for public houses. Police said the men had been advised to make their own way to Lunacy House, in Croydon, Surrey, where they will be given accommodation, welfare benefits and advice on obtaining a British passport.

In Norfolk, the siege surrounding a group of German para-troopers who occupied a church and took dozens of civilians hostage has ended peacefully. The paratroopers were taken by charabanc to a nearby hotel, where they have been billeted while they speak to lawyers from the leading London chambers, Nazis 'R' Us, which was founded by the prime minister's wife, Mrs W. W. Churchill. All are expected to be granted exceptional leave to remain in Britain.

In Finsbury Park, police closed roads and provided an armed escort to allow Sir Oswald Mosley, leader of the British Union of Fascists, to preach hatred of the Jews to hundreds of followers in black shirts.

After an incident which destroyed Coventry Cathedral, the Archbishop of Canterbury has urged worshippers to reach out to members of the Nazi community and to understand the root causes of their grievances.

In the Middle East, the planned assault on El Alamein by Field Marshal Montgomery has been aborted amid concerns that it could inflame the Arab Street.

RAF fighter squadrons have been grounded following accusations that air crew are hideously white and male. The Macpherson Report into the RAF has concluded that despite a smattering of Commonwealth personnel, the service is institutionally racist. The very term 'Battle of Britain' is in itself racist, said the report. Campaigners also say it is outrageous that Squadron Leader Douglas Bader is the only differently abled pilot on active duty and are demanding the immediate recruitment of more women, paraplegics, homosexuals and members of the ethnic minorities.

The War Office has ordered Air Marshal Arthur 'Incident' Harris to cease operations over Germany following fears that this will only drive more impressionable young recruits into joining the Waffen SS.

The proposed 'Dambusters' raid has been cancelled on the instructions of health and safety officials following a risk assessment. The news was broken today to Wing Commander Guy Gibson, who was accompanied to the ministry by his faithful dog, Visible Ethnic Minority.

Throughout Britain, local authorities have banned the flying of the Union Flag because it could be considered offensive to members of the Nazi community.

In Romford, a pensioner who painted the words 'Up Yours Adolf' on the roof of his house has been arrested by police and charged with incitement to racial hatred.

Three British men caught by US forces spying for the Germans in North Africa are to be returned to Britain without charge. The men, dubbed 'The Gornal Gestapo' by the *News Chronicle* will be interviewed at Dock Green police station before being released back into the community. They are expected to receive substantial compensation.

Schoolchildren in Haringey, North London, have been banned from singing a nursery rhyme which makes fun of Herr Hitler's alleged deficiency in the trouser department. The song makes similar mockery of Herr Himmler and other German dignitaries. Education chiefs say the rhyme is inappropriate.

That is the BBC news for tonight. Good evening and Heil Hitler!

*

Now I'm not suggesting that the BBC reverts to the Reithian approach, whereby ministers were invited by obsequious interviewers to address a grateful nation. I'm all for them getting a verbal kicking at every opportunity. But because of the modern obsession with 'balance' and 'neutrality' and the desire for confrontation, even when it's not called for, the Beeb sometimes loses sight of the real story. I bow to no one in my admiration for John Humphrys – he's far and away the BBC's best current affairs interviewer. So I couldn't help wondering what might have happened if Humphrys had been around during Second World War.

*

'Good morning. It's eight o'clock on 19 June, 1940. You're listening to *Today* on the BBC Home Service. Joining me from our wireless car in Downing Street is the prime minister, Winston Churchill. Good morning, Prime Minister.'

'Good morning, Mr Humphrys.'

'You said in the House of Commons that if the British Empire lasts for a thousand years, men will say: "This was their finest hour." Where's your evidence for that?'

'I—'

'What about Agincourt, Mr Churchill? Many would argue that was a fine hour, too.'

'Er—'

'You also said recently that you had nothing to offer but blood, toil, tears and sweat. What sort of message does that send out?'

'If I may—'

'It's going to take more than blood, toil, sweat and tears, with respect.'

'No one can guarantee success in war, but—'

'So you're saying we're going to lose. Isn't that a bit reckless?'

'We shall not flag or fail. We shall go on to the end. We shall fight in France, we shall fight in the seas and oceans—'

'I'm sorry but I'm going to have to interrupt you there, Prime Minister. How can you say "We shall fight in France"? The French government in Vichy has welcomed the intervention of Herr Hitler. The Americans remain neutral. There has been no second resolution at the League of Nations.'

'We shall fight with growing confidence and growing strength in the air, we shall defend our island—'

'And that's why you're locking up asylum seekers, is it?'

'We have found it necessary to take measures of increasing stringency, not only against enemy aliens and suspicious characters of other nationalities, but also against British subjects who may become a danger or a nuisance should the war be transported to the United Kingdom.'

'But that is a clear breach of the League of Nation's charter on human rights.'

'We shall defend our island, whatever the cost may be.'

'Even without a second resolution?'

'We shall fight on the beaches, we shall fight on the landing grounds, we shall fight in the fields and in the streets.'

'On whose authority? What beaches? What landing grounds? What fields? Which streets do you have in mind? The British people have a right to know. What about civilian casualties?'

'We shall fight in the hills. We shall never surrender.'

'Come off it, Prime Minister. How can you possibly say you will never surrender? What is your policy?'

'What is our policy? To wage war against a monstrous tyranny, never surpassed in the dark, lamentable catalogue of human crime.'

'You have no proof to back up that statement. Why haven't you given the inspectors more time? Where is the evidence that Herr Hitler has in his possession any weapons of mass destruction? What on earth are you hoping to achieve?'

'Victory, victory at all costs. Victory in spite of all terror. Victory, however long the road may be, for without victory there is no survival.'

'And how do you hope to achieve that? You have failed in your attempts to build even a coalition of the willing. The French and Belgians are siding with the Germans. So are the Italians. There is no precedent in international law for taking this country to war. A recent opinion poll in the *Manchester Guardian*—'

'When I warned the French government that Britain would fight on alone whatever they did, their generals told their prime minister and his divided cabinet that in three weeks England will have her head wrung like a chicken. Some chicken! Some neck!'

'How long can we expect this illegal war to last, Prime Minister? What is your exit strategy? Can we have your assurance that this will soon end?'

'Now is not the end. It is not even the beginning of the end. But it is, perhaps, the end of the beginning.'

'Prime Minister, when are you going to resign?'

44 | Good Morning, Mr Ripper

The BBC is determined not to be 'judgemental'. Last year the *Today* programme on Radio 4 even gave a platform to fraudster William Gibson to explain why he should not have been hounded out of his job at the Porchester School, in Bournemouth, after his conviction for indecently assaulting a fifteen-year-old girl came to light. The day before, it invited a former primary school headmaster to tell us why he should be free to resume his career despite serving a three-month sentence for downloading child pornography. Where would they draw the line?

*

'Good morning. You're listening to the *Today* programme on BBC Radio 4 with me, James Naughtie. All this week we've been asking whether sex offenders should be allowed to work as teachers. Today the BBC has learnt of another victim of the current witch-hunt. Jack the Ripper has been suspended from his job as a biology teacher at the Osama Bin Laden Middle School, in Whitechapel, East London, even though his appointment was approved by the education secretary, Ruth Kelly. It has been revealed that Mr Ripper has been on the sex offenders' register for the past 117 years after being linked to up to eighteen gruesome murders of young women in the East End. But Miss Kelly decided, on the recommendation of civil servants, that he no longer represented a threat. Mr Ripper joins me now from our radio car. Good morning to you, Mr Ripper.'

'Call me Jack, Jim.'

'Very well, Jack. You were responsible for the savage killing of at least five women and suspected of murdering thirteen more. Do you think that in itself should mark someone out to be unsuitable to teach in a school or not?'

'In my case, Jim, I am suggesting it should not. I mean, these girls were prostitutes—'

'Let me just interrupt you, Jack. We don't say "prostitutes" any more, we say "sex workers".'

'Sex workers, common whores, whatever. The point I'm making is that they were quite happy selling their bodies.'

'But they had a right – did they not? – to expect to conduct their business in safety. Do you accept that in killing them and slicing them up your behaviour may, in some quarters, be considered inappropriate?'

'No doubt there are some people who would say that, Jim. But the point here is: there was no suggestion of a sexual relationship.'

'So you're saying you should never have been on the sex offenders' register in the first place?'

'Took the words out of my mouth, boss.'

'Interesting. But, forgive me for pressing you on this, can you see – and I'm not passing judgement here – how murdering and dismembering at least five sex workers – who, after all, are victims of society and only forced into pros— er, the sexual services sector, which is, er, why the government this week introduced new laws designed—'

'Is there a question in there somewhere, Jim?'

'I do the interrupting on this programme, Jack.'

'Fair enough, Jim.'

'What I was going to say was: don't you think that, at the very least, there was an element of, well, misjudgement on your part?'

'I accept that there was an error of judgement on my part, yes. But you have to understand that it was all a long time ago. I was depressed and I'd been working too hard. That was a different Jack the Ripper back then from the Jack the Ripper speaking to you today.'

'I take your point that you were depressed at the time, but you do agree that you – if this isn't too harsh a word – transgressed?'

'Absolutely.'

'And if I understand your position, it is that this error of judgement, this transgression, occurred a very long time ago, that you have not killed or dismembered anyone since 1888, and that therefore the school should accept that this was an isolated misjudgement and that it shouldn't now be held against you or bar you from working as a teacher.'

'A bit long-winded, Jim, but, yes, you've got it in one.'

'On a broader issue, Jack, the word "psychopath" is bandied about very loosely these days – and we must be careful not to cause offence to members of the psychopathic community – but would you agree that in your case the term "psychopath" would be – sorry, would have been – appropriate?'

'Absolutely, Jim. Psychopath, yes. Paedophile, no. It's not as if I was looking at dirty pictures or nuffink. We didn't have the Internet in 1888.'

'So you believe that the education secretary in your case was correct in allowing you, as a self-confessed psychopath, to work in schools?'

'Absolutely.'

'And what is your position on letting paedophiles back into the classroom?'

'Never, Jim. Those people disgust me. They shouldn't be allowed anywhere near vulnerable kiddies. I'll tell you what I'd do to them – I'd slice their—'

'Jack the Ripper, thank you very much. And coming up next: *Thought For The Day*. Today's speaker is Gary Glitter.'

45 | Frankie Goes to Hartlepool II

Peter Mandelson probably thinks he's worth a whole book documenting his pivotal contribution to the success of New Labour.

He isn't.

By the time Mandy turned up with his pretty little red rose, the battle against Militant and the rest of the hard left had already been won. The heavy lifting was done by hairy-arsed trades unionists – Terry Duffy, of the engineers; Brian Nicholson, of the transport workers; Jack Henry and Jack Rogers of the construction workers; Eric Hammond and John Spellar, of the electricians. These were hard, physical, often violent battles, not the Molly House posturing of Mandy, who turned up to take the credit.

I first encountered Mandelson in 1986, shortly after he joined the payroll of the Labour Party, after a pretty undistinguished career as a TV researcher at LWT. I was working on a story for the *Evening Standard* about the Labour Party in Bermondsey and thought I'd do him the courtesy of a call.

He lied to me.

I ran the story anyway.

He rang up and screamed at me. I was never going to work in this town again – you know, the usual bollo. I told him to sod off.

Mandy then rang John Leese, my editor and one of my journalistic heroes. John told him to sod off, too.

It was a trick Mandelson always pulled. 'Don't you know who I am? I'm a personal friend of your editor. You're finished.' Half the time it worked. I never understood why. For some unknown reason, Mandelson became know as the Prince of Darkness.

He probably coined it himself, a bit like Paul Ince, who used to play for West Ham and Manchester United, and who anointed himself The Guv'nor.

There's a line in the movie *The Usual Suspects*, about the best trick the devil ever pulled was convincing people he didn't exist. (You might have thought that would have registered with Mandy, given his personal closeness to the star of the film, Kevin Spacey.) But whenever one of his little schemes went the shape of the pear, far from vanishing from the scene, Mandy could always be found at the scene with his trousers round his ankles – smoking gun in one hand, plonker in the other.

That's why he was bundled off to Brussels, rather than luxuriating in the House of Lords (although at the time of writing we haven't had the resignation honours yet. Don't bet again on Mandy being on the lavender list).

When he arrived in Brussels, he told Euro MPs that his time as a minister in Britain was 'shorter than I would have wished'. And he explained that the reason he was forced to resign twice from the cabinet was nothing more than a 'set of unfortunate circumstances'.

In a sense, I suppose it's true. I'm sure his time in cabinet was shorter than he would have wished. And from where he's sitting the reasons for his truncated tenure were, er, 'unfortunate'.

What was actually unfortunate from his point of view was not what he did but the fact that he got found out.

He failed to tell his building society that fellow minister, Geoffrey Robinson was bankrolling the bulk of the purchase money with a £373,000 loan. He didn't tell the prime minister, nor did he tell his own civil servants at the DTI.

Mandelson was lucky not to have been prosecuted. End of story.

But he slimed his way out of it and after an indecently short interval was reinstated as a minister.

You might have thought that once bitten and all that. No such luck.

He then did it all over again.

When he bought his next property, he insisted the price was registered as £249,000, even though the estate agent involved in the deal maintained subsequently that the actual amount paid was 'a shade over a quarter of a million'.

Perhaps it was merely a happy coincidence that in pegging the purchase price under £250,000 and making up the difference by 'apportioning' a couple of grand for fixtures and fittings, he managed to save around £3,700 in tax. (Above £250,000, the rate of stamp duty payable rises sharply.)

Mandy hadn't done anything illegal. Just stupid. Given his track record in the property market, Mandelson must have realised that his next purchase would have to be cleaner than a nun's knickers. It was always going to be subjected to forensic scrutiny by Fleet Street.

So although pegging the price below the threshold and 'apportioning' the balance is a perfectly legitimate method of avoiding stamp duty, it certainly flew in the face of the spirit of the law. As a cabinet colleague of Gordon Brown, Mandy would have known that the chancellor has twice raised the level of stamp duty above the £250,000 threshold.

Of course, for £249,000, Mandy could have bought a perfectly decent house in most respectable London suburbs. But, as a dedicated follower of fashion, he just had to live in supercool Notting Hill. They seek him here, they seek him there, in Ladbroke Grove and Powis Square.

Frankly, I never understood all the fuss over Notting Hill. I used to drive through it every day on my way to LBC and it always struck me as a bit of a dump.

Notting Hill is for people who can't afford to live in Holland Park.

Bandit country begins at the Westway.

The houses are pretty enough, but like a lot of nineteenth century speculative building, they have impressive facades disguising shallow foundations and flimsy construction. Come to think of it, at the time Notting Hill was a perfect home for one of the so-called architects of New Labour. It is exactly the sort of place you would expect Peter Mandelson to live. His other house (the one he couldn't afford and should never have bought) was described as a 'triumph of minimalism' – presumably because he couldn't afford any furniture.

The next flat was 'barely habitable', according to the nephew of the previous occupant. Whatever Mandy paid for 'fixtures and fittings' he was robbed. 'The kitchen is no more than a cupboard. No one in their right mind would pay that kind of money for it.' It cost Mandy another £100,000 for renovations before he could move in.

He must have known he would get found out. 'Trust me, I'm an estate agent,' is not an expression you hear often. For all his 'political skills', yet again Mandy presented his critics with an open goal. That didn't stop Blair hurrying him back into government.

Mandelson was soon up to his old tricks again, helping to obtain passports for the Millennium dome donors, the billionaire Hinduja brothers. When he was caught red-handed, it was group hug and bye-bye Mandy time again. How terribly 'unfortunate'.

In addition, it was never explained on what basis his Brazilian boyfriend Reinaldo was granted a visa extension to live in Britain. This is a legitimate question.

But we're asked to believe that the only reason his time in government wasn't as long as he may have wished was because of 'unfortunate circumstances'.

That's rather like Harold Shipman claiming that his time as a GP was cut short because of a set of unfortunate circumstances. Or Mad Frankie Fraser explaining that his career as a dentist wasn't as long as he would have liked because of unfortunate circumstances: ie, getting banged up for a 30-year stretch.

Mandelson is one thoroughly bad bastard.

Yet Tony Blair thinks he is a fit and proper person to represent Britain as a commissioner in Brussels, that superannuated retirement home for disgraced grifters, ne'er-do-wells, has-beens and never-wases, where he lives to this day with Reinaldo in the beautifully appropriate rue des Jeunes Garcons.

Which tells you all you need to know about the contempt Blair has always held for the people who pay his wages.

The Roman emperor Caligula made his horse a pro-consul, because he could, just to show the hoi polloi who was boss. Mandelson is Blair's equivalent of Caligula's horse. Yet it hasn't stopped him from climbing both the greasy pole and the property ladder. In November 2006 he bought a mansion in London's trendy Primrose Hill for £2.4 million – on a salary of £160,000 a year. As the Americans say, go figure.

My abiding image of Mandy dates back to his re-election as member for Hartlepool in 2001. On regaining his seat at the 2001, Mandy announced in his best Gloria Gaynor 'I Will Survive' fashion, that: 'I'm a fighter, not a quitter.' He then dropped in to a local bar where a talent contest was taking place. Soon he was on stage, delivering his rendition of Frank Sinatra's 'My Way'.

Although I wasn't there that night, I've since managed to obtain an exclusive live recording of Mandy's brand-new version of the Old Blue Eyes signature tune. It was last performed in public at the launch party to mark the publication of my novel, *To Hell In A Handcart*, at Gerry's Club, in Soho.

You may sing along if you wish.

> And now
> The end is near
> Or are you just
> Pleased to see me?
>
> My friends,
> I'll say it clear
> But don't expect
> That you'll believe me.

> I've lived
> In a great big house
> I've travelled First
> I like to lord it.
> But more, much more than this
> I can't afford it.

Regrets
They'll have a few.
When I find out
Who bloody shopped me.

I did
What I had to do
It's not my fault
That no one stopped me.

I borrowed big
From Uncle Geoff.
I told some fibs
But then we all do.
But what I did, I did it all
For my Reinaldo.

Yes there were times
I'm sure you knew.
When I blew off
More than I could chew.
But through it all
When there was doubt
I took care to spit it out.
I had my fill
In Notting Hill and
Rio de Janeiro.

I've bluffed
I've told some lies.
I've been a shaker
And a mover.
I built the Greenwich Dome
And sold passports
To the Hindujas.

To think
I had all that
A cabinet seat
An Irish castle.
And still, I'd have it all
But I'm such an arsehole.

For what is a man?
What does he have?
If not a home
With a stainless steel lav.
I had my friends
So rich and funky
A chauffeured car,
A team of flunkies.
And now I'm back
In Hartlepool, where
 They hanged a monkey.

(Available as a twelve-inch on Stiff Records, price £373,000.)

46 | Blessed are the Child Molesters

Dare I venture to suggest that one word which will enter the vocabulary in the next couple of years is 'paedophobe'? This will be used as a term of abuse for anyone who dares to criticise child molesters, in much the same way as those who voice even the mildest reservations at the more outlandish behaviour of some members of the gay 'community' are routinely smeared as a 'homophobes'.

Now that the legal age at which a boy or girl can be buggered has been lowered to sixteen, campaigners are already pushing for a further reduction to fourteen.

It can't be long before the Wicked Witch and her sidekicks at Nonces 'R' Us takes on a case arguing that it is the 'human right' of a paedophile to enjoy sexual relations with children. They may even argue that any age of consent is an infringement of the 'human rights' of children to explore their sexuality.

And given past evidence, would you bet against such an action succeeding?

In the USA, the American Man/Boy Love Association is already agitating for child-molesting to be legalised. And a bunch of lunatics calling themselves 'Zoosexuals' are lobbying for the recognition of bestiality as a proper way to behave. Gives a whole new meaning to 'doggy fashion', doesn't it?

The softening-up process is well under way over here. Sexualisation of even prepubescent youngsters is rampant in adverts, magazines and TV programmes.

Rather than condemn paedophiles, we are increasingly being encouraged to understand them, to accept that their urges are perfectly natural and their intentions honourable.

A friend of mine went to a Christmas carol service at Christ

Church, Little Heath, just outside Potters Bar, Hertfordshire. After a quick burst of 'While Shepherds Watch' and 'Silent Night', he settled back to listen to the sermon, which was delivered by the Rev James Robson, a tutor at the Oak Hill Theological College.

My friend was expecting an innocuous celebration of the family, a bit of peace on earth and goodwill to all men, a few bars of 'O Come All Ye Faithful' and everybody off to the boozer for a couple of large ones.

What he and everyone else in church got was an extraordinary lecture about how God's love even extended to paedophiles.

Blessed are the Child Molesters.

Quite why the Rev Robson thought this was an appropriate topic for a family audience, including many young children, only he knows. My friend and the rest of the congregation were horrified. Few of them will be going back.

When the Church of England next wonders why attendances are plummeting, it may consider the Rev Robson's tasteless and offensive sermon.

But it does serve to illustrate just how far the game has moved on. Soon pleas for understanding and forgiveness will give way to a militant campaign for acceptance and legalisation.

Child sex is the final frontier. Anyone who objects to greater tolerance for child molesters will be denounced as a 'paedophobe'.

Just remember, you read it here first.

*

Footnote: the week after I raised the possibility that 'paedophobia' would soon be lining up alongside 'homophobia' and 'Islamophobia' as terms of abuse, the *Independent* – the *Guardian* without the jobs adverts – carried a long piece by a gay activist called Johann Hari, headlined: 'Remember: Paedophiles are people, too.'

We have to accept, he argued, that 'paedophilia is an intractable sexual orientation, like heterosexuality or homosexuality, that cannot be "trained out" of a person'.

Horrible right-wingers like me must realise that paedophiles are victims, too. We must understand, not condemn.

He didn't actually use the word 'paedophobe', but only because he hasn't thought of it yet.

47 | Phew, What a Scorcher!

You may not need a weatherman to know which way the wind blows. But apparently you do need a weatherman to tell you which suntan lotion to wear. They don't only deliver the forecast, they've started handing out advice on what factor suncream you should be using.

This was the latest brainwave to emerge from the BBC and the Rubber Johnny Police, aka the Health Education Authority, as part of the government's safe sunbathing campaign.

Skin cancer is the new Aids. Next they'll be hanging bottles of Ambre Solaire alongside the condoms on trees in public parks. Ministers are already calling on suncream manufacturers to cut their prices, despite claims by the chief medical officer, Sir Kenneth Calman, that suntan lotions actually contribute to skin cancer by encouraging people to sunbathe for longer than they should.

How long before councils start employing sunburn counsellors and it becomes a criminal offence to take off your shirt on a beach?

David Dickinson will be banned from our screens for setting a bad example.

There is no element of human activity in which politicians and self-appointed busybodies are not prepared to meddle. The moment the sun comes out, the sirens start howling and the entire apparatus of the nanny state swings into action. When are they going to stop treating us all like mentally-retarded two-year-olds? We should be allowed to watch the weather forecast in peace, without being forced to listen to a lecture.

Most of us are intelligent enough to be aware of the risks of over-exposure to the sun. That's why we buy suncream in the first place, wear hats and sit under umbrellas. There are always a few chimps who will peg themselves out in the heat of the day until they are done to a crisp. It's their own stupid fault if they end up looking and suffering like survivors of a meltdown at Windscale. It is absolutely nothing to do with the Rubber Johnny Police, the BBC or the Met Office.

I suspect the real reason they want to interfere is not because they give a stuff about the incidence of skin cancer but because they can't bear the idea of anyone enjoying themselves. Lolling around in the sun is one of the few free pleasures we have left. That's why the authorities have to exaggerate the dangers. If we are allowed to get away with sunbathing, the next thing you know we'll be putting T-bone steaks on the barbeque and drinking more than two units of lager.

Consider for a moment the audacity and sheer stupidity of weather girls dispensing advice on which sunblock to wear. The BBC now has a sliding index based on the intensity of the sun's rays. Nine, for instance, will call for factor eight. Only the combined great minds of the BBC and the Health Education Authority could come up with an index in which nine equates to eight.

If you are going to do something this daft, then at least index mark eight should equal suncream factor eight. But that's not the point. One man's factor eight is another man's factor six. And another man's factor twenty-four. It all depends on your skin type and how long you spend in the sun.

I can't wait for the first case of someone suing the BBC for compensation after getting sunburned.

'M'lud, my client slapped on factor eight in good faith on the advice of the weather forecaster on BBC1, yet it now appears that she should have been using factor sixteen. As a result she suffered severe distress and her marriage is at an end. Not only did her husband tell her she was a silly cow for spending the entire day spreadeagled on their ornamental patio wearing nothing but her bikini bottoms, but attempts at reconciliation that evening in the form of vigorous sexual intercourse proved impossible because her sunburn made intimacy too painful. I ask the court to award exemplary damages.'

If the BBC really wants to do something useful, it could go back to giving us the weather in English, instead of Celsius.

Most of us know what 80 degrees in the shade means. Very few have the faintest idea how hot 23°C is in old money. I believe there's some formula which involves multiplying by thirty and dividing by two, or something. But I can never remember.

And, anyway, we shouldn't have to do it in the first place. Fahrenheit is a far more precise measure. If it's in the 30s, it's a bit parky. If it's in the 80s, it's Phew, What A Scorcher and fried eggs on the pavement time. Even those who have had Celsius drummed into them in school, will still tell you it's in the 70s today, not somewhere between 18 and 21.

My mum once tried converting the temperature in Sellotape into Fahrenheit and worked out that it was 107 degrees, even though it was snowing outside.

Most of the time the weather forecasters don't even get the weather right, so how the hell can they reliably issue instructions on what suncream to wear?

I live a few miles away from Lord's cricket ground. I have lost count of the number of times I've been lying in the garden in glorious sunshine listening to *Test Match Special* only to be told that rain has stopped play at Lord's.

The only thing you can guarantee is that by the time you've covered yourself in factor twenty-four, it will be chucking it down.

48 | Hijack a Plane, Win a Council House!

In the week a hijacked Afghan airliner was diverted at gun-point to Stansted, I invented a spoof game show called *ASYLUM!* It appeared in my column in February 2000 under the headline: 'HIJACK A PLANE, WIN A COUNCIL HOUSE'. It was a throwaway piece at the bottom of the page.

Most columns end up wrapping chips, but this one had legs. Someone must have liked it, because it was circulated on the Internet. In fact, after it turned up on the web, dozens of people sent it to me wondering whether I'd like to use it in my column.

Another 'columnist' actually did reproduce it, downloading it from the net and attempting to pass it off as all her own work. She went on to become editor of the *Daily Star*.

Readers wrote to me saying it had been run off and handed round their pub or workplace. I also slipped a version of it into my novel, *To Hell In A Handcart*. Waste not, want not. Don't let anyone accuse me of not doing my bit for the planet. If you can't recycle your own stuff . . . Here it is.

*

Good morning and welcome to a brand-new episode of ASYLUM!

Today's programme features another chance to take part in our exciting competition: hijack an airliner and win a council house. We've already given away hundreds of millions of pounds and thousands of dream homes, courtesy of our sponsor, the British taxpayer. And, don't forget, we're now the fastest-growing game on the planet.

Anyone can play, provided they don't already hold a valid British passport. You only need one word of English: ASYLUM!

Prizes include all-expenses paid accommodation, cash benefits starting at £180 a week and the chance to earn thousands more begging, mugging and accosting drivers at traffic lights. The competition is open to everyone buying a ticket or stowing away on one of our partner airlines, ferry companies or Eurostar. No application ever refused, reasonable or unreasonable.

All you have to do is destroy all your papers and remember the magic password: ASYLUM!

Only this week 140 members of the Taliban family from Afghanistan were flown Goat Class from Kabul to our international gateway at Stansted, where local law enforcement officers were on hand to fast-track them to their luxury £200-a-night rooms in the fabulous four star Hilton hotel. They join tens of thousands of other lucky winners already staying in hotels all over Britain.

Our most popular destinations include the White Cliffs of Dover, the world famous Toddington Services Area in historic Bedfordshire and the Money Tree at Croydon.

If you still don't understand the rules, don't forget there's no need to phone a friend or ask the audience, just apply for legal aid. Hundreds of lawyers, social workers and counsellors are waiting to help. It won't cost you a penny. So play today. It could change your life for ever.

Iraqi terrorists, Afghan dissidents, Albanian gangsters, pro-Pinochet activists, anti-Pinochet activists, Kosovan drug smugglers, Tamil Tigers, bogus Bosnians, Rwandan mass murderers, Somali guerrillas.

COME ON DOWN!

Get along to the airport. Get along to the lorry park. Get along to the ferry terminal. Don't stop in Germany or France. Go straight to Britain. And you are guaranteed to be one of tens of thousands of lucky winners in the softest game on earth.

Roll up, roll up my friends, for the game that never ends. Everyone's a winner, when they play: ASYLUM!

★

Eventually *ASYLUM!* turned up in a publication called *ADvantage*, a local giveaway shopping and services magazine, based in Verwood,

Dorset. Someone gave it to the editor, who chuckled and thought it deserved a wider audience. He received one letter of complaint from a humourless harridan, accusing him of stirring up racism, and another from a reader who found it funny.

And that was the last he heard until 8.30pm one night three months later, when there was a knock on the door of the *ADvantage* office.

There stood two police officers from Dorchester CID who demanded to see the editor.

When he asked what it was all about, they brandished a copy of the offending article and informed him that for the past three months the magazine had been under investigation by the police, the race relations commission, the Wiltshire and Dorset Race Relations Council and the Director of Public Prosecutions.

He was told: 'The lawyers have decided that you have done nothing wrong, but it has got to stop.' They insisted he give them his name. He refused, saying if he had done nothing wrong they had no right to demand his name. At this, they warned him to 'be careful' in future otherwise he would be arrested for 'inciting racial hatred'.

The editor told them to leave. All this took place in front of a witness, the owner of the house in which *ADvantage* is produced.

After coming across *ASYLUM!* in *To Hell In A Handcart*, the editor wrote to me wondering if I had been similarly threatened. He hadn't realised that it originally appeared in my column.

He has asked me not to identify him because he is worried the police will be back. He admits annoying the local Plod by regularly using the magazine as a platform to criticise the police over speed cameras and their surrender to burglars and vandals and believes they were using *ASYLUM!* to get back at him.

When we rang Dorset Police, the press office was helpful and promised to look into it. But when they rang back their attitude had changed and they said they wouldn't help unless we showed them a copy of the signed letter from the editor, sent to me in confidence.

Maybe he's got a point in wishing to remain anonymous. But as

I keep reminding you, just because you're paranoid it doesn't mean they're not out to get you.

I asked him if he'd ever published anything else which could be accused of inciting racial hatred. He said he'd expressed doubts about the scale of bogus asylum claims but had done nothing illegal.

Since the DPP obviously agreed, I took his word for it.

Just to be on the safe side, I thought I'd check out the magazine to make sure it wasn't a front for right-wing extremists, hell-bent on fomenting race riots in Dorset. If it is, it disguises it well. The magazine runs adverts for poultry farms, dairies, specialist food suppliers, garden sheds, pine furniture and notices on behalf of local cancer charities and coffee mornings.

The Verwood Friends of Guides' Duck Race – £1 a duck – and Car Boot Sale sounds harmless enough. I scoured 'From the Potting Shed' by 'Pandora' for cryptic instructions to Ku Klux Klan sleepers in between advice on dealing with ground elder, fuchias and geraniums. I could find no obvious evidence of racism, although the author does reveal a prejudice against 'gaudily painted garden gnomes'. Could this be it? I wondered. Has 'gnomism' been added to the crimes of racism and sexism? But then Pandora says in the next sentence 'Sorry, Gnome Lovers', so no threat there.

I scanned the Solent Coaches' advert for cut-price trips to a festival of firebombing in Oldham, but to no avail. Nothing more seditious than an outing to the Hampton Court Flower Show. One of the answers to the previous month's ADquiz was Yasser Arafat, but since the question wasn't republished, I gave the editor the benefit of the doubt.

So what was the justification for spending three months and involving four government agencies in investigating a 4,000-circulation freesheet over a harmless, knockabout piece of non-sense which had already appeared in Britain's biggest-selling daily newspaper? We keep being told this war on terrorism is in defence of our way of life, our liberties, including our right to freedom of expression, which is why the mad mullahs spewing hatred and murder against America, Britain and Israel on the streets of London have rarely been prosecuted.

Far easier to bully a defenceless Middle England magazine editor for reproducing a knockabout spoof game show even though he had committed no offence.

Well done, Dorchester CID.

Incidentally, the week after *ASYLUM!* appeared, I warned that anyone who thought that the hijackers would be prosecuted and banged up, before being speedily extradited, was deluding themseles. They'd still be here five years hence. The judges would see to that. Some of them were charged, but the trials collapsed and they were freed. After a legal battle which cost the British taxpayer £15 million, in August 2006 the Court of Appeal ruled that they could all stay. Although they were denied refugee status, they were told they could remain in Britain on 'discretionary leave' for 'human rights' reasons and would be entitled to work and given the rights to free council housing and a full range of benefits worth tens of thousands of pounds.

Come on down!

49 | Counting Crows – in Fourteen Different Languages

An exciting leaflet dropped through my letter box from Enfield Council, designed to help me understand the planning process. On the off-chance that I couldn't read English, the council helpfully offered translations into a number of different languages, many of them scribble.

Enfield has an admirable reputation for going the extra mile (perhaps that should be kilometre) to communicate with its multi-cultural residents. For many years there has been a sign under the railway bridge between Arnos Grove and Southgate Tube stations exhorting residents in at least half a dozen languages not to feed the birds. And in case anyone is in any doubt, or not fluent in English, Greek, Turkish, Hindi or Graffiti, the notice also features a rather handsome crow (it could be a rook) with a cross through it.

It has obviously proved effective. In twenty-five years, I have never seen anyone, from any ethnic background, standing under that particular bridge with a bag of millet surrounded by starving starlings or hungry hawks.

Which may explain why the birds are forced to scavenge for food in the overflowing rubbish bins outside the local kebab shops.

But times have moved on and half a dozen languages are no longer sufficient to cater for the linguistic requirements of the diverse population of the London Borough of Enfield.

Indeed, it may even be racist.

It was revealed recently that the tower block next to Arnos Grove station, where a couple of the 21 July would-be London homicide bombers lived at the expense of the British taxpayer, is home to twenty-three different nationalities. (Or it could have been twenty-five. But you get the picture.) It is a veritable Tower of Babel.

I can't help wondering whether the impressionable young Muslim men who set out to slaughter hundreds of commuters on 21 July were driven into the arms of extremists by that very Do Not Feed The Birds sign.

We know for a fact that they liked to play football in Arnos Park, where I used to play with my kids when they were younger, so it is likely that they would have come face to face with that notice.

Is it possible that they stared at the sign but were unable to understand any of the languages featured? And in that moment was encapsulated their exclusion from mainstream British society. How can they have been expected to play a full part in the life of the nation if they are unable to read something as simple as a Do Not Feed The Birds notice?

This was typical of the imperialism of the infidel. And therefore their only recourse was to blow themselves and hundreds of others to smithereens on the Piccadilly Line.

Clearly, I am not the only person to whom this horrifying thought has occurred. They must be haunted by it at Enfield Civic Centre.

Which would explain why the new leaflet on planning applications is available in fourteen different languages, including Tigrinya, which is a new one on me.

Apparently, Tigrinya is widely spoken in Eritrea. I know I should get out more, but I wasn't aware we had a sizeable Eritrean community in Enfield. You don't get many Eritreans in the West Stand at White Hart Lane, although with the size of our squad there may be one or two in the reserves.

The leaflet has also been translated into Tamil, just in case the Tamil Tigers have an active service unit squirreled away above a chip shop in Oakwood and they wish to take exception to one of their neighbours sticking an Edwardian-style conservatory on the back of a perfectly innocent 1930s Metroland semi.

And why not? Don't want to create any new grievances, do we? We've got enough to be going on with as it is.

I am, however, puzzled not only by the box marked BRAILLE (how can you tick it if you can't see it?) but also by the box marked OTHER. This reads: 'Please say which language you would like this leaflet in.'

Eh? If you can't read any of the fourteen languages on offer, you won't be able to read the box marked OTHER, either.

Nor can I help wondering why translation is also available into Italian, Greek and Turkish. In the quarter-century I have lived in North London I don't think I have ever met any Italian, Greek or Turk who can't speak perfectly good English. Still, it is commendable the lengths to which Enfield Council is prepared to go to reach out to all the residents of our vibrant, diverse suburban borough. Anything inner London boroughs like Islington can do, Enfield is determined to prove it can do better. It surely can't be long before the Steam Fair in Trent Park is recognised as one of Europe's leading celebrations of multi-culturalism, dwarfing even the Notting Hill Carnival. We can be proud that Enfield is now at the cutting edge of inclusivity, determined that even Eritreans are part of the planning process.

It is a pity, therefore, that Enfield Council can't be bothered to include its wider community of council-tax payers in its planning decisions. For some years, a developer has been applying for permission to turn an attractive family home at the top of our road into a block of flats in the teeth of widespread local opposition. Multiple applications have been made, some approved, some turned down.

When the most recent application for a development twice the size of the existing property was put forward we assumed it would be rejected, not least because a plan for a smaller development on the site had previously been turned down.

Enfield Council asked for observations. Just about everyone from the local councillors, through local residents and the conservation society objected.

Yet the council simply ignored local opinion. The application was nodded through on the recommendation of unaccountable planning officers and the development went ahead regardless.

Quite why Enfield bothers to print leaflets explaining the planning process when it has no intention of taking any notice of what the people who pay its wages have to say is a matter of bewilderment. But at least now it can tell local residents to get stuffed in fourteen different languages.

Including Tigrinya.

50 | The Immigration Game

Following his triumphant return to BBC1 on *Have I Got News For You*, Bruce Forsyth was lined up for a new prime time TV show, modelled on *The Generation Game*.

The format was inspired by the news that human-rights lawyers were touting for business among asylum seekers by offering them free mobile phones, videos, meals and trips to London. I was lucky enough to get my hands on a tape of the pilot episode.

*

(Announcer): 'Laydeez and gen-ul-men, live from Dover, it's the Immigration Game. Heeeere's BROOOOOC-EEEE!'

'All right, my loves. Good game, good game. Nice to see you, to see you . . .'

'NICE!'

'Let's meet our first contestants, from Afghanistan. Give a big Immigration Game welcome to the Talibans.'

(Wild applause.)

'Mother and son. That's nice. Abdul it says here that your hobby is stoning women to death. I'll make a note of that. A bit impetuous. And mum, you once came second in a beauty contest in Kabul. We'll just have to take your word for it, seeing as you won't take your burka off. Nice eyes, though. A wink's as good as a nod. OK, good game. Let's bring on our second contestants who want to play the Immigration Game tonight. Please welcome brothers Ilie and Billie Pikea, from Romania. At least, that's what it says here. Now then, according to this, you only arrived here in Dover this evening. Nice to see you, to see you . . .'

'NICE!'

'And I'm told you came across the Channel in a paddling pool. I'll make a note of that, too. Mad as a fish. Right. Ilie, it says here that back home in Albania—'

'Romania.'

'Same thing. Albania, Romania, who cares? It says you are a qualified brain surgeon. Very good. Do you know anything about backs? I've got this twinge, see. Oh, never mind.'

(Laughter.)

'And Billie, it says here you specialise in extortion and prostitution. We'll have to watch this one. Could be trouble. Now don't forget, every time you hear the word "Croydon" . . .'

'CROYDON!'

'You're ahead of me already. Every time you hear "Croydon" . . .'

'CROYDON!'

'All right, settle down. Every time you hear "Croy—"'

'CROYDON!'

'Wait for it, wait for it. Every time you hear that word, it means someone else has qualified for an all-expenses-paid life in Britain. So, let's play the Immigration Game. And to show us how it's done, please welcome, from the top human-rights firm Nonces 'R' Us, barrister Charles Claims-Direct. Nice to see you, Charles, To see you . . .'

'NICE!'

'Now then, you're going to demonstrate just how easy it is to claim asylum in Britain.'

'Yes, I am Bruce. It's quite simple, all you have to do is get here. When you arrive, you'll be met by one of our representatives with a welcome pack, which includes a mobile phone and my telephone number. Just ring me up and I'll give you the directions to Croydon . . .'

'CROYDON!'

'. . . and we'll take it from there. We recommend that before you arrive you destroy all your papers, passports, that sort of thing.'

'Does it help if you can speak English?'

'Definitely not. Even if you can speak English, we recommend you keep your mouth shut. We've got a team of trained interpreters to handle that side of things.'

'Anything else?'

'A notifiable disease is a bonus.'

'A Brucie bonus!!'

'If you like, Bruce. Aids always comes in handy. It can help you miss out Croydon . . .'

'CROYDON!'

'. . . altogether. We've got specially reserved NHS rooms for anyone with a communicable disease.'

'That's nice.'

'And that's basically it, Bruce. Once you're here, you're in for life. Just give me a call, collect your prize, and away you go. The British taxpayer takes care of all the rest. And don't forget the magic word "asylum".'

'Super, super. Now then, contestants, that's all there is to it. So let's play the Immigration Game. Before we give you your First Class rail tickets to Croydon . . .'

'CROYDON!'

'. . . we'll go straight to the conveyor belt, where you can choose your prizes courtesy of our good friends at the British government.'

(Annoucer): 'And on the conveyor belt tonight, a mobile phone, a video recorder, a toaster, a council house, free NHS treatment, social security, unemployment benefit, legal aid, driving lessons, a seaside holiday, cuddly toy . . .'

'CUDDLY TOY!'

'Didn't they do well?'

In Derbyshire, a theatre group renamed *The Hunchback of Notre-Dame* after consultations with disabled-rights activists. It became *The Bell-ringer of Notre-Dame*.

Elli Mackenzie, of Oddsocks Productions, explained: 'We wanted to treat the situation sensitively, to avoid anything which might be offensive and we did not want to exclude any of our audience. It is clear that "hunchback" would have been offensive and we are happy to change the title and we make no apologies for that. The content of the play, though our own interpretation, remains exactly the same and we do not shy away from the fact that one of the main characters has a deformity.'

It's difficult to know where to start. On the face of it this is just another piece of nonsense. But when you've stopped chuckling, it's worth taking a few moments to delve into the thought process behind it.

Having decided to stage *The Hunchback of Notre-Dame*, who thought it was a good idea to consult a disablity adviser to check whether or not the title might cause offence? It's not difficult to imagine the tortured debate about the use of the word 'hunchback'.

'Through the chair, I must object that this production could be deemed offensive to members of the, er, hunch– er, stooped, er, differently, um, you know, er, dis– no, um . . . some members of our diverse, inclusive community.'

I don't know how many hunchbacks there are living in Derby these days. Or how many of them would take offence. Very few, if any, I guess.

The reason *The Hunchback of Notre-Dame* is called *The Hunchback of Notre-Dame* is because it's about a hunchback who, er, lives in Notre-Dame Cathedral.

If the producers found the title of the play so offensive why didn't they just put on something else – for instance, *Snow White and The Seven Dwarfs*?

No, forget that. Snow White sounds a bit racist. And I'm not sure you can call dwarfs dwarfs any more. I believe the correct expression is Persons of Restricted Growth. But somehow *Mixed-Race Female and The Seven Persons of Restricted Growth* doesn't quite have the same ring to it.

What would Oddsocks make of two of my boyhood heroes – Hopalong Cassidy and Limpalong Leslie? Presumably any remake would be called *Differently Abled Cassidy*.

Why stop there? *Les Misérables* is clearly a deliberate insult to sufferers from chronic depression. *Robin Hood and His Merry Men* is a calculated affront to those affected by seasonal affliction disorder.

I thought all this madness had gone out with the last century. It reached its peak in the early 1990s when the municipal maniacs were busily rewriting school books to make them more 'appropriate'. We all had a lot of fun with it at the time, columnists competing to invent the most ridiculous name change. I seem to remember Keith Waterhouse coming up with Noddy and Socially Challenged Ears.

I don't suppose Black Beauty is a runner any more. And where, or rather how, does Long John Silver stand these days? That peg leg will have to go. And the eyepatch. Long John will have been fitted out with a proper prosthetic limb and a glass eye – or better still had laser surgery to restore his 20/20 vision. Meet Tall But Perfectly Formed Silver.

Captain Hook will have been flown by the NHS to Germany for an artificial hand. And I look forward to the forthcoming production of *Jeffrey Bernard Is Right As Rain*. *A Christmas Carol* goes straight out of the window, replaced by *A Diwali Tune*. *Crime and Punishment* gives way to *Social Exclusion and Rehabilitation*. *The Beggar's Opera* is a non-starter. Judgemental and elitist. Make that *The Big Issue Seller's Rap*. The list is endless.

Now don't get me wrong. There are some words which are now so offensive they should be avoided in polite society. They were absolutely right to change the name of Agatha Christie's *Ten Little Niggers* to *Ten Little Indians* – even though rappers have now reappropriated the N-word.

But now someone is objecting to the use of the word 'Indians'.

Coming soon to a theatre near you – Agatha Christie's *Ten Little Native Americans*.

Just a hunch.

52 | Eglish as
    # a Scond Language

By the start of the autumn term in 2006, more than half of all schoolchildren in inner London had English as a second language. Nationally, one in five had a different mother tongue and English speakers were in a minority in many schools.

This came as no great surprise to me. A couple of years earlier I stumbled across a newspaper advertisement for two classroom assistants in East London. It contained twenty spelling, grammar and punctuation errors, not counting an assortment of rogue capital letters. It was headed 'Cyril Jackson Primary School' and gave its address as Limehouse Causeway, Lonon E14.

That's right, Lonon not London. Not an encouraging start.

Wages were 'Scale 2 – ponts' (points?) '11–13 dependng' (depending, I assume) 'on experience and qualifications' (no full stop).

It went on:

Could you make a differnce [*difference*] for a primary child who needs your? [*Your what?*]

if [*no capital letter*] you think you have the skills to support childrens [*no apostrophe*] learning including those children for whom English is a Scond [*Second*] language we want to here [*hear*] from you.

You need to have GCSE at leval [*level*] A–C in Eglish [*English*] and Mathematics [*again, no full stop*]

You are invited to send for an appliation [*application*] pack although late applications will not beaccepted [*all one word*].

This being the London Borough of Tower Hamlets, Investors in People, fairness and equal opportunities thoughout [*throughout*] the workforce and inservice [*no, me neither*] is ensured and appliations [*applications*?] are welcomed from sutiably [*suitably*] skilled candidates regardless of ethniity [*ethnicity, I would imagine*].

Tower Hamlets wants a workforce to reflect the community commited [*committed*] to positive action.

So there you have it. If you fancied supporting children for whom Eglish is a Scond language and believed you could make a differnce and were sutiably skilled, regardless of your etniity, all you had to do was send your appliation to Lonon E14.

The advert sounded as if it had been written by someone with Eglish as a Scond language. But how the hell did it ever make it into print. Didn't anyone read it? Don't they have a spellchecker on their word processor? The name of the headmaster, Peter Sawyer, was on it. Didn't he give it the once-over?

OK, so mistakes happen. Typos, literals and the odd spelling error still manage to creep into even the most carefully scrutinised documents. They say that if you sit a monkey down in front of a typewriter it will eventually come up with Shakespeare. Maybe this was the first draft of *As You Like It*.

I suppose there's always the possibility that they don't teach proper spelling and grammar in schools any more because they don't want to be judgemental (or judgmental, depending on your preference). But this is just mental.

How on earth can anyone teach kids English if you think it's spelled Eglish, and can't even spell the name of our capital city correctly? Maybe it's because I'm a Lononer. How does someone with such a limited command of the English language get put in charge of drafting adverts for classroom assistants?

When Tower Hamlets says it welcomes appliations from sutiably skilled candidates regardless of ethniity, gender, disability, etc., does it have a deliberate policy of hiring as school secretaries the semi-literate, the dyslexic and those who have Eglish as a Scond language? What chance have the poor kids got? And it gets worse.

If ths buk woz rit lyk kdz cmunyk8 2dy u wd thnk I woz on drgz or hd tkn lEv of my snsz.

Incredibly, the above sentence would not count against me if it were submitted as part of a modern English paper. Never mind Eglish as a Scond language, text speak is now acceptable in school exams. In 2005 schools were being told by the Department of Education that fourteen-year-old pupils should not be penalised for poor spelling. Even elementary mistakes will go unpunished.

This from a government which swept into office proclaiming its number one priority as 'education, education, education'. Perhaps that should be amended to 'ejukashun, ejukashun, ejukashun'.

Call me old-fashioned, but isn't the primary function of teaching English to ensure that pupils can read, write and spell properly? And with the proliferation of sloppy, semi-literate text messaging, isn't that even more important than ever?

There was a profoundly depressing snapshot of modern educational standards in 2005 at the shrine to Mary-Ann Leneghan, who was brutally murdered near Reading in the week the new diktat was revealed. Amid the usual flowers and teddy bears were scrawled messages of sympathy which bore little resemblance to English. They were a crass mixture of abbreviations, numbers, symbols and misspellings. It might have been a epitaph for an entire generation shamefully denied the means of expression.

How can we expect youngsters to go on to lead rounded, fulfilling, rewarding lives if they can't even communicate in their mother tongue? What kind of careers are they being prepared for? This disgraceful betrayal has been perpetrated by cynical politicians and bureaucrats, all university graduates who themselves benefited from a traditional education. In a blatant exercise designed to meet government targets for exam passes, standards have not so much been lowered as dropped down a borehole and cemented over.

The English language is our greatest gift to the world. Yet our own young people are growing up unable to read or write it correctly. Foreign students receive better instruction in English than pupils in most of Britain's state schools.

If you don't believe me, just compare the fluent post-match interviews with foreign footballers in the Premiership with the

Neanderthal gruntings of, say, Lee Bowyer, one of the yeomen of England.

I just don't understand the thinking behind a policy which deliberately turns out a generation of illiterate, inarticulate, ignorant school leavers.

You can bet your house, though, that there's no such dereliction of duty at the London Oratory and the other elite schools to which Blair and some of his ministerial colleagues tend to send their children.

But this isn't about class or wealth. My late grandmother grew up in the East End and had little formal education. She went into service at an early age. But her handwriting, grammar and spelling were immaculate.

Sending a school leaver into the world without the tools to communicate is like asking a plumber to install a central heating system with his bare hands.

Blair has spent ten years banging on about 'respect'. But how are kids expected to show any respect if they haven't any self-respect? And how can they respect themselves if they haven't been taught to read, write and speak their own language properly? Is it any wonder they spend their days hanging round shopping arcades, hiding their heads under hoodies, rather than perusing the shelves of the local library?

Labour ministers are always boasting about how education standards are rising.

Bllx.

53 | 1966 and All That

So little proper British history is taught in our schools that seven out of ten children have never heard of Guy Fawkes and think Bonfire Night is something imported from America. They haven't been taught that 5 November is one of the most important dates in British history – marking the Catholic plot in 1605 to blow up Parliament.

Since it came to power in 1997, this government has done its utmost to destroy any concept of Britishness. It has tried to tear up the past, to rubbish or ignore our history, to destroy the whole concept of Britain. Labour has built on thirty years of post-colonial, guilt-ridden propaganda in schools, universities, broadcasting and the left-wing media. British history is constantly painted in the worst possible light. Schoolchildren are taught that the Empire was a racist, slave-mongering tyranny, for which we should all be deeply ashamed. This completely ignores the enlightenment, advancement, prosperity, rule of law, democracy and liberty which the Empire, and subsequently the Commonwealth, brought to the world.

How many pupils know, for instance, that it was the British Navy which brought about the end of the slave trade? We are told that mud huts and wood carvings are the equal of St Paul's and Shakespeare. Even when they bother to teach the history of the Second World War, they now proclaim that the bombing of Germany in self-defence was a war crime on a par with the Holocaust.

The entire teaching of history in state schools is designed to denigrate our achievements, one of the greatest of which is the Union itself. Britain has always been greater than the sum of its parts. It has enabled us to punch above our weight on the international stage, whether in trade or war.

How much do you know about our history? Take this simple, multiple choice test.

1)   Which battle took place in July 1690?
a)   Battle of the Boyne.
b)   Battle of the Bulge.
c)   Battle of the Bottle.

2)   Who was Britain's first Labour prime minister?
a)   Ramsay MacDonald.
b)   Trevor McDonald.
c)   Ronald McDonald.

3)   What happened in 1066?
a)   England was invaded by the Normans.
b)   England was invaded by asylum seekers.
c)   England won the World Cup.

4)   Who was voted our greatest-ever Briton?
a)   Winston Churchill.
b)   Winston Smith.
c)   Winston Silcott.

5)   Who said: 'I may have the body of a weak and feeble woman . . .'?
a)   Elizabeth I.
b)   Elizabeth II.
c)   Elizabeth Hurley.

6)   Who won the battle of Trafalgar?
a)   Lord Nelson.
b)   Trevor Nelson.
c)   Nelson Mandela.

7)   Who was Catherine Howard?
a)   Henry VIII's fifth wife.
b)   Frankie Howerd's wife.
c)   Michael Howard's wife.

8) Who laid out the gardens at Blenheim Palace?
a) Capability Brown.
b) Gordon Brown.
c) Alan Titchmarsh.

9) Where did the famous massacre take place in 1819?
a) Peterloo.
b) Portaloo.
c) Portillo.

10) Who was Britain's youngest prime minister?
a) William Pitt the Younger.
b) Brad Pitt.
c) Cess Pitt.

11) Who led the famous charge at Sebastopol?
a) The Light Brigade.
b) The Fire Brigade.
c) The Angry Brigade.

12) Who wrote *The Communist Manifesto*?
a) Karl Marx.
b) Howard Marks.
c) Harpo Marx.

13) Who discovered the Victoria Falls?
a) David Livingstone.
b) Ken Livingstone.
c) Victoria Beckham.

14) Who discovered Australia?
a) Captain Cook.
b) Thomas Cook.
c) Ready, Steady, Cook.

15) Who founded the Boy Scouts?
a) Baden-Powell.
b) Enoch Powell.
c) Cozy Powell.

16) Who became prime minister in 1916?

a) Lloyd George.

b) Charlie George.

c) Boy George.

17) Who was evacuated from Dunkirk in 1940?

a) British Army.

b) Salvation Army.

c) Barmy Army.

18) Who began his diary in 1660?

a) Samuel Pepys.

b) Samuel Smiles.

c) Nigel Dempster.

19) In 1649, who banned Christmas?

a) Oliver Cromwell.

b) Oliver Twist.

c) Oliver Letwin.

20) Who said: 'I'm just going outside and may be some time'?

a) Captain Oates.

b) Captain Peacock.

c) Captain Birdseye.

If you answered:

Mostly (a): London Oratory.

Mostly (b): Hogwart's.

Mostly (c): Bog-standard comprehensive.

54 | Sexual Outercourse

Ever wondered what they teach in schools these days? I'm not going to analyse the whole curriculum, but here's a couple of examples.

In Cornwall, swearing lessons are now part of the syllabus. Pupils aged eleven to sixteen at the Callington Community College were encouraged to write down as many swear words as they can think of as part of their Personal, Social and Health Education module, whatever the hell that is. When I was at school we had reading, writing and 'rithmetic, not Personal, Social and Health Education. And a module was Twiggy.

Now they have courses covering sex, drugs, smoking and 'relationships'. This is back-of-the-bike-sheds stuff. Since when have youngsters needed tuition in sex, drugs and smoking? We managed quite well without any help from Mr Chips. I was better at sex, drugs and smoking than geography. By the time I was fifteen, I could have passed A-level smoking standing on my head.

I was knocking out Haliborange tablets eight for a quid to gullible classmates convinced they were pep pills. I got richer and they got healthier by the handful.

By the fifth form we had the condom concession sewn up, courtesy of one of the lads who had a Saturday job sweeping up in a barber's, though most of them passed their perish-by date long before they saw active service. Now they probably hand out rubber johnnies like school milk.

Is any of this really necessary, especially in an age when a significant number of pupils leave school functionally illiterate and innumerate?

I've got a couple of old mates from my schooldays. One of them was called Spot, on account of his moonscape acne. The other still answers to the name of Torch, even though his flame hair has long since turned grey and largely fallen out. We were reflecting over Guinness on whether kids are allowed nicknames any more. Surely calling someone Spot would be seen as an unfair attack on the dermatologically challenged and would inevitably lead to expulsion and a letter from Claims Direct.

Giving someone a moniker on account of their physical characteristics would probably be considered a form of racism today.

So what's behind the swearing lessons? 'The object is to get pupils to look at their language and see if they know what they are saying. A lot of swear words are homophobic, racist and offensive to women,' said teacher Phil Gibson. Ah ha. That explains it.

Of course we should discourage children from gratuitous abuse. But an obsession with homophobia, racism and sexism has been elevated to a religion in many schools to the point where actually teaching pupils to read and write comes a distant second.

So now they get lessons in subjects which would have got them expelled a few years ago. In Devon, I discovered schoolchildren were being given lessons in mutual masturbation. I don't know about you, but that's something most of us manage to work out for ourselves. Practical instruction used to take place at playtime behind the bike sheds. They've even got a fancy new name for it – outercourse. I wonder how long it will be before that expression enters the language.

The referee's an outercourser.

We live in a country where thousands of kids leave school without even learning to read and write properly. Yet someone thought it worthwhile taking time out of the school curriculum to deliver tuition in hand relief to fourteen- and fifteen-year-old boys and girls. Now pay attention, children. Here's something I tossed off earlier. At least it won't be difficult getting them to do their homework.

'Tracey, what do you think you're doing?'

'I'm just helping Wayne with his revision, Mum.'

It's the only subject where you get a prize for coming last. I wonder what my old English master, Spud Taylor, would have made of it. We wouldn't be allowed to call him Spud, for a start. Tuberist. But I am trying to imagine his reaction if I had put my hand up in class.

'Yes, Littlejohn. What is it now?'

'Excuse me, sir, I was just wondering.'

'Come on boy, spit it out, we haven't got all day.'

'Well, sir, it's, um . . .'

'Get on with it, boy.'

'Er, pardon me, sir, but how many 'l's are there in bollocks?'

55 | Sex 'n' Drugs 'n' the Eleven-plus

When I was at school, tests were pretty mundane and routine. There was never any suggestion that they should be made 'relevant' to the spotty oiks in 4G. They were often designed to be as obscure and difficult as possible. For instance:

'If it takes a man a week to walk a fortnight, how long will it take him to skin an elephant down to a whippet? Ten minutes, no talking at the back.'

That, of course, was before the fad for 'child-centred' education. Under Labour, primary schools are urged to use drama, role play and quizzes to teach under-elevens about drugs and alcohol. Among the recommendations to schools from the Qualifications and Curriculum Agency was that children should be asked to imagine that someone has dropped a bag of drugs and then draw what is inside.

I tried to imagine a typical exam paper for eleven-year-olds.

1)   Johnny has ten grams of crack. If he cuts them into one-gram deals and sells them outside the tuck shop for £1 a wrap, what can he expect?

a)   £5 profit.

b)   £10 profit.

c)   An Uzi up his nose.

2)   Jill has unprotected sex with nine different boys in twenty-one days. What will she get?

a)   Triplets.

b)   Triple-Sec.

c)   A council house.

3)   Billy is found face down in the Boys' toilets at playtime, with vomit dribbling from his mouth. What is wrong with him?

a)   Measles.

b)   Mumps.

c)   Fifteen bottles of Smirnoff Ice.

4)   What does Father O'Hara give for sex behind the bike sheds?

a)   Three Hail Marys.

b)   Three Bloody Marys.

c)   A packet of sweets.

5)   Teacher gives you a hundred lines after school. How would you do them?

a)   With a pencil and lined paper.

b)   With a pen, plain paper and ruler.

c)   With a mirror and a rolled-up tenner.

(Time allowed, one hour. Last orders on the bell, with twenty minutes drinking-up time.)

56 | Going for Gold

'Good evening and welcome to tonight's edition of *Going for Gold*. I'm Jeremy Paxman. Fingers on buzzers. No conferring. Here's your starter for ten. In the 1981 film *Chariots of Fire*, in which Cambridge college do the actors Ben Cross and Nigel Havers recreate the famous race around the courtyard between Olympic champion Harold Abrahams and Lord Burghley?'

'Swot, Wolfson.'

'Trinity College.'

'Correct. Your bonus questions for five points. In which year did that famous race take place? You can confer.'

'Er, was it 1925?'

'No, close, it was 1927. Who won?'

'Ben Cross?'

'I'm going to need more than that.'

'Harold Abrahams.'

'Correct, in the film version, although in real life it was Nigel Havers – er, I mean Lord Burghley. And for another five points, in which year was the race banned because the runners might slip over and hurt themselves?'

(Mumble, mumble, mumble.)

'Come on, I'm going to have to hurry you.'

(Mumble, mumble, mumble.)

'Oh, DO come on!'

'Sorry, we don't know.'

'You don't KNOW? What's the matter with you? The correct answer is 2005.'

That was the year in which a twenty-six-year-old English International middle-distance runner called Neil Speight requested permission to run around Great Court at Trinity College, Cambridge, to recreate the famous scene in *Chariots of Fire* in order to publicise the following year's Commonwealth Games to be held in Australia.

Traditionally, the Great Court Run – to give it its official title – was held on Matriculation Day and competitors raced against each other and the chimes of the college clock at noon, which last approximately forty-three seconds. In 1927, Harold Abrahams, played by Ben Cross in the movie, raced against Lord Burghley, played by Nigel Havers. Abrahams had won a 100-yards gold medal at the 1924 Olympics. Burghley went on to win gold in the 400-yards hurdles in 1928.

But the twenty-first century college authorities prevented Speight from running around Great Court because he wasn't insured and they were afraid he might trip on the cobbles and sue for compensation.

Bodes well for London hosting the Olympics in 2012, doesn't it?

By the time the Health and Safety Executive has finished there won't be a Games worthy of the name. Running is obviously not a runner in case anyone trips. Plus, spikes.

Hurdles? Don't be daft.

Javelin? Sharp pointy thing being hurled in the air at 70mph an hour? You must be joking.

Discus? Ditto.

Long jump? Someone could fall on their jacksie and sue for millions.

High jump? Do me a favour.

Triple jump? Trebles all round.

Modern pentathlon? Five times the risk.

Decathlon? Think we're made of money?

Shooting? Does the word 'Dunblane' ring any bells?

Diving? Why do you think we've taken the diving boards out of every public baths?

Swimming? Don't even go there – we've already banned school-children from wearing goggles in case they snap back and hurt themselves. Not to mention drowning.

Cycling? Piles.

Boxing? Brain damage.

Horse jumping? Might frighten foxy-woxy.

Tiddlywinks? Broken fingernails.

Well, that's that, then, unless they can persuade every competitor to dress up in an *It's A Knockout* Mr Blobby suit.

Here's your starter for ten. Which government, led by a lawyer married to a lawyer, introduced 'no win, no fee' and opened the way for a flood of frivolous compensation claims?

Oh, DO come ON!

57 | Is That The Chattanooga Choo-Choo?

Britain's national rail enquiries operation decided to follow banks and insurance companies and move their call centre to India to save money. Rail chiefs announced that passengers (sorry, customers) would be redirected to operators in three Indian cities. I decided to put it to the test.

★

'Thank you for calling British Rail Inquiries. You are being held in a queue. Your business is important to us. If you have a touch-tone phone, please press the star button now.'

'Hello?'

'For InterCity services, press 1. For local services, press 2. For all other inquiries, press 3.'

'Hello?'

'Thank you for pressing 3. All our operators are busy assisting other passengers. Please hold.'

'Hello? Is that British Rail Inquiries?'

'No mate, this is Mumbai Minicabs. You want my brother.'

'Can you transfer me?'

'Sorry, I'm POB at the moment. Try ringing back in ten minutes.'

(Ring, ring.)

'Thank you for calling British Rail Inquiries. You are being held in a . . .'

Yeah, yeah.

'Your business is important to us. For 200mph, luxury tilting trains, please press 1 and wait for ten years. For fifty-year-old, clapped out slam-door cattle trucks, please replace your receiver and ring Network South-East. To be transferred to someone who barely speaks English, press 3.'

'Hello?'

'Train inquiries, Mahatma speaking.'

'At last. I'd like to go from London to Glasgow tomorrow morning, please. Can you give me some details?'

'Oh, yes indeed. Finchley Central is two and sixpence from Golders Green on the Northern Line.'

'No, London to GLASGOW. How do I get there?'

'So sorry. It goes from St Louis down to Missouri, Oklahoma City looks oh so pretty, you'll see Amarillo, Gallup, New Mexico, Flagstaff, Arizona, don't forget Winona, Kingman, Barstow, San Bernadino.'

'LONDON to GLASGOW!'

'Oh, you want the last train to Clarksville?'

'Not Clarksville, GLASGOW!'

'Sorry, there must be leaves on the line. Just transferring you to a supervisor.'

'Hello?'

'Thank you for calling British Rail Inquiries. All our operators are on strike at the moment. Please wait while you are transferred to Kolkata.'

'Hello?'

'If you have a hash button, please press it now. If you want to wait three hours on a rain-lashed platform for a train that never comes, press 1. If you want to pay a week's wages for a First Class ticket, only to be kicked off at Watford and put on a replacement bus service which gets stuck in roadworks outside Milton Keynes, press 2. To remain holding, press 3, and your call will be answered when one of our assistants stops talking about the legover on Big Brother last night and bothers to pick up the phone. If you'd rather speak to someone who doesn't know the difference between Peterhead and Peterborough and for whom English is a second language, press 4.'

'Hello?'

'Vijay speaking, how can I help you?'

'Thank heavens, I've been waiting for ages.'

'So sorry, but my chef is off sick today and I'm doing my best. Are you the madras chicken, pilau rice and double keema naan for Acacia Avenue?'

'No, London to GLASGOW.'

'Oh, I am so sorry, sir. But we don't deliver that far, only within a five-mile radius of Southall. Why don't you ring my cousin at Raj's Revenge in Sauchiehall Street?'

(Click. Redial button.)

'Oh, it's you again. If you are having a panic attack, press 1. If you are suffering from stress, press 2. If you are suffering from heat exhaustion, press 3. If you want trauma counselling, press 4. If you want to get anywhere by train, on time, replace your handset and move to India.'

58 | Cry God for Harry, Ing-er-land and St George

By the time of the 2002 World Cup in France, football fever had even engulfed the Royal Family. In an attempt to rehabilitate his image after the death of Lady Di and burnish his populist credentials, Prince Charles bought tickets for England's game against Colombia in Lens.

Nick Hornby's success with his novel *Fever Pitch*, chronicling his obsession with Arsenal, made football respectable in literary circles. Hornby moved to Reading, in Berkshire, with his mum after his parents split up. His dad would take him to Arsenal on the weekends he had access. Hornby was soon hooked and the book explores his relationship with his father and follows him from childhood to Arsenal's championship-winning season in 1988–9.

I couldn't help wondering if one day in the future, Prince Harry might emulate Hornby and write his own best-seller, *Playing Away*, drawing on his experiences of going to football with his dad.

CHAPTER ONE

My parents separated in 1994. My father had met someone else and moved out. I lived with my mum in our house in Kensington. After she died I went to live in Berkshire with my dad.

These were difficult times. Often we would sit through meals in complete silence. I sometimes got the impression Dad would rather be talking to his plants.

He did his best, taking me shooting and skiing. He even fixed for the Spice Girls to come and visit us one day. It was as if he was trying to make up for the loss of my mum, though he drew the line at McDonald's.

Then one day he suggested football. The World Cup was

taking place in France and Dad had got his hands on a couple of tickets for England's game against Colombia in Lens. He'd never shown any interest in football before. Whenever anyone sent him two together at Wembley he always gave them to the Duke and Duchess of Kent.

To be honest, I thought that if he supported anyone it would be Wales. He was prince of the place, after all, even though he spent half his time in Scotland.

But I suppose it was only natural that we should follow England. All my life I had been surrounded by men with three lions on their shirts. Soldiers, most of them. And footmen. Never stopped them dreaming, though.

Dad was determined that I experience all the big-match build-up and atmosphere. He said we would be travelling just like all the other ordinary fans.

In the morning I climbed the battlements, hauled down the flag of St George which was flying above the castle and stuffed it in my duffel bag. I found some of Dad's friend Camilla's red lipstick in the bathroom and painted a cross on my face.

Dad was waiting downstairs. I'd never seen him look like this before. He was wearing a white England shirt under his tweed jacket and a plastic bowler hat. Unfortunately, his kilt rather spoiled the effect. I suggested that unless he wanted to get his head kicked in he should change. He ordered one of the bodyguards to hand over his trousers.

We headed off to Waterloo in the Daimler, just like any other ordinary fan, stopping briefly at Oddbins in Chiswick to load up with forty-eight cans of lager, a crate of Hooch and a packet of crisps for the journey.

The Eurostar terminal was a sea of red, white and blue. The red and white were the England fans, the blue was the Tactical Support Group, laying into them with batons and riot shields.

When Dad tried to jump the queue, a mounted policeman bundled him to the ground. 'Who the hell do you think you are?' he bawled. 'The Prince of bleedin' Wales?' Dad's protestation that, yes, actually, he was, cut no ice.

We picked our way through the puddles of vomit, boarded the train and made for our carriage. We reached our First Class seats, only to find them occupied by two large gentlemen in shell suits.

Dad explained to them that they were sitting in our seats and asked them to move. The larger of the two men, who had an earring through his nose and 'HATE' tattooed on his forehead, looked at my father as if he was speaking a foreign language.

He picked up Dad by the throat and headbutted him. His companion grabbed my father by the ears and ran up and down the corridor pretending he was holding the World Cup.

Eventually the bodyguards rescued him and we were able to settle back and enjoy the journey. There was no hot food available because something called the InterCity Firm had ransacked the buffet and thrown the steward out of the window as we passed Catford. There was a party atmosphere on board and we soon picked up the traditional songs being sung by our fellow passengers. I especially liked the one where we were invited to stand up if we hated the scum.

Even the bodyguards entered into the spirit of the occasion when we emerged from the tunnel into France and the whole train burst into a spontaneous chorus of 'Where Were You In '42?' At Calais, passport officials boarded the train and were greeted with a rousing rendition of 'If It Wasn't For The British You'd Be Krauts'.

We were joined at our table by a man who said he was one of the Chelsea headhunters. Dad said he had heard the recruitment industry was very interesting. The man asked if father liked hospital food.

The misunderstanding was resolved over several cans of Special Brew and we sealed our new friendship with a few verses of 'One Man Went To Mow', although not the version I learned in prep school.

A chap from Tottenham told us his old man had said 'Be an Arsenal fan', but he had politely declined.

Even to this day I can still smell the exhilarating aroma of the marijuana smoke, the beer, the puke and acrid stench of stale urine which filled the carriage. Unfortunately, the toilet was out of order all the way to Lens. Someone had stuffed the ticket collector's head down it.

We left the train at Lens and stampeded along the platform, turning over the tobacco stands and the newspaper stalls as we ran. Outside the station we discovered that the road was blocked by striking lorry drivers and our official car laid on by the British embassy has been set on fire.

There was no alternative but to walk to the ground, a red and white army on the march. Dad said it must have been like this at Agincourt. 'Cry God for Harry, England and St George', he shouted as he clambered on top of a Citroen to urge us once more unto the breach.

One of our fellow supporters said he wasn't at Agincourt but he did go to Anderlecht with Spurs a few years ago and that was a bit of a grin, even if one geezer did get shot.

Dad really seemed to be enjoying himself, especially when we rushed the gates at the ground, only to be repelled by the French riot police.

It turned out that our tickets were forgeries. When I asked Dad where he had got them from, he said he had a contact in Downing Street who had promised him they were kosher.

Still, it didn't seem to matter. We were bonding, me and Dad. I don't remember much about the football. We watched it on TV in a nearby bar, although we didn't get to see the end because someone threw a petrol bomb at the screen when Colombia went 2–0 up and Gazza was sent off.

I can still picture my dad's face as the CRS handcuffed him and drove him off to jail in their van.

So this is what real life is like, I thought to myself. Brilliant. I was hooked.

C'mon, Ing-er-land.

59 | Porridge

Despite prison overcrowding, there is no doubt that the penal system has got softer under Labour. We now take you over to Slade Prison for a brand-new episode of *Porridge 2007*. Fletch is lying on the bed in his cell as Mr Mackay marches in.

*

''Ten-shun. On your feet when an officer enters the cell, Fletcher.'

'Oh, there you are, Mr Mackay. We wasn't expecting you back yet. I thought you was away having your Chalfonts fixed.'

'For your information, Fletcher, the operation was cancelled six times while I was in hospital and eventually they sent me home. Not that my haemorrhoids are any of your business, Fletcher.'

'Just curious, that's all. We was hoping that once you'd had your Farmer Giles trimmed you might be in a better frame of mind.'

'Don't be impudent. I am always in a perfectly reasonable frame of mind, Fletcher.'

'Still, what do you expect from the NHS? I wouldn't be seen dead on the National Health. Or, more likely, I would, what with all that YMCA bug, or whatever they call it.'

'MRSA, Fletcher.'

'That's the one. Criminal, innit? You should have gone private, Mr Mackay.'

'You must be joking. Me, go private? On a prison officer's salary?'

'Haven't you got PPP?'

'PPP?'

'Private Prisoners Plan, Mr Mackay, sir. All us guests of Her Majesty have. Gives us access to priority private medical treatment. Now if you'd been on PPP you'd have been back on your feet in a jiffy. Sorry, that's why you're on your feet, innit?'

'PPP? Never heard of it.'

'Introduced while you was away awaiting the surgeon's knife in some godforsaken Victorian sanatorium, Mr Mackay. Something to do with yer Yuman Rights Act, apparently.'

'Human rights? Prisoners don't have human rights.'

'That's where you're wrong, Mr Mackay. Just because we is behind bars, it don't mean we don't have yuman rights. It's all thanks to the prime minister's wife, the one what that Littlejohn bloke in the paper calls the Wicked Wossname.'

'Poppycock.'

'Speaking of poppycock, Lukewarm's put in for gender reassignment. He's been on the turn ever since he shared that cell with that nonce in, where was it?'

'Strangeways?'

'He does have some strange ways, does Lukewarm, I grant you. No, I was thinking of Brixton.'

'Enough of this nonsense, Fletcher. I came to see Godber. Where is he?'

'Young Lenny is currently in the flotation tank before his Ayurvedic detox treatment.'

'Ayur-what?'

'A traditional Indian healing method based on the use of herbs, nutrition, panchakarma cleansing, acupressure massage, yoga, Sanskrit, and Jyotish astrology, Mr Mackay, sir.'

'I know what it is, Fletcher. I read about it in one of Mrs Mackay's magazines. But what the hell is it doing at Slade Prison?'

'It was Mr Barrowclough's idea, sir, while you was away. He came up with it after reading what they was doing in other prisons.'

'What other prisons?'

'Well, take Peterborough, for a start. They've just hired two holistic therapists on £18,000 a year to help inmates relax.'

'Relax? Prisoners aren't inside to relax. They're here to be punished.'

'Wrong again, Mr Mackay. This isn't the Dark Ages. This is the New Ages. Prisoners is people, too, and as such is entitled to all the same yuman rights as those on the out.'

'I've never heard anything so ridiculous.'

'Wait until you hear what they're offering over in B-wing, Mr Mackay.'

'What are you talking about, Fletch?'

'Indian head massage, Japanese reiki, shiatsu, that sort of thing. Did I tell you my Ingrid was working as a masseuse in a sauna in Crouch End? Doing very well, by all accounts. Giving French lessons, too. Funny, 'cos I didn't know she spoke French. Maybe there's an opening for her here at Slade Prison. You could have a word with the governor.'

'I shall do no such thing, Fletcher. Where is Mr Barrowclough?'

'What time is it?'

'Just after 3.30.'

'In that case, he'll be taking the ashtanga yoga and dance class in the exercise yard.'

'What?'

'Ashtanga yoghurt. Very popular with all yer Hollywood stars. And now with armed robbers and burglars, too.'

'Why aren't you there, then, Fletcher?'

'Not with my feet, Mr Mackay. I'm excused yoga.'

'You should get them seen to, Fletcher. That would stop your malingering.'

'That's exactly what I am going to do. It's all fixed up on PPP. The chiropodist will be over later today after he's finished cutting the toenails of that Captain Hook geezer what was transferred here from Belmarsh last week.'

'I don't know what this prison's coming to. I can't turn my back for five minutes. Where is everyone?'

'You'll find Genial Harry Grout in his dingly dell. Tuesday's his manicure day. And he's having SkyPlus installed this afternoon.'

'Warren?'

'Facial, followed by a full body aromatherapy massage. It's all the go at Bristol Prison. Here, in the papers, see for yourself.'

'Unbelievable.'

'I'd like to sit here all day talking to you, Mr Mackay, but I'm having the cell feng shui-ed in half an hour. Will that be all, sir?'

'No, where's 'Orrible Ives?'

'Gone into town to get his PlayStation fixed.'

'McLaren?'

'He's with his Zen counsellor, sir. He was down for an Indian head massage, only as soon as the masseur laid hands on him, Jock snapped and threw him off the landing. Still, they say with a little meditation and a few drops of ylang-ylang oil he'll be right as rain.'

'What, after being thrown off a thirty-foot-high landing?'

'Oh, no, not the masseur. He's in intensive care, poor sod. McLaren. His therapist says all he needs to do is get in touch with his feminine side.'

'I'll give him feminine side.'

'Now now, Mr Mackay. Temper temper. That won't get you very far in today's modern prison service. Don't think of us as prisoners, think of us as customers.'

'Customers, my arse.'

'Speaking of your arse, Mr Mackay, perhaps you should try the acupuncture session on C-wing. It might do wonders for your Chalfonts.'

60 | The Mother of All Parliaments

The British left went into paroxysms of rage when George W. Bush won the 2000 US presidential election after the Supreme Court ruled in his favour following the 'hanging chad' fiasco in Florida.

Whichever way you cut it, Bush became president despite narrowly losing the popular vote to his Democrat rival, Al Gore. He made it into the White House because of the USA's electoral college system.

What the British left refused to acknowledge was that their darling Bill Clinton was elected president on just two-fifths of the popular vote. That was because of the intervention of independent candidate Ross Perot, who turned the contest into a three-way race, reminiscent of a traditional British general election.

As I pointed out when I appeared on a live BBC *Question Time* from Miami before the 2004 presidential election, we have our own electoral college system in Britain. It's called the House of Commons and for the last three elections it worked heavily in Labour's favour. Blair won a landslide in 1997 despite polling fewer votes than John Major in 1992.

By 2005, Labour only received the support of a quarter of those eligible to vote. They actually lost the popular vote in England, which makes up eighty per cent of the United Kingdom. But thanks to skewed constituency boundaries, which favour Labour's inner-city boroughs, and the party's dominance in Scotland and Wales, Blair was returned with another comfortable majority, even though he had already announced he would be standing down sometime in the new Parliament.

Try explaining that to the Americans. Imagine a US news network attempting to unravel Britain's 2005 general election.

'Good evening, you're watching *Eyewitness News*, live from Palm Beach, Florida. I'm Chad Hanging, reporting on the British general election. Let's go over to our special correspondent in London, Brit Limey, who is standing beside the famous Nelson Mandela's Column.'

'Chad, this is an historic day in Englandland. President Tony Blair has just won a third term.'

'Third term? He can do that?'

'Yes, Chad, unlike the USA, British presidents can go on and on.'

'So Blair could be there for life, Brit?'

'No, he's already announced that he's going to resign.'

'What, straight after being elected?'

'Before, actually.'

'So these crazy Brits voted for a guy who says he's going to quit, Brit?'

'That's an affirmative, Chad.'

'Blair's a Conservative, right?'

'No, he's Labour.'

'But I thought he was big buddies with George W. Bush.'

'He is, Chad, and before that he was a kissin' cousin of Bill Clinton.'

'So who takes over when Blair goes?'

'A guy called Brown, like the gillie who was having an affair with Queen Victoria.'

'He's the vice-president, like Cheney, yeah?'

'No, that's a fat guy called Two Jags, used to be a waiter on the cruise ships.'

'Two Jags? He's, like, a Native American?'

'No, that's his nickname. It's short for Two Jag-wars.'

'Who came up with that, Brit?'

'Don't ask me, Chad.'

'So who's this Brown?'

'He's, like, the Treasury guy, from Scotlandland.'

'So Englandland gets a president from Scotlandland, who they haven't voted for?'

'That's right. In actual fact, without Scotlandland Blair wouldn't be able to govern, which he isn't going to for much longer.'

'How's that, Brit?'

'Well, Chad, the Conservatives won the popular vote in Englandland by a 60,000 margin.'

'So why didn't a Conservative become president?'

'That's because of the electoral college system called the House of Commons, which means that even though Blair got 60,000 fewer votes in Englandland he still got 92 more seats in Parliament.'

'Hang on, Brit, weren't these the guys who claimed that Bush wasn't legitimately elected in 2000?'

'That's correct, Chad. But Blair also won in Scotlandland, too. In fact, he relies on his MPs from Scotlandland to get through legislation in Englandland.'

'Doesn't Scotlandland have its own parliament?'

'That's right, Chad, but Scottish MPs in Englandland can't vote on stuff like education and health in Scotlandland, so they decide what happens in Englandland instead, even though no one in Englandland has voted for them.'

'Run that by me again, Brit. Isn't that a bit like the USA being run by Canada?'

'I guess so, Chad.'

'Aren't the Conservatives challenging that? Who was their candidate?'

'A guy called Howard.'

'What, the Australian?'

'No, that's Crosby.'

'But he's just teamed up with Stills and Nash again. I saw them in Miami a couple of weeks ago.'

'Different guy, Chad. The Aussie Howard's called John. This one's called Michael, from Walesland.'

'How can a guy from Walesland be leader of the Conservatives in Englandland?'

'He's not, Chad.'

'Not what, Brit?'

'Not leader any more. He's resigned too.'

'So there's a president who's resigning and a leader of the opposition who's also resigning, Brit?'

'Got it in one, Chad.'

'But we keep hearing how popular Blair is. Why would he go?'

'Actually, Chad, everyone here hates him. Labour only got thirty-six per cent of those who bothered to vote. Taking abstentions into account, fewer than one in four voted for Blair.'

'Yet still he won, Brit?'

'Go figure, Chad.'

'Still, the soldiers in Iraq must have voted for him.'

'Not exactly, Chad. They didn't get a vote. Their postal votes got lost in the post. There's been a bit of a problem with postal voting this time. In fact, the police have made a number of arrests. It seems some political activists were applying for postal votes in other people's names then filling them in themselves. It even happened to a guy from the BBC called Humphrys, Englandland's answer to Dan Rather.'

'I thought Englandland prided itself on being the cradle of democracy, Brit. Mother of Parliaments and all that.'

'Not any more, Chad. A judge recently described Englandland's voting system as something which would shame a banana republic.'

'So if Blair's going and this Howard guy is going, who else is there?'

'There's a chubby guy called Kennedy, for the Liberals. Likes a drink.'

'What, Ted Kennedy's standing in Englandland?'

'No, Charles Kennedy. He's from Scotlandland, too.'

'We're running out of satellite time, Brit. Just help me out here. What we're talking about is a president being elected even though he lost the popular vote in Englandland because Englandland is now run from Scotlandland?'

'Affirmative, Chad.'

'And people vote for him knowing that he's going to resign?'

'Check.'

'And you're telling me that the voting system is so corrupt that a judge says it would disgrace a banana republic?'

'That's a big ten-four, Chad.'

'And they have the nerve to tell us that we can't run a democratic election. This is Chad Hanging signing off from Palm Beach County. Have a nice day.'

61 | How Clean Is Your Hospital?

In December 2003, the Department of Health announced it was launching a new digital television channel for patients called NHS Direct TV. This was the first day's schedule, as it appeared in my column.

6.00am   **Breakfast With Frost** (T)
> Live from the Robert Mugabe Wing of Haringey Memorial Hospital. Patients shiver to death while being served plates of cold bacon, congealed eggs and salmonella.

7.00am   **Superbug** (R)
> Popular children's cartoon series in which a flying teddy bear contracts MRSA and dies after visiting Outpatients for removal of an ingrowing toenail.

8.00am   **RISE**
> Barbara Windsor distributes Viagra to inmates on the Erectile Dysfunction Ward at Hattie Jacques General.

9.00am   **ER**
> Her Majesty the Queen undergoes keyhole surgery on her knee at the Princess Grace Hospital. (Available only to BUPA subscribers.)

10.00am   **Teletubbies**
> Pro Celebrity dieting clinic from the Slimfast Arena, Bromsgrove. Presented by Marjorie Dawes and the late Dr Robert Atkins.

11.00am   **Casualty** (T) (R)
> Accident and Emergency patients queue for up to twenty-three hours to see a doctor. Presented by Stuart Hall.

12.00pm   **Doctors** (P)
> A routine gall bladder operation goes horribly wrong with hilarious consequences. Stars Dr Robert Winston and Jim Dale.

12.30pm **Celebrity Ready, Steady, Cook**

Live from the kitchens at the Nelson Mandela Clinic, Gateshead. Fern Britton and her guests rustle up a delicious lunch of botulism out of old bandages and amputated body parts, garnished with used syringes. With special guest star, Swampy.

1.00pm **Film: Fever**

An outbreak of Legionnaires' Disease at a multi-screen cinema in Chipping Sodbury results in 300 deaths, following the closure of the local cottage hospital.

1.30pm **Wallace and Gromit** (R)

A repeat of the popular episode in which our hero goes in for an ear operation.

2.00pm **Film: Carry On Up The Khyber**

Medical drama. Chuckle at the side-splitting goings-on in the colonoscopy department of the Bournville Boulevard Health Centre. Stars Kenneth Williams and Chris Bryant MP. Sponsored by Cadbury's.

3.30pm **Celebrity Kidney Swap** (T)

Linda Barker and Neil Hamilton go under the knife to exchange organs. Presented by Ant and Dec.

4.00pm **Fifteen-To-One**

The odds of anyone getting a hip operation this side of the year 2525.

4.30pm **A Place In The Sun** (R)

Thousands of critically ill NHS patients fly to Ibiza for routine operations to beat three-year waiting lists in Britain. Presented by Judith Chalmers, with special guest stars Frank and Nesta Bough.

5.00pm **Richard and Judy** (T) (P)

Live from their new studio at the Priory Clinic. Today's topics include battling alcoholism. Featuring Michael Barrymore and Paula Hamilton.

6.00pm **The News** (R)

Special report on the success of the NHS under New Labour. Presented by Dr John Reid and the Brothers Grimm.

6.30pm   **How Clean Is Your Hospital?**
Kim Woodburn and Aggie MacKenzie take on a modern inner-city hospital where the managers, doctors and nurses don't seem to mind the filth and squalor.

7.30pm   **EastEnders** (T)
Pauline and the bloke who used to be in *Dad's Army* go to the Royal London Hospital, Whitechapel, to visit Dot, only to discover her routine operation has been cancelled because her surgeon is doing a private job.

8.00pm   **Holby City** (R) (T) (P)
A pensioner is taken on a 300-mile round trip in search of a bed after the geriatric ward is closed because of spending cuts.

9.00pm   **The Million Pound Property Experiment**
Dozens of local hospitals are shut down and sold off to developers of yuppie flats. Presented by Four Poofs and a Piano.

9.30pm   **Changing Rooms**
Dozens of NHS patients are kicked out of their beds to make way for asylum seekers.

10.00pm   **HIV Graham Norton** (R)
Graham's guests tonight include the late Freddie Mercury and Kenny Everett.

10.30pm   **Newsnight** (T)
Cherie Blair refuses to discuss whether or not Damien has had the MMR jab. Presented by Andrew Gilligan and Alastair Campbell.

11.00pm   **Parkinson** (R)
Mike and his special guests, Dean Martin, George Melly and Neil Kinnock talk about their vasectomies.

11.30pm   **The Office** (R) (T)
David Brent gets a new £50,000 job with the NHS as a Five-A-Day Smoking Cessation Outreach Co-ordination Facilitation Monitoring Manager. He immediately sets about closing down wards to make room for the thousands of new bureaucrats being hired out of the *Guardian*.

NHS Direct TV was the genuine article. My schedule was wholly fictitious. Or so I thought. I refer you to:

6.30pm   How Clean Is Your Hospital?

Kim Woodburn and Aggie MacKenzie take on a modern inner-city hospital where the managers, doctors and nurses don't seem to mind the filth and squalor.

For the uninitiated, Kim and Aggie are a couple of charladies who have carved out a successful television career scrubbing up the homes of the slovenly and insanitary in programmes such as *How Clean Is Your House?* and *Too Posh To Wash*. My imaginary show *How Clean Is Your Hospital?* was meant to be a joke.

I should have known better. In August 2006, Kim and Aggie took part in a real-life programme on Channel 4 from Ealing Hospital, in West London, a unit that had the third worst rate of MRSA infection in the UK.

Its title: *How Clean Is Your Hospital?*

No doubt *Celebrity Kidney Swap* is on its way to a small screen near you any day now.

62 | Squeals on Wheels

Under an enlightened New Labour health policy, the NHS is now providing prostitutes for disabled men.

Just in case you didn't quite take it in first time, I'll repeat that sentence. The NHS is now providing prostitutes for disabled men.

According to a report by Dr Sarah Earle, of Coventry University, social workers are acting as 'sexual matchmakers' for men confined to wheelchairs.

The Royal College of Nursing issued guidelines giving support to 'carers' who arrange sexual liaisons for their disabled clients.

'Sex is a key issue: many carers describe it as a want, which can be a matter of choice, while the disabled regard it as a need that should be accommodated as part of the carer's job description,' wrote Dr Earle in the journal *Disability & Society*.

Elsewhere it was revealed that social workers in Luton were buying pornographic magazines for the disabled and helping them to masturbate – which I'd have thought falls squarely into the category of What's The Worst Job You Ever Had?

If you accept that as a fit and proper way to make a living, then fixing them up with prostitutes is merely a natural progression.

All part of the service. Squeals on wheels.

One of the men interviewed by Dr Earle described how he had graduated from porn to prostitutes with the help of his social worker, who negotiated a rate for the job (£20, since you ask).

Another disabled man, who happened to be homosexual, asked his carer to help him undress so he could have sex with his boyfriend.

There's more, but that's probably too much information already. You get the general picture. I'm not for a moment denying that the disabled have a right to a sex life. But whether it's the job of the NHS to provide it is another matter entirely. This is not, after all, a question of equality. There is no matching service for the able-bodied. Not so far as I know, but I could be wrong.

'Good morning, Mr Jones, and what seems to be the matter with you this morning?'

'Well, to tell the truth, Doctor, it's me leg.'

'Your leg?'

'Yes, Doctor, I'm not getting it over enough.'

'Very well, Mr Jones. Go home and lie down and I'll send a couple of hookers round. That should do the trick.'

'Thanks, Doc, you're a real gent.'

Where do the social workers find the prostitutes? Do they go kerb-crawling in the interests of research? Do they pinch tarts' cards out of phone boxes?

I'm all for compassion but you have to draw the line some-where. NHS 'resources' are finite. And, all other considerations aside, to the best of my knowledge, procuring prostitutes is still a criminal offence. Since when has pimping been regarded as part of a social worker's job description?

It was later revealed that the NHS helped a mentally ill woman get a job as a pole dancer. Dr Rachel Perkins, of St George's Hospital in London, said it was part of a programme to help vulnerable people regain their confidence.

Some might argue that getting your kit off and gyrating in front of a team of braying, drunken City spivs is good for your self-esteem. But since when did the NHS act as an employment agency for strippers?

Spearmint Rhino – you don't have to be mad to work here, but it helps.

63 | Herrings on Prescription

In Scotland GPs started dishing out fish on prescription. Patients with heart trouble are as likely to be given a bucket of herrings as a bottle of pills. The Orkney surgery has a fridge stocked with marinated fish.

It's well known that a diet rich in oily fish can help ward off heart disease. But quite why herrings are available on the NHS is completely beyond me. There's a world of difference between doctors giving healthy-eating advice and actually handing out fish. Where's it all going to end?

'Doctor, it's my feet again.'

'What I want you to do is take three sardines, twice a day, with a little fresh tagliatelle in a squid ink and basil jus, some rocket dressed in virgin olive oil and ground pepper, and a kumquat with a loganberry coulis.'

'Thank you very much, Doctor. Any chance of a nice bit of skate for my husband?'

'Certainly. Wing or middle?'

'Wing would be lovely, if you could see your way clear.'

'No problem. Fresh off the boat this morning. But go easy on the black butter.'

'You wouldn't have a bit of parsley, would you, save me going to the shops?'

'I think we can run to that, Mrs McGregor. I'll get my receptionist to tie you up a bouquet garni. And come back and see me in a week. Nurse will give you some wet haddock and a pint of whelks on the way out.'

Madness. Herrings on prescription. Sounds like an old Frank Zappa LP.

Red wine is supposed to ward off cancer. Are we going to have doctors dispensing bottles of Beaujolais?

This could change the whole nature of hospital dramas on TV. Imagine someone being wheeled into casualty at Holby General.

'It's a minor cardiac infarction, Doctor.'

'Get him into the kitchen, nurse. And help me scrub up. We may need to fillet the herrings.'

I'm sorry, I know this is founded on the best intentions. But I really don't think this is what Beveridge had in mind. There are people dying on trolleys in corridors, waiting lists the length of the Great Wall of China and meanwhile doctors are spending taxpayers' money doling out halibut on prescription. Let them eat fish, by all means. But let them buy it themselves.

Then they might not have so much money to spend on deep-fried Mars bars.

64 | If Your Ears Are Bleeding, Press 3

Another gimmick introduced by the health service was NHS Direct, a telephone helpline aimed at cutting waiting lists. On the face of it, anything which stops waiting rooms and accident and emergency departments being clogged up with malingerers and those with minor ailments makes good sense. But when *Which?* magazine tested the service the results were frightening.

Researchers made thirty-three calls to eleven different NHS Direct centres. Seven times they had to wait more than thirty minutes for a nurse to ring back. The target was for ninety per cent of inquiries to be handled in five minutes.

They also found failure to diagnose symptoms ranging from an angina attack to an ectopic pregnancy.

To confirm these were not freak results, I decided to conduct my own research by calling an NHS Direct line chosen at random.

This is what happened.

*

'Thank you for calling NHS Direct. All our operators are busy assisting other patients. Your health is important to us. You are being held in a queue and your call will be answered at the earliest available opportunity.'

'Hello?'

'NHS Direct offers a range of diagnoses to suit all illnesses. If you would like a brochure, press 1. For all other inquiries, please hold.'

'Hello?'

'This call is being monitored for training purposes. For details of our privacy protection policy, press 2. To continue holding, press three.'

'Hello?'

'Thank you for holding. If you have a headache, press 1. If you have cut yourself, press 2. If you have a nosebleed, press 3. For all other symptoms, press 4.'

'Hello?'

'NHS Direct appreciates your call. Did you know that New Labour has increased spending on health by £20 billion? If you think you have high blood pressure, press 1. If you have pains in your chest, press 2. If you have injured your hand slamming your fist into the wall or have broken your toe kicking the cat, press 3. For all other symptoms, press 4.'

'Hello?'

'Thank you for pressing 4. If you are foaming at the mouth, press 1. If you are vomitting uncontrollably, press 2. If your ears are bleeding, press 3. If you wish to speak to a nurse, press 4.'

'Hello?'

'All our nurses are busy, getting ready to go out dancing for the evening. If you think your appendix has exploded, press 1. If you are having a heart attack, press 2. If you have got stomach cramps, you shouldn't have eaten that chicken madras, should you?'

'Hello?'

'If you've got acute angina, press 1. If you've got big breaths and you're only thirteen, press UK Gold on your Sky digital remote. If you haven't already lost the will to live, press 3.

'Hello?'

'Thank you for holding. If your contractions are coming every five minutes, press 1. If your waters have broken, press 2. If you are a lesbian and would like details of artificial insemination available on the NHS and a free turkey baster, please press 3.'

'Hello?'

'If you are interested in tattoo removal, press 1. If you would like a sex-change operation, press 2 and your call will be answered immediately.'

'Hello?'

'If you are an old age pensioner, please hang up and don't waste our time. If you are a newly arrived asylum seeker and would like treatment for Aids or any other contagious disease, please ask your interpreter to press 3 and you will be put through to a consultant who will make arrangements for you to be admitted to a private room.'

'Hello?'

'Thank you for calling NHS Direct. All our medical staff are busy treating drunks, drug addicts and illegal immigrants, or filling in forms. If you are already dead, please hang up.'

65 | The Man Who Stole Your Old Age

The mobile rang. It was Charlie Whelan, Gordon Brown's mouthpiece. I've known Charlie for twenty-five years, ever since I was a young industrial correspondent on the *Evening Standard* and his job was to go to the bar for the late Jimmy Airlie, the engineering union official who brought you the Upper Clyde shipbuilders' strike.

For years Charlie sat two rows behind me at White Hart Lane. When Gordon became Shadow Chancellor, the union lent him Charlie to help him polish his dour Scottish public image. Gordon needed all the help he could get.

After Gordon became Chancellor of the Exchequer in 1997, the arrangement was formalised and Charlie went on the payroll as press secretary. It was always going to be a seat-of-the-pants operation.

After one of Gordon's early speeches to City businessmen at the Mansion House, I remember writing that the whole thing sounded as if it had been written in the back of the cab on the way there. The following morning Charlie phoned and said: 'How did you know? That's exactly what happened.'

Charlie had a habit of making policy on the hoof without consulting Gordon, usually from the downstairs bar of the Red Lion, on Whitehall. I can remember one night after a Spurs home game against Chelsea, I was drinking in the Starting Gate, an Edwardian boozer near Alexandra Palace, North London, with Charlie and Suggs, the lead singer of the group Madness.

As you do.

Our deconstruction of another home defeat kept being interrupted by Charlie's mobile phone going off. There was some crisis in the financial markets and the political correspondents wanted the chancellor's reaction.

Not to worry, Charlie reassured them. He had it on good authority that the Bank of England's monetary committee would be putting interest rates up (or down, I forget which, they'd called last orders) the following day.

'You can't do that, Charlie,' I told him. 'You might just have wiped billions off the stock market and caused a run on the pound.'

'No problem,' said Charlie, ordering another pint of Guinness. 'It's all bollocks, anyway. It'll sort itself out in the morning.'

Madness.

But I've always had a soft spot for Charlie, even though politically we agree on practically nothing. So when he rang to say: 'Gordon and Sarah would like you and Wendy to come for a drink at the flat,' I decided to suspend my rule about hobnobbing with politicians.

I'd met Gordon a few times over the years and found him far more personable than his public image. And I figured that anyone who'd keep a scruffy wide boy like Charlie on the strength in the stuffed-shirt world of Whitehall couldn't be all bad. Especially someone who harboured a pathological hatred of Peter Mandelson. I also knew Sarah, through her brother Sean, on old friend of mine, so what the hell.

Anyway, Gordon is big enough and ugly enough to know that a few convivial glasses of wine wouldn't stop me giving him a kicking in print whenever the occasion presented itself. And Charlie wouldn't have expected it otherwise.

Although Gordon's official residence was 11 Downing Street, his flat was above Number 10.

Also invited were Stuart Higgins, then editor of the *Sun*, and his wife and Penny Smith, who read the news on TV-mayhem, or whatever it calls itself these days.

There were no flunkeys. Gordon opened the wine himself and Sarah handed round the nibbles. I'd love to tell you what we talked about, but little of it sticks in my mind.

What I do remember is that about halfway through the evening, Gordon had to slope off to the Commons to vote in a division, but insisted on us staying. Like Arnie, he'd be back.

In his absence, Charlie, Stuart and me opened another couple of bottles and talked football. Sarah took the women on a tour of the flat. In the bedroom, Penny Smith flung open the wardrobe to find half a dozen identical dark suits, half a dozen identical plain blue shirts and half a dozen identical red ties.

But the *pièce de résistance* was in the bathroom. On the side of the bath there was a pair of full-sized swimming goggles, to keep the Grecian 2000 out of Gordon's good eye.

We also got an invitation to the Browns' wedding reception, which I couldn't resist, either, even though it meant walking into a room full of people I regularly ridiculed and abused in Britain's biggest-selling newspaper.

It was at some trendy art gallery, south of the river. I enjoy going south of the river about as much as I like mixing with politicians, but I thought it might be a bit of a scream. It was worth it just to see the look on the Wicked Witch's face when she spotted me chuckling away with Charlie. I don't know which one of us she hates most.

The first person I saw was the Labour MP Diane Abbott, with whom I'd done a few shows over the years. She gave me a hug before stepping back and saying: 'Hang on a minute, you're not New Labour.'

'Neither are you Diane,' I replied. We roared with laughter. Diane's got a fantastic, infectious giggle, as anyone who watches her on the Andrew Neil show will be aware.

'And,' I added, 'neither are half the people here.'

It was true. The reception was divided into Blairites and Brownites even then, glaring at each other over the wine and canapes like Cavaliers and Roundheads lining up before a battle during the civil war.

That war came to a head at the 2006 Labour conference when Brown finally forced Blair to announce that he was standing down. As any fule kno, Gordon has always felt that he was cheated of the leadership when John Smith died in 1994. And he believes Blair reneged on the famous Granita restaurant agreement.

History has it that Gordon agreed to stand aside in exchange for control of the domestic agenda and a promise that Tony would hand over the reins during his second term.

I've never been so sure, even though Blair tells everyone what they want to hear and is the kind of man who can paint himself into a corner and then walk out over the paint. The plain fact is that if it had gone to a vote Gordon would have lost. He bottled it, just as he's bottled just about every single major decision in his career.

By the time this book is published, Gordon may well be prime minister, but he's already damaged goods. I think one of the reasons Blair hung on so long is that he knows Gordon's a loser, especially in Middle England.

That's why last summer Gordon embarked on a cynical, capped-teeth charm offensive, garnished with mawkish sentimentality. Once fiercely protective of his personality, he couldn't stop talking about his childhood, his marriage and the tragic death of his daughter.

Frankly, I preferred Mr Grumpy to the 'inner' Gordon. There's something unsettling about that kiddie-fiddler grin. If you saw him beaming from ear to ear while approaching a children's playground with a packet of sweets, you'd call the police.

He even invited the *Mail on Sunday* drinking team to Number 11 to watch the 2006 World Cup in a cynical attempt to convince the English that he's One Of Us. No doubt it seemed like a good idea at the time.

He sat there, sipping lo-cal, lo-carb lager, about three feet from the screen, pretending to support Becks and the boys against Trinidad and Tobago.

You'd have to have a complete sense of humour bypass not to see the total absurdity of it all. If you ever doubted that politicians are from another planet, here was the conclusive evidence.

The rest of the country watched the game sprawled on a sofa, on a big screen, or down the pub. Dress code ran from red replica shirt to chain mail. Gordon was probably the only England 'fan' to watch the game wearing a pink tie.

We all have our own match day checklist – kettle chips, cold beer, phone off the hook. How many of us turned to our loved ones and said: 'There's something missing here. I know, let's get the chaps from the Mail on Sunday round'? Only a politician on the make would think to invite a newspaper to watch him watching the football.

This was the Dunkirk of charm offensives. The *MoS* did him up like an Arbroath smokie. Gordon was determined to shake off his image as a miserable, Scottish control freak. He figured that if he makes an ostentatious show of supporting England in the World Cup, we will all come to love him.

How daft does he think we are?

Forget football. If he sincerely wanted Sven's men to succeed in Germany, it will be about the only time he's ever supported England in anything. Gordon spends every waking moment working out how to screw the English. His entire economic philosophy is predicated on robbing the English blind. His taxation strategy has concentrated on fleecing England – and the South of England in particular. His larcenous rates of stamp duty and his disgraceful, confiscatory attack on inheritance have little impact north of the border, where few properties and estates fall foul of the thresholds.

He might make speeches designed to portray him as a British patriot, but I've yet to hear him address the democratic deficit which subjugates the English to rule by a Scottish Raj.

We don't actually care if he backs England at football. We would like him to explain why England should be run by a Scottish prime minister who is able to pass laws affecting us which do not apply to his own constituents. Gordon could dress up as World Cup Willie and paint a St George's flag on his face but we still won't forgive him for stealing our pensions. The crass stunt of inviting a news-paper to watch him cheering on England's footballers smacks as much of desperation as opportunism.

The Tories won the popular vote in England last time. If 14,000 had voted the other way in 2005, there would have been a hung parliament. Call Me Dave has every reason to feel confident going into the next election, whenever it comes. People are increasingly coming to resent Gordon's belief that the keys to Number 10 should be his by divine right. Voters are looking at their rocketing tax bills and their dwindling pension funds and are aware where the blame lies.

The West Lothian question is no longer confined to arcane conversations between political anoraks. And three lions on his shirt won't save him.

It's not just England where Gordon is struggling. The shine is coming off north of the border, too. In 2006, Labour lost the seat next to Gordon's to the SNP, even though the chancellor campaigned there heavily. Not all his own constituents are in thrall to him.

All politics is local, they say, but most MPs would rather it wasn't. Few went into politics to spend their days worrying about drains, potholes or the leaking roof at the Nelson Mandela Resource Centre.

Cultivating a constituency is merely establishing a base camp on the road to greater glory. Gordon didn't become an MP simply to deal with the parochial problems of Dunfermline East. His ambitions lay hundreds of miles south in Downing Street.

His formidable mind has always been on the application of post neo-classical endogenous growth theory, screwing the last penny out of the hated middle classes, and sticking pins in a clay model of that bastard Blair.

But Gordon has to give the impression of caring about his constituents, too. So, like all MPs, he is forced to press the flesh, to meet the proles from time to time.

He appears to handle it with all the characteristic grace that he employs when caught dissembling over his latest stealth tax. A *Daily Mail* reader kindly sent me a letter from Gordon's local paper, the *Courier & Advertiser*. It was written by one of a group of ex-soldiers from the Black Watch, who went to meet the chancellor when he paid a state visit to a community centre in Lochgelly.

They hoped to question him on the government's decision to kill off the county regiment; to ask why he reneged on his promise to reassign work to the dockyard at Rosyth; to have him explain why he had not attended the funerals of local soldiers killed in Iraq; and to draw his attention to the rising level of unemployment in the area.

'Needless to say he ran past us so fast that by the time he hit the front door of the centre he was so out of breath he could not, or would not, answer. We are a fair group of people so we gave him the benefit of the doubt and waited until his meeting was over. He emerged, flanked by his minders, and, yes, we asked him the same questions again. Unfortunately we got the same answer. Nothing. I then asked him how could he ask us to trust him with the country when we can't even trust him to look after his own county? Again, there was no answer.'

If all politics really is local, think of the callous, pig-ignorant way Brown tramples over old soldiers in his own constituency. As the ex-Black Watch member wrote to the local paper: I only hope that the country takes on board the kind of person he really is.'

Hide your wives and daughters, hide your savings, too. Great Statesman Gordon coming through. He might be hailed as the Iron Chancellor, but to my mind his record doesn't stack up.

For instance, Labour used to sneer at the Tories for 'selling off the family silver'. That was when Mrs Thatcher was returning lumbering, inefficient nationalised industries to private ownership.

Gordon literally sold off the family gold, putting half Britain's gold reserves on the market at an all-time low price of \$275 an ounce. The money was split forty per cent in dollars, forty per cent in euros and twenty per cent in Japanese yen.

Holding reserves in dollars and yen was a reasonably safe bet. Both currencies have a fairly reliable track record. Gambling on the euro was utterly irresponsible.

The euro was just four months old. Experts now think it won't be around in four or five years' time.

This decision was sneaked out on a Friday afternoon, when the news was dominated by reports of the bombing of the Chinese embassy in Belgrade during the Balkans War.

Gordon argued that the value of gold has fallen. Indeed it has. But it has been around as a measure of wealth for 3,000 years, not five minutes like the euro. It exists. You can touch it, you can weigh it. And they're not making any more, even though there is still plenty left to be mined.

The value of gold does not depend on anyone's promise to pay, unlike the euro, which can be undermined instantly by an ill-judged statement from the Greek minister of finance following a dodgy olive harvest.

Investing in the euro was an act of political faith, not a prudent economic decision. He might just as well have bet the farm on some of the modern South Sea Bubble companies floating around the Internet.

Imagine him going to the House and informing MPs that he just punted £4 billion on an Internet start-up.

But then he didn't consult the House, and apparently ignored the advice of Eddie George, then governor of the Bank of England.

By January 2007, gold had risen to $609 an ounce. At these prices, Gordon's recklessness cost Britain £2.8 billion. Nice one, Prudence.

You don't hear him boasting about that when he's lauding his own 'prudence' and economic genius.

But it is in the area of pensions that Gordon's record is despicable. Not for nothing did I christen him the Man Who Stole Your Old Age.

Here's the deal. If in 1997, Gordon had promised to steal your pension and make you work until you're seventy, would you still have voted Labour? Especially if he said that the money he took from you would be used to hire hundreds of thousands of utterly useless and superfluous public sector workers?

And while you could look forward to a miserable old age living on bread and scrape, all these new inspectors, co-ordinators and outreachers would be guaranteed gold plated, index-linked pensions of their own – paid for out of your taxes?

Well, that's what's happened. As soon as he got his feet under the table of Number 11, Gordon mounted a smash-and-grab raid on pension funds. Back then, it raked in £5 billion a year. Today, it's £8 billion and rising. Britain is facing a pensions black hole of over

£60 billion – a large slice of which is down to Gordon's greed, which has cost us getting on for £50 billion.

The rest is because of a collapse in the stock market. And why has that happened? It's in large part down to Gordon's tax raid, which has discouraged pension funds from investing. So while foreign stock markets have risen by up to forty-five per cent, Britain's stagnated.

Result: We're all poorer.

Correction: We're not *all* poorer. Only those of us who rely on private pensions or the basic state pension. Those who work for the state are quids in. If you're lucky enough to be employed by the civil service, or the NHS, or your local town hall, reach for those Saga brochures and start planning your round-the-world cruise right now.

A state employee can expect twice the pension of someone in the private sector making the same contributions all their working life. As of 2006, someone aged thirty, earning £30,000 in the private sector was looking at a fixed pension of just under £10,500 at today's prices. Over the years the value of that will dwindle.

Someone else, same age, same salary, in the public sector, can expect a pension of £22,000 on retirement, index-linked against inflation.

The difference is that private firms contribute around four per cent of earnings, while public employers are more generous, chipping in on average 11.5 per cent.

But hang on a minute. Public sector employers don't have any money. It belongs to the British taxpayer. What gives them the right to be so generous with our hard-earned?

It used to be argued that public sector workers got better job security and pensions in exchange for far lower wages than they could earn in private industry. But that went out of the window years ago. Most of the jobs advertised every week in the *Guardian* offer salaries at least equal to those outside – and often higher.

As I detail in 'Nice Work If You Can Get It', thanks to Gordon's largesse with our taxes, we've now got £115,000-a-year NHS diversity supremos and £26,500-a-year cotton nappy co-ordinators. I don't know how we managed without them up to now.

In 2005, MPs voted themselves £25 million of our money to make up their pension shortfall. You would need a fund of at least £1 million to get anywhere near the kind of pension one of our elected representatives can look forward to.

Dream on.

An MP on £57,000 today can expect an index-linked pension of £93,000 in twenty-six years. A private sector employee, same age, same salary, same contributions, will be lucky to get £22,300.

Politicians know how to look after themselves. Derry Irvine, Blair's old boss, trousered a pension fund worth £2.3million after just five years as Lord Chancellor – all courtesy of the taxpayer.

No chance of any of Labour's cronies ending up selling the *Big Issue* in the Strand, with a dog on a piece of string, or huddled round one bar of an electric fire, dining on a tin of Whiskas.

Britain's pension industry was once the envy of the world until Gordon got his hands on it. There hasn't been a swindle like this since Robert Maxwell. At least Captain Bob had the decency to top himself when he got found out.

Brown's daylight robbery is compounded by the fact that he has done all he can to make the system as complicated as possible, so that very few people can understand it.

That's because of his control freakery. Gordon's like the swot in the maths class who sat at the back hunched over his work with his arm round his exercise book, terrified anyone else would get a peek. At the first sight of someone approaching, he'd hide it in his desk and throw his body over it.

It shouldn't be like this. Pensions should be fairly straight-forward. You save up every month, invest your money and years later when you retire, you get a pension. Governments can offer tax incentives here and there, but that's about it.

Instead Gordon goes out of his way to confuse and confound with a Byzantine system of rules, regulations, credits and a dozen other hurdles, which means you need a degree in higher economics – or Klingon – to make head or tail of it.

And for what? So that most of us, after years of saving and paying our National Insurance contributions on the dot, will end up with thirty per cent less than we were led to believe we had coming. And the only way out of it, we're now told, is to pay even more tax or work till we drop. The retirement age is going up to sixty-eight – except for public employees, Gordon's client base, who can still put their feet up at sixty.

The Man Who Stole Your Old Age can himself look forward to a retirement income of around £100,000, index-linked, courtesy of the British taxpayer. That would need a pot of over £3 million in the private sector. But, of course, even the select few who could amass such a fund would be insane to do so, given that Gordon sneaked through a usurious tax of fifty-five per cent on everything over £1.5 million.

Naturally, that supertax doesn't apply to the pensions of prime ministers. And Gordon has always believed it was his divine right to inherit the keys to Number 10 without bothering to trouble the electorate first.

He may have eschewed many of the perks of office, but he can look forward to a comfortable and secure old age – unlike millions of his fellow citizens. And the platinum-plated pension will come on top of directorships, book deals and lecture tours.

At last year's Labour conference, he gave it the full Prime Minister In Waiting routine. As Charlie Whelan would say, it was all bollocks. Gordon's speech was an object lesson in duplicity and denial.

Here was the man who once told Tony Blair 'there is nothing you could say to me now that I could possibly believe' ladling praise upon the prime minister's head like a short-order chef pouring hollandaise sauce over eggs Benedict.

Gordon's gofers have been peddling poison about Blair for as long as I can remember, ever since the infamous Granita deal. Having convinced himself he wuz robbed, Gordon has spent thirteen years in a vengeful sulk. Never has the distinction between a ray of sunshine and a Scotsman with a grievance been more pronounced.

In politics, judge a man by what he does, not what he says. On that basis, his speech was a symphony of mendacity.

The Man Who Stole Your Old Age had the nerve to stand on the platform and speak about his commitment to reducing poverty. He talked about a new partnership between government and the voluntary sector but refuses tax breaks on charitable giving. He boasts of his intention to solve the housing crisis – which he has exacerbated by colluding in mass, uncontrolled immigration – while at the same time presiding over an inheritance-tax regime which means thousands of vulnerable people will have to sell their homes to pay his punitive death duties.

And what about all those elderly folk in England and Wales who are having to sell their houses to finance long-term care? If they lived in Scotland they wouldn't have to.

North of the border, long-term care is free, thanks to lavish subsidies paid out of English taxes. Same with university tuition fees, which the Scots don't pay either.

Gordon talks about equality in education yet used his political muscle to force through tuition fees for everyone else in Britain. So when the chancellor promises a constitutional revolution, I don't know whether to laugh or cry. We've had a constitutional revolution under Labour – and as a result the English are now second-class citizens in a so-called United Kingdom, of which they comprise eighty per cent of the population and pay the lion's share. All for selfish, sectarian political advantage, since Labour relies on Scottish votes to rule.

The fact is that Gordon has been the most powerful member of the cabinet and he has controlled the purse strings. Every major decision of the past ten years – including the war in Iraq – has his fingerprints on it.

We've been told repeatedly that Gordon is the 'real' prime minister. Now we're asked to forget all that and swallow the idea that he's the new broom. If he wants a different kind of Britain, he's had ten years to make it happen. Why tell us now?

That speech was supposed to be Gordon's Agincourt moment. My guess is that it will be the start of his swansong. (Even if, as seems likely, by the time you read this, Gordon has graduated from 'real' Prime Minister to real Prime Minister.)

He even managed to get himself upstaged by the Wicked Witch, who stole the headlines the following day. She was standing by a TV monitor watching the speech. When Gordon got to the part where he was telling the delegates what a privilege it had been working with her husband, the WW barked 'That's a lie' and stomped off.

For once in my life, I agreed with the Wicked Witch.

66 | Nice Work II

Speaking of nice work, if you're looking for a cushy, lucrative line of employment you could do worse than consider a career in politics.

On the latest figures available, last year Westminster MPs pocketed an average of £204,000 in pay and perks – equivalent to £124 for every hour they, er, 'work'.

The 646 Members of Parliament claimed £86.7 million in expenses and office allowances, on top of their £60,000 basic salaries. Cabinet ministers cost us £115,000 in housing allowances alone, even though many of them have grace-and-favour homes which cost them nothing.

The housing allowance is one of the biggest rackets going. For instance, Mike Gapes, the Labour MP for Ilford North, a short train ride from central London, claimed £21,584.

This isn't a party political point. Michael Trend, the Tory MP for Windsor, Berkshire, had to stand down at the last election after an investigation into allegations that he falsely claimed up to £100,000. Trend had been receiving a generous London living allowance even though most nights he returns to his wife and family at his constituency home in Windsor. Since he entered Parliament in 1992 his claims for the 'additional costs allowance' ran into six figures.

This money was supposed to be available to all MPs with constituencies outside inner London. It is supposed to be used to pay for accommodation and can be put towards hotel bills, rent or mortgage payments.

Windsor is twenty-five miles from Westminster. Trend claimed he was entitled to the allowance because he keeps an address in London despite regularly commuting from home.

During the Major years there were endless late nights for

MPs. But since Labour adopted more 'family friendly' hours and marginalised the Commons, there's very little for them to do at Westminster.

Under parliamentary rules, the allowance is available to anyone who faces an 'unreasonably lengthy' journey home. These days that applies to just about everyone who lives outside a five-mile radius of Westminster.

To his credit, Mr Trend chose to brave the M4 bus-lane madness rather than go out on the razzle. But this must be the first time an MP has found himself all over the papers for going home to his wife rather than staying in his London flat and knocking off his secretary.

This kind of fiddle has been going on for years. There are legendary stories of Scottish MPs travelling four and five to a car and then all claiming the cost of a First Class rail ticket back to their constituencies.

They must have got the idea from their student days, when it was all the rage to see how many people you could cram into a Mini.

There was a tale doing the rounds in Westminster about a West Country MP who paid his children's school fees by falsely claiming to drive back and forth to Cornwall every weekend.

After the Trend episode, an inquiry was set up into MPs' expenses claims. Shortly before the report was due to be published, it was reported a number of members had been rushing to repay money which had been, er, claimed in error. In other words, they wanted to get in sharpish before they got their collars felt.

I am reminded of an episode of *Minder* in which Arthur broke into a warehouse to replace a consignment of dodgy wine before Mr Morley could charge him with half-inching it.

Upstairs from the Commons, Tony's cronies in the House of Lords are able to claim £320 a day simply for turning up. They don't have to spend more than a few minutes in the chamber. Once they've been signed in, they're free to do as they please – go home, go to sleep, go to the bar. It's entirely a matter for them.

Their walking-about money bears no relation to the amount of work they actually do. Main beneficiaries are all the placemen and brown-nosers Blair has stuffed into the Lords since scrapping most of the hereditaries, few of whom bothered claiming their expenses.

Whatever you think of the hereditary principle – and I'm against it – those peers at least went to the Lords out of a sense of public duty, not out of party loyalty and personal advancement.

Still, alongside the European Parliament, the scams at Westminster are small beer. According to the authors of *The Bumper Book Of Government Waste*, every single MEP costs a staggering £2.4 million a year.

Neil Kinnock, who was laughed out of Britain, only to be rewarded for his failure with as a European Commissioner, is estimated to have earned £1.5 million in pay and expenses alone from the EU. According to the *Mail on Sunday*, his annual expenses in the year before he retired included £24,000 for a housekeeper, a £7,000 entertainment allowance, and his perks included a subsidised mortgage, special low European tax rates and a chauffeur-driven car. His pension package would cost at least £2.3 million on the open market.

Over ten years it all added up to around £4 million for Kinnochio, whose main achievement in Brussels was an abject failure to tackle corruption. Meanwhile it was estimated that his wife Glenys must have made around £1 million since going to Brussels as an MEP.

In April 2005, MEPs rejected a further series of tighter controls to stop them fiddling their pension contributions, their lavish office allowances and forcing them to produce travel receipts. The Liberal Democrats' leader in the European Parliament, Chris Davies, said his colleagues were giving themselves 'the all-clear to embezzlement'.

More to the point, what do they do for it? Can you name your MEP? In the interests of open government, I managed to obtain a typical week's expenses claim. The name has been blanked out to protect the guilty.

European Parliament Expenses Claim
W/e 12 Dec, 2003.

XXXXXX MEP, XXXXX XXXX Constituency

OFFICE
25 x Paperclips (A4) €200
20 x Rulers (metric) €120
50 x Coathangers (unisex) €200
12 x Furry Gonks €120
20 x Novelty Mouse Pads €100

SUNDRIES
Tea and Coffee €250
Biscuits (Bourbon) €100
Newspapers and Magazines (*Le Monde*, the *Sun*, *Les Grandes Bazookas Pour Hommes*) €300

TRAVEL
First Class Airfare (Brussels, London, Strasbourg) €3,000
Taxi (Office–Brussels Airport) €50
Taxi (Heathrow–The Ivy, wait and return) €250
Taxi (Strasbourg Airport–Foie Gras D'Or Restaurant) €120

ACCOMMODATION
Hotel Splendide, Strasbourg (Hamilton Suite) €1,500
Minibar €250
Fifi la Coco Escort Service (x2) €2,000

TOTAL: €8,560 (call it €9,000 for cash).

*NB: Sorry, no receipts (eaten by dog).

67 | No Income Tax, No VAT, Dave

After winning the Conservative Party leadership, Call Me Dave announced an A-list of candidates to be parachuted into winnable seats. He wanted more women, gays and members of the ethnic minorities to reinforce the Tories' new commitment to diverse, multicultural Britain.

But where, I wondered, did that leave the down-to-earth, working class Conservative voters who were the backbone of Mrs Thatcher's victories in the 1980s? Who would speak for Essex Man?

That was when I was invited to sit in on the Tory selection process in Peckham, which Cameron himself decided to chair.

*

'Good morning, Mr Trotter. I'm David Cameron, but you can call me Dave.'

'Awight, Dave. And you can call me Del Boy.'

'Tell me, why do you want to be a Conservative candidate?'

'Vote Blue, Go Green, Dave. You're talking my language.'

'Excellent, the environment is the great challenge for our generation, don't you agree?'

'Oh, absolu-ment, Dave. And I think I can help you out there.'

'In what respect?'

'I know where I can lay my hands on a few dozen tins of green emulsion, RUC surplus stock. Could come in very handy with the old rebranding, eh? I could let you have the lot for a pony.'

'A pony?'

'Fair enough, Dave. You drive a hard bargain. Twenty notes and the paint's yours. I'll have Rodney bring it round to Central Office in the morning.'

'This isn't about paint, Mr Trotter, it's about the future of our planet, sustainable energy, global warming.'

'Mange-tout, Dave. Why didn't you say? It just so happens that I have a job lot of sun-damaged solar panels back at the lock-up.'

'I think we're in danger of getting away from the wider issues. We must think global, act local.'

'That's the motto of Trotter's Independent Traders – New York, Paris, Peckham. It doesn't get more "think global, act local" than that.'

'No, I mean we should all do what we can in our own backyards. For instance, I get on my bike whenever I can.'

'I thought Boycey sold you a Lexus.'

'He did, but it keeps breaking down. That's why I bought a bike. What do you do to cut road use?'

'I drive a three-wheeled van, Dave.'

'Is it a hybrid?'

'No, none of that Korean rubbish. It's a Reliant.'

'Do you have a bike?'

'Bain-marie, Dave. Do I have a bike? I've got a couple of dozen flood-damaged Dutch mountain bikes going cheap. Why don't you buy them for the shadow cabinet?'

'I didn't think there were any mountains in Holland.'

'He's razor sharp, this boy. There aren't – that's why they're going cheap.'

'I don't think so, Del.'

'How about a genuine, wind-damaged windmill? From Old Amsterdam.'

'I've already got one.'

'Can I interest you in an environmentally friendly, thermal, polar anorak, made in Mogadishu, as worn by Captain Oates?'

'I bought one when I went to see the glaciers.'

'What, those Americans who bought Manchester United? I thought they lived in Florida.'

'No, not the Glaziers. Have you ever been to the frozen North?'

'I've been to Hull and back.'

'This is getting us nowhere. Let's talk fiscal policy.'

'You'd be better off asking my Uncle Albert. He was on the trawlers before he joined the navy. During the war—'

'Not fisheries – fiscal. Taxes, economic policy.'

'I'm against them.'

'Against what?'

'No income tax, no VAT. There's a vote-winning slogan for you. Luvvly jubbly.'

'Don't you think the voters would consider that a tad irresponsible?'

'Not in Peckham, Dave. No one pays taxes round here. They're either independent entrepreneurs like myself or they're on the old rock and roll.'

'Where do you stand on party funding?'

'Boycey says if you could see your way clear to getting him into the New Year's honours list, you're looking at fifty grand in Nelson Eddys, no questions asked. Marlene's always fancied herself as a lady. There'll be a nice little drink it for you, too. We can clean up selling peerages and knighthoods, just like Maggie flogged off the gas board, British Telecom and everything else which wasn't nailed down. Stick with me, Dave, and this time next year we'll be millionaires.'

'I'm already a millionaire, Del. On your bike. Next.'

(Enter next prospective candidate.)

'Good morning Mr Trigger. I'm David Cameron, but you can call me Dave.'

'Awight, Rodney.'

68 | The Fastest Pushbike in the West

Shortly after becoming Tory leader, 'Call Me Dave' Cameron, was invited onto *Desert Island Discs*. Among the songs he nominated was Benny Hill's 'Ernie, the Fastest Milkman in the West', which was number one when Dave was five. I couldn't resist bringing it up to date.

You could hear his tyres pound,
As they raced across the ground,
And the clatter of the wheels,
As they spun round and round,
And he pedalled into Westminster,
His helmet on his head,
His name was Davey,
And he rode the fastest pushbike in the West.

Now Davey had a chauffeur,
A fella known as Bill,
He followed Davey in the car,
From his home in Notting Hill.
They said Davey was a hypocrite,
For cycling into work,
With his bags and clothes in a Lexus,
The two-faced little berk.
They called him Davey,
And he rode the fastest pushbike in the West.

He said he'd save the planet,
And if you want the proof,
Davey jetted off to Greenland,
And put a windmill on his roof.
He said I'll bring you happiness,
'Cos happiness is best,
We said Davey we'll be happy,
If you'll just tax us less.
And that flustered young Davey,
(Day-vey),
And he rode the fastest pushbike in the West.

Now Davey had a rival,
An evil-looking lad,
Called Gordon Brown from Kirkaldy Town,
And he drove the voters mad.
He tempted them with his benefits,
And his fancy jobs for life,
In his desperate run at Number 10,
He even took a wife.
And though they swooned at the Cameroons,
Gordon said if you vote for me,
I'll index-link your pensions,
And give you eyesight tests for free.
He thought they'd fall for his new capped teeth,
And his sultry Scottish charm,
But what put them off was he bit his nails,
Halfway down his arm.
Not like young Davey,
(Day-vey).
And he rode the fastest pushbike in the West.

But Gordon had a rival too,
His name was Tony Blair,
It tormented him from dawn to dusk,
That Tony was still there.
He yelled: 'If you don't get out now,
Then I'll be in my grave,
And sitting here in Downing Street,
Will be bloody Call Me Dave.'
And that tickled old Tony,
(To-ney)
And he had the biggest mortgage in the West.

Our Tony had a missus,
A money-grabbing bitch,
She bought a house in Connaught Square,
And was called the Wicked Witch.
Our Davey knew that human rights,
Had made this woman rich,
But when he saw the size
Of her meaty thighs,
He rode straight in the ditch.
Her name was Cherr-ee,
(Cherr-eeee!)
And she rode the fastest broomstick in the West.

Now Tony had a deputy,
He wasn't any good.
But he had a flat in Admiralty Arch,
And a house in Dorneywood.
He thought he was a ladies' man,
They didn't come much smarter,
But behind his back the whole world laughed,
At the size of his chipolata.
They called him Two Jags,
(Two-Jags)
And he drove the fastest limo in the West.

Young Davey had an A-list,
To get the Tories back.
He'd only choose from candidates,
Who were female, gay or black.
No more old blokes in pinstriped suits,
Called Norman, Geoff or Maurice,
Just metrosexuals who ride bikes,
And Etonians like Boris.
You all know Boris,
(Bor-is)
And he pulled the fastest women in the West.

Dave was only thirty-nine,
He didn't think he'd win.
He could only hope that Tone and Gord,
Would do each other in.
Dave couldn't know that Mr Plod,
Would feel old Tony's collar,
For flogging seats in the House of Lords,
For a suitcase full of dollars.
And so, at last, came Gordon's turn,
But as he stepped up to the mike,
He turned to see a man in green,
Approaching on a bike.
His head was down, his legs a blur,
Veins bulging in his neck.
Before Gordon knew what hit him,
He was lying on the deck.
As Gordon lay there dying,
The cyclist gave a wave,
Racing home to prepare for government,
Pedalled Call Me Dave.
They won't forget Davey,
(Day-vey)
And he rode the fastest pushbike in the West.

A few days later, Call Me Dave sent me an email requesting a copy of the original page, complete with Gary's brilliant cartoon. More than happy to oblige, we sent him a framed copy, which I'm told hangs in his office at Tory Central Office.

I subsequently learned that Dave had telephoned the editor raving about the column and suggesting that the song should be recorded and put up on the newspaper's website.

Unfortunately, the editor in question was not Paul Dacre, of the *Daily Mail*, but Rebekah Wade, the flame-haired editor of the *Sun* – the paper I'd left in 'amicable' circumstances six months earlier to rejoin the *Mail*.

69 | At Last – The Truth!

Hungary was plunged into turmoil in autumn 2006 after a leaked tape was broadcast in which the prime minister, Ferenc Gyurcsany, admitted his socialist government had lied morning, evening and night to win re-election.

'It was perfectly clear that what we were saying was untrue and in the meantime we did absolutely nothing for the past four years,' he confessed.

More than 10,000 demonstrators clashed with police in Budapest but Mr Gyurcsany said he had no intention of resigning.

The following day I received this extraordinary, unexpurgated recording of a candid meeting between Tony Blair and his cabinet colleagues.

Hey, guys. Have you seen the riots in Hungary on the news? All because the prime minister decided to tell the truth for once. What got into him?

I mean, everyone knows we've been lying through our teeth for years, but that's no reason to admit it. How I've got away with the pretty-straight-kind-of-guy act for so long is a mystery. The first time I wheeled it out, over the Formula One fiasco, John Humphrys and I kept getting a fit of the giggles. We had to do three takes.

Remember 'Twenty-four hours to save the NHS'? That was a laugh. We've spent billions and the health service is still a complete shambles.

Don't interrupt, Patricia. We all know your statistics are a work of fiction. We're having to bale out hospitals in marginals just to keep them open. Patients are dying like flies from MRSA. You stand more chance of getting out of Basra alive.

And that's another thing. Can you believe anyone ever fell for that WMD rubbish cobbled together off the internet? As for the idea that we were all going to be attacked in forty-five minutes, well, I ask you. I don't know how I kept a straight face.

Dubya decided to attack Iraq long before 9/11, just to get even for his dad. First time I met him, he took me to one side and said: 'Yo, Blair! We're going into Iraq to kick ass. I'm expecting you to step up to the plate because we can't rely on those cheese-eating surrender monkeys.' What could I do? I couldn't risk missing out on the book deal and the American lecture circuit. Cherie would have killed me.

I don't have to tell you guys how much we need the money. Connaught Square, don't even go there. And those flats in Bristol. Why did I ever agree to that? Anyone could see that Peter Foster coming a mile off, but you know Cherie when she gets an idea in her head.

Have you seen the price of everything these days? I don't know how the hell we get away with pretending that inflation is at an all-time low.

Even though we wangled the kids into selective schools, it still costs a fortune putting them through college. When I said education, education, education was my priority, I only meant Euan's education, Nicky's education and Kathryn's education. We didn't even have the other one in '97. Then there was the MMR-jab business, of course it's not safe, but I could hardly say that, could I?

I don't know what you're laughing about, Tessa. Only a halfwit would swallow the line about you not knowing anything about your seven mortgages or your husband's business dealings in Italy. How daft do you think people are? You'll be telling me next that Dr Kelly really did commit suicide.

What is it with us and mortgages? Look at the mess Peter got himself into, just because he couldn't bring himself to tell the truth to his building society. Or his permanent secretary. Or me, for that matter. Still, he lies about everything else, so no change there.

Tough on crime, tough on the causes of crime. That was a belter. It's like the Wild West out there. The police are useless and thanks to Cherie's beloved Human Rights Act — which I only brought in so she could make a few bob out of it — the courts can't do anything about terrorists.

Mind you, we've got to find them first. We haven't got the faintest idea who's living here. Managed immigration? Don't make me laugh. For all I know, Osama Bin Laden could be holed up in Bradford, claiming benefits.

And no, John, please don't tell me that were tightening up the borders, because you know it isn't true. The punters might fall for it, but you're talking to me now. For a start, Cherie and her friends in the legal profession wouldn't let us.

We can't even be bothered to prosecute those nutters running round the streets of London calling for anyone who disagrees with them to be beheaded. What's the point? There's no room in the prisons, anyway.

While we're telling the truth about the Home Office, why do we maintain the fiction that ID cards are the solution to everything? We all know the technology doesn't work properly.

About the only things which do work are all those speed cameras, which we keep saying are there to save lives but everyone knows are just there to raise money.

And so much for our integrated transport system. Still, it's probably my fault for putting Two Jags in charge of it all those years. I knew perfectly well he'd spend his life gallivanting round the world, scuba-diving, taking helicopter rides and chasing skirt like Warren Beatty on Viagra. The man can barely read and write, for heaven's sake. What was I thinking of when I made him deputy prime minister? I must have been on drugs.

And speaking of drugs, who thought it was a good idea to legalise cannabis while at the same time banning smoking? Probably the same idiot who thought the measured response to the foot-and-mouth scare was to set fire to every cow and sheep in the country.

Don't even mention the bloody Dome. We should have strangled that at birth instead of falling for all that phoney Cool Britannia guff.

Thank goodness I didn't get away with signing us up to the euro.

What is it, Gordon? Don't give me prudence. We've doubled public spending and all we've got to show for it is another few hundred thousand civil servants sitting around on their backsides doing the Sudoko in the *Guardian* and a government deficit bigger than Elton John's florist's bill. No wonder taxes have gone through the roof.

And what's the use in importing all these people from Eastern Europe when we've got about five million unemployed of our own, whatever the figures say?

Frankly, the past nine and a half years have been a complete and utter waste of time, a squandered opportunity. What's my legacy? British troops bogged down in Iraq and Afghanistan? The M4 bus lane?

No, I shall just have to stay on until I achieve something – anything.

Calm down, Gordon. When I said I was standing down next year, you didn't actually believe me, did you? What can I say?

I lied.